BENVENUTO CELLINI

BENVENUTO CELLINI

SEXUALITY, MASCULINITY, AND ARTISTIC IDENTITY IN RENAISSANCE ITALY

MARGARET A. GALLUCCI

BENVENUTO CELLINI
© Margaret A. Gallucci, 2003.

First published in hardcover in 2003 by Palgrave Macmillan
First PALGRAVE MACMILLAN™ paperback edition: March 2005
175 Fifth Avenue, New York, N.Y. 10010 and
Houndmills, Basingstoke, Hampshire, England RG21 6XS
Companies and representatives throughout the world.

PALGRAVE MACMILLAN is the global academic imprint of
the Palgrave Macmillan division of St. Martin's Press, LLC and of
Palgrave Macmillan Ltd. Macmillan® is a registered trademark in the
United States, United Kingdom and other countries. Palgrave is
a registered trademark in the European Union and other countries.

Cloth ISBN 1–4039–6107–7
Paperback ISBN 1–4039–6896–9

Library of Congress Cataloging-in-Publication Data

Gallucci, Margaret A.
    Benvenuto Cellini : sexuality, masculinity, and artistic identity in
Renaissance Italy / by Margaret A. Gallucci.
        p. cm.
    Includes bibliographical references and index.
    Cloth ISBN 1–4039–6107–7
    Paperback ISBN 1–4039–6896–9
        1. Cellini, Benvenuto, 1500–1571—Criticism and interpretation.
    2. Artists as authors—Italy. 3. Renaissance—Italy. I. Title.

NB623.C3G35 2003
808'.0092—dc21   2003041307

A catalogue record for this book is available from the British Library.

Design by Newgen Imaging Systems (P) Ltd., Chennai, India.

First PALGRAVE MACMILLAN paperback edition: March, 2005

10 9 8 7 6 5 4 3 2 1

Printed in the United States of America.

For my parents,
Charlotte O'Connor Gallucci and Donald Thomas Gallucci,
who inspired me

TABLE OF CONTENTS

Acknowledgments

This book had its beginnings in a Renaissance history course at the University of Connecticut when Guido Ruggiero challenged me to go beyond misogyny in attempting to explain Benvenuto Cellini's violent boasting. Guido has been a consummate mentor and friend whose groundbreaking work on gender and crime has paved the way for a generation of younger scholars like me. I have been lucky to have his constant support, guidance, and friendship.

Teachers at many institutions shared their enthusiasm and passion for literature, history, and ideas with me. At the University of Connecticut, I want to thank Joseph Cary, Jack Davis, and the late Robert S. Dombroski for their friendship and for providing ongoing encouragement, advice, and rigorous critical assistance through the years. My undergraduate advisor Robert Dombroski was a model mentor, teacher, and friend whose critical acumen, deep political commitment, and sense of humor made him a rare and special person. He was, without question, *il miglior fabbro*. Teachers in far-flung places like Naugatuck, Connecticut, especially Patricia Pawlak and Mary Eileen Galliette, stimulated my curiosity at a young age and laid the foundations for my passion for literature and languages.

This book draws on research from my dissertation. My dissertation adviser Louise George Clubb gave me the freedom and courage to work on Cellini, considered a major artist but minor writer. I want to thank her for her unwavering support, encouragement, and critical acumen. She has been a model mentor, scholar, and friend whose pioneering work in the Renaissance continues to serve as a model for me to follow and emulate. Randolph Starn challenged the limits of my theoretical boundaries and helped me to conceptualize a crucial aspect of my project when it was just an intuitive thought of mine that legal matters provided a grid through which writers like Cellini viewed their world. Randy has provided unwavering support and encouragement at every stage and has become a cherished friend. Gavriel Moses provided unstinting encouragement and acute critical judgments at the earliest stages of my work. The University of California at Berkeley offered financial support and an unrivaled community of scholars and friends.

Research for this book has been supported by grants and fellowships from the Fulbright Commission, the National Endowment for the Humanities, which sponsored my participation at the Newberry Library Summer Institute in the Italian Archival Sciences in 1993, the Gladys Krieble Delmas Foundation, and the Renaissance Society of America. New York University hosted me as a Visiting Scholar in 1997; a special thanks to Francesco Erspamer who organized my stay there. I also wish to express my gratitude to the directors and personnel of the Archivio di Stato, Florence, the Archivio della Confraternità dei Buonuomini di San Martino, Florence, the Biblioteca Riccardiana, Florence, the Biblioteca Moreniana, Florence, the Biblioteca Medicea Laurenziana, Florence, the Biblioteca Nazionale Centrale, Florence, the Biblioteca Nazionale Marciana, Venice, as well as the Pierpont Morgan Library in New York, the Houghton Library at Harvard University, the Newberry Library, the Bobst Library at New York University, Butler Library at Columbia University, and the Rare Book and Manuscript Library at Columbia University without whose collective resources and assistance this book could not have been written. To the staff of all these organizations and institutions I am deeply grateful.

In particular, I want to thank Dottoressa Anna Lenzuni at the Biblioteca Medicea Laurenziana, Florence, for allowing me to study the part-autograph manuscript of Cellini's *Vita*, Dr. Alberto Brini of the Confraternity of the Buonuomini di San Martino, Florence, Dr. Carlo Picchietti of the Biblioteca Nazionale Centrale, Florence, and Dottoressa Paola Benigni of the Soprintendenza Archivistica per la Toscana for permission to consult documents and manuscripts.

Thanks are due to Robert Dunkin at Art Resource, Mary Corliss at The Museum of Modern Art Film Stills Archive, the Biblioteca Nazionale Centrale in Florence, and the Pierpont Morgan Library in New York for granting permissions to reproduce texts or images from their collections.

Friends and fellow scholars read and commented on various portions of the manuscript, including James Amelang, Albert Russell Ascoli, Marvin Becker, John Brackett, Ross Chambers, Timothy Hampton, Dennis Looney, Ronald Martinez, Michael Rocke, Guido Ruggiero, Peter Sahlins, James Saslow, Randolph Starn, and Ruggero Stefanini. Franca Petrucci Nardelli and Armando Petrucci helped me with the transcriptions and continue to provide friendship, encouragement, and critical judgments about matters paleographic and codicologic.

Laura Giannetti Ruggiero helped me with the English translations. Any errors, however, remain my own. To all of them I am deeply indebted.

Gloria Allaire acted informally as my copy editor when this project was merely an unruly dissertation and has provided friendship and encouragement at every stage since we met as fellow Fulbrighters in 1990. Gloria is my model of rigorous scholarship and genuine friendship. To her, a special and deep thanks.

I want to thank members of my extended family, especially Amelia Viola Gallucci-Cirio, who contributed toward the completion of this project in ways too complex to enumerate. I also want to remember the late Joseph L. Gallucci, the late Margaret T. O'Connor, and the late Aldo Cirio who helped along the way in more ways than they know but who did not live to see the completion of this project.

Kristi Long, my editor at Palgrave, was a joy to work with. All of the staff at Palgrave, especially her assistant Roee Raz, was knowledgeable and helpful at every stage.

A very special thank you is owed to David Finn who generously provided his beautiful and incomparable photographs of Cellini's art for half of the illustrations that appear in this book as well as the jacket design. I am grateful to him and to his wonderful assistant Rosie Lue for helping make my book so much better than it was.

Without the support of Michael Rotondi the years I spent working on this project would have been much less successful and happy.

My family—parents, sisters Carole and Mary, brother Joe—provided a lifetime of support of every kind. My parents, Charlotte O'Connor Gallucci and Donald Thomas Gallucci, both public schoolteachers, set the example of teaching as a vocation and a passion, and for this and so many other things I am deeply indebted. Among those so many other things, my parents taught me intellectual curiosity, a passion for living abroad among strangers, and a love of reading. As a wholly inadequate gesture of my appreciation for their ongoing love, constant support, and intellectual guidance, I dedicate this book to them.

List of Abbreviations

ACBF	Archivio della Confraternità dei Buonuomini di San Martino, Florence
ASF	Archivio di Stato, Florence
BMLF	Biblioteca Medicea Laurenziana, Florence
BNCF	Biblioteca Nazionale Centrale, Florence
BNMV	Biblioteca Nazionale Marciana, Venice
BRF	Biblioteca Riccardiana, Florence

FOREWORD

Where indicated, I have provided my own modernized transcriptions of all texts from archival documents and manuscripts. By modernized transcription, I mean a *trascrizione interpretativa* rather than *diplomatica* as defined by Franca Petrucci Nardelli in "Riproduzione o interpretazione? Note sull'edizione dei documenti," *Arte Documento* 4 (1992): 266–67. I am following the conventions for modernized transcriptions set out by Giampaolo Tognetti in his "Criteri per la trascrizione di testi medievali latini e italiani," *Quaderni della Rassegna degli Archivi di Stato* 51 (1982): 1–66. In general, this involves employing capitals, adding punctuation, accents, and apostrophes, expanding abbreviations, dividing words logically, with the exception that in appendix 1 I have retained Cellini's spellings of words as well as *et* for *e*.

All dates have been modernized to reflect the "new style." Until 1725 in Italy, the new year began on 25 March, so dates that fall between 1 January and 24 March have been changed from "old style" to "new style."

Unless otherwise noted, English translations are mine with the exception that I utilized George Bull's 1956 translation of the *Vita* but modified it at my discretion. I have provided literal English translations for passages but have added explanatory material in square brackets for the nonspecialist reader to clarify what I believe to be the implied meaning.

I gratefully acknowledge permission to reprint two previously published articles, re-titled and in different form. Material in chapter 2 was published in "Cellini's Trial for Sodomy: Power and Patronage at the Court of Cosimo I," © *The Cultural Politics of Duke Cosimo I de' Medici*, Konrad Eisenbichler, 2001, Ashgate. Portions of chapter 3 appeared in "A New Look at Benvenuto Cellini's Poetry," *Forum Italicum* 34, no. 2 (2000): 343–71.

To avoid what Randolph Starn has dubbed "the early modern muddle," I have primarily used the terms "medieval," "Renaissance," and "sixteenth century" throughout this book to characterize my historical timeline. There is no consensus among literary scholars, nor is there agreement between literary scholars, historians, and historians of art, as to when early modernity in Italy begins and ends. At times, I distinguish between medieval and Renaissance Italy to show a kind of evolution of values (for instance, medieval prosecutions of sodomy or medieval conceptions of honor vs. Renaissance ones), which I believe allows for both continuity and radical change. Occasionally, I employ the term "sixteenth century" to situate Cellini firmly in the society and culture of his time. At times, but rarely, I use the term "early modern" to emphasize the links between Cellini's world and our own modern/postmodern one, such as in the artist's tendency to address the reader directly as "gentle readers" in his *Vita*.

Figure 1   Benvenuto Cellini, Saltcellar of Francis I. Vienna, Kunsthistorisches Museum. Photo: David Finn

Figure 2   Benvenuto Cellini, Nymph of Fontainebleau. Paris, Louvre. Photo: Giraudon/ Art Resource, NY

Figure 3 Benvenuto Cellini, Nymph of Fontainebleau, detail. Paris, Louvre. Photo: David Finn

Figure 4   Benvenuto Cellini, Bust of Cosimo I. Florence, Bargello. Photo: David Finn

Figure 5 Benvenuto Cellini, Ganymede. Florence, Bargello. Photo: David Finn

Figure 6 Benvenuto Cellini, Ganymede, detail. Florence, Bargello. Photo: David Finn

Figure 7 Benvenuto Cellini, Apollo and Hyacinth. Florence, Bargello. Photo: David Finn

Figure 8   Benvenuto Cellini, Narcissus. Florence, Bargello. Photo: David Finn

Figure 9 Benvenuto Cellini, Perseus (restored). Florence, Loggia dei Lanzi. Photo: Scala/Art Resource, NY

Figure 10   Benvenuto Cellini, Perseus (restored). Florence, Loggia dei Lanzi. Photo: Scala/Art Resource, NY

Figure 11 Benvenuto Cellini, Crucifix. El Escorial, Monastery of San Lorenzo el Real. Photo: David Finn

Figure 12 Giorgio Vasari, "The Forge of Vulcan." Florence, Uffizi. Photo: Alinari/Art Resource, NY

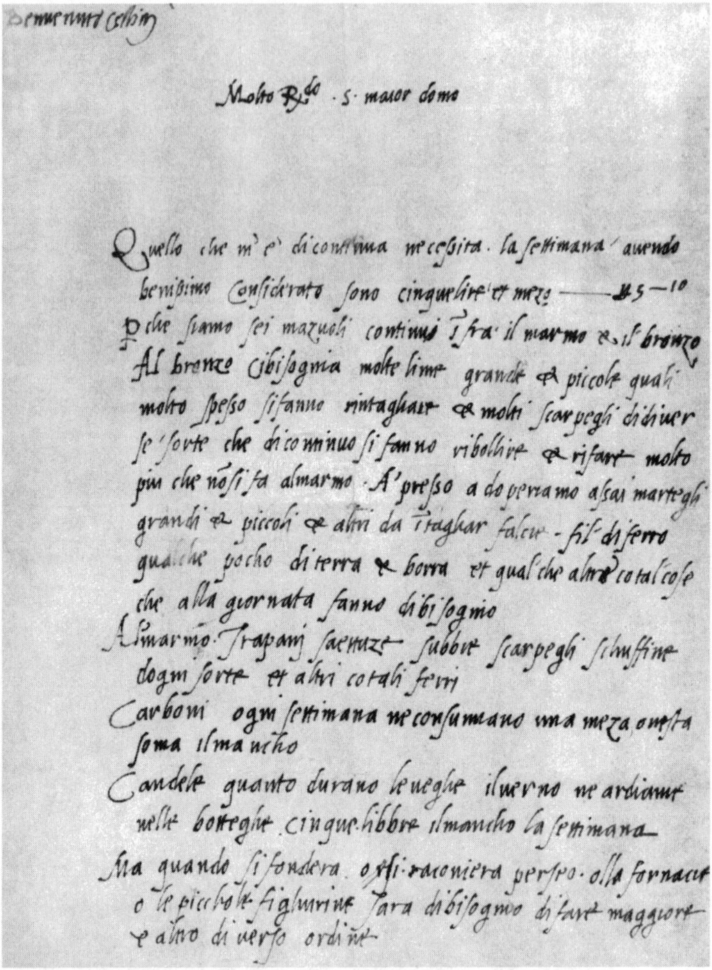

Benuenuto Cellini

Molto R.do · S· maior domo

Quello che m'e' di continua necessita. la settimana auendo
benissimo Consid'rato sono cinquelire et mezo ———— ₰5—10
p che siamo sei mazuoli continui i fra il marmo et il bronzo
Al bronzo Cibisognia molte lime grande et piccole quali
molto spesso si fanno rintagliare et molti scarpegli di bjuer
se sorte che di continuo si fanno ribollire et rifare molto
piu che no si fa al marmo A'presso a doperiamo assai martegli
grandi et piccoli et altri da tragliar falce · fil di ferro
qualche pocho di terra et borra et qualche altre cotal cose
che alla giornata fanno di bisognio
Al marmo · Trapani saettuze subbie scarpegli schuffine
dogni sorte et altri cotali ferri
Carboni ogni settimana ne consumiano una meza oueta
soma il mancho
Candele quanto durano le vegle il uerno ne ardiamo
nelle botteghe cinque libbre il mancho la settimana
Ma quando si fondera o ssi raconiera per fso o lla fornace
o le piccole figliurine sara di bisognio di tare maggiore
e altro di uerso ordine

Figure 13   Autograph letter of Benvenuto Cellini. The Pierpont Morgan Library,
New York. MA 973, f. 2

Figure 14 Fredric March and Constance Bennett in "The Affairs of Cellini." Photo: The Museum of Modern Art/Film Stills Archive

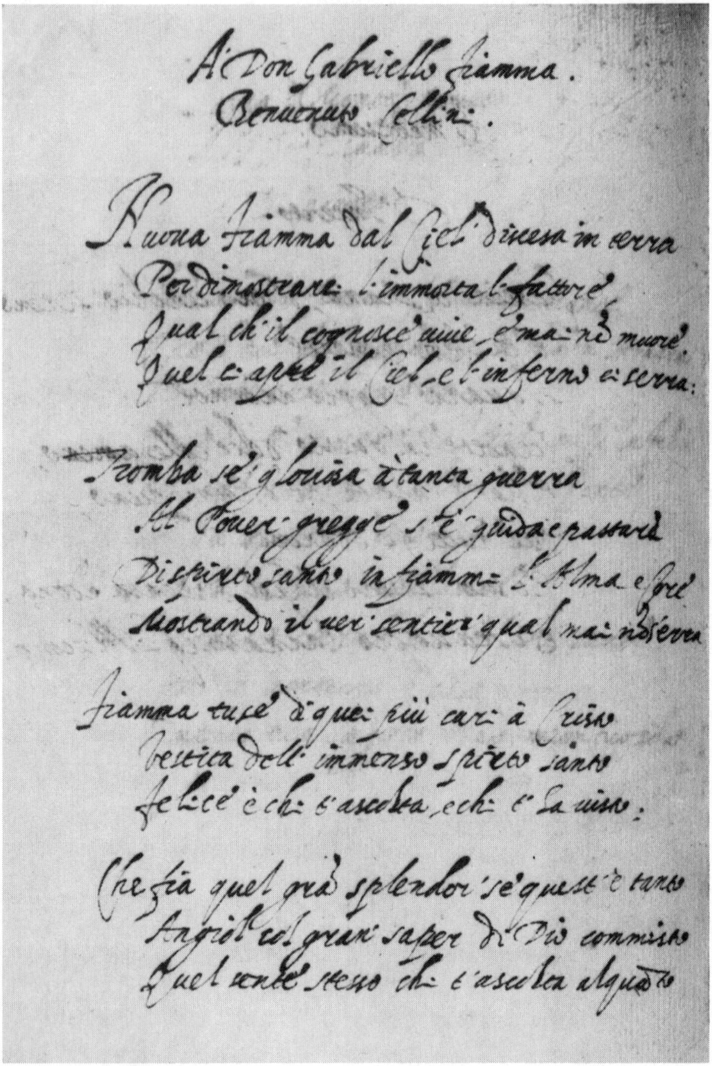

Figure 15 Unedited Sonnet Attributed to Benvenuto Cellini. Florence, Biblioteca Nazionale Centrale. Conv. Soppr., B 8 1657, fol. 252v. Courtesy of the Ministero per i Beni e le Attività Culturali. Used by permission. Reproduction or duplication prohibited

Figure 16 Joseph Schildkraut as Benvenuto Cellini in "The Firebrand" (undated).
Photo: The Museum of the City of New York

INTRODUCTION

On 15 February 1571 Benvenuto Cellini was buried in the church of the Santissima Annunziata in Florence. Amid glittering pomp and ceremony, members of the prestigious Academy of Design stood solemnly with members of the congregation as Cellini's body was carried from his house to the church. The procession wound its way slowly through the narrow cobblestone streets, followed by nearly all of Florence, nobleman and commoner alike, until it arrived at the steps of the church, where throngs packed the church hoping to catch a final glimpse of the great artist. There, in the numinous glow of a galaxy of candles, four members of the Academy raised the coffin and transported it to the altar. When Cellini's body was set down and all honored guests seated, a Servite friar rose, ascended to the pulpit, and gave a powerful, moving oration praising Cellini, the fine disposition of his body and soul, and his incomparably virtuous work and life.[1]

As is often the case, however, history yields a different memory: remembered at death for a life of virtue, Cellini is notorious today for his life full of vice.

Oscar Wilde referred to Cellini's *Vita* (Life) as the book in which "the supreme scoundrel of the Renaissance relates the story of his splendour and his shame."[2] The splendor for Wilde most likely refers to Cellini's artistic triumphs in Italy and France; the shame, his violent boastings, his misogyny, or his many run-ins with the law for crimes ranging from murder to sodomy. Although Cellini's reputation may be due in part to sensationalist readings by Victorian Englishmen, this notion is founded on his actual sexual behavior. Cellini is notorious for being the only major artist during the Italian Renaissance tried, convicted, and imprisoned for the sex crime of sodomy. In 1557, more than a decade before his death, the Florentine criminal court convicted him for committing repeated acts of sodomy with Fernando, a youth who worked as an apprentice in his goldsmith's shop in Florence. The magistrates sentenced Cellini to serve a four-year prison term, imposed a fine, and stripped him of the privilege of holding public office. Outside the courtroom his contemporaries, including his mortal enemy Baccio Bandinelli and rival artist Giorgio Vasari, accused him of a wide variety of transgressions. Paradoxically, even after his conviction and public humiliation, rather than attempting to cover up the rumors of his sodomitical practices, Cellini instead chose to defiantly and proudly proclaim himself a sodomite, celebrating male love and masculine beauty in his writings. Cellini's bold declarations stand in stark contrast to Michelangelo's frequent proclamations of orthodoxy and, it appears, life of total sexual abstinence.

A celebrated goldsmith and sculptor of the Italian Renaissance, Benvenuto Cellini (1500–71) fits the conventional image of the Renaissance man: a skillful virtuoso and courtier; an artist who worked in marble, bronze, and gold; and a writer. He is famous for a large statue in bronze, the *Perseus* (completed 1554) commissioned by Duke Cosimo I de' Medici, and infamous for his outrageous *Vita* in which he recounts acts of assault and narrates tales of murder with a disarming nonchalance. Cellini's *Vita*, composed between 1558 and 1566 and titled *La Vita di Benvenuto di Maestro Giovanni Cellini fiorentino scritta per lui medesimo in Firenze*, is one of the earliest surviving autobiographies, and its author's self-presentation as a swashbuckling rebel has been the subject of a long line of romantic novels and biographies. The *Vita* was printed posthumously in 1728; it had limited circulation in manuscript form prior to its first appearance in print. Gabriele D'Annunzio praised Cellini's *Vita* as one of his three favorite books, calling it "the book of my freedom and pleasure."[3]

In his autobiography when Cellini is not holding a chisel, he is usually clutching a dagger. The popular image of the artist as fearless adventurer and shameless seducer anticipates Don Juan and Casanova. Cellini appears frequently in anthologies of gay literature as a major figure in the tradition.[4] Although known as a central figure in the artistic culture of Medicean Florence, Cellini crossed the boundaries between art and literature.

This book concentrates on Cellini's literary as opposed to artistic oeuvre. A central concern is to discern why Cellini, lacking a formal education, wrote so much, so well, and in such different genres. In addition to his *Vita*, he penned art treatises and discourses, account books, diaries, sonnets, and letters.[5] Why, in the case of Cellini, was writing so closely allied with the identity of an artist? The majority of his writings—literary, artistic, and poetic—were written after his prosecution and conviction for sodomy, and it was under house arrest that Cellini began to write the story of his life. One of the goals of this book is to establish precisely, and for the first time in English, the nature of Cellini's poetics. In this book, I use the term "poetics" to signify his writing style, themes, and motifs in his literary output as a whole, in his poetry as well as his prose.

This book assumes that literary texts and historical documents illuminate each other, and draws upon the methodologies of New Historicism and gender studies.[6] New historicist studies locate literary texts in a context of contemporary discourses and practices. These normally include nonliterary texts as well as institutions and social relations of power. Gender theory when applied to Cellini analyzes, for instance, male sexuality and gender restrictions on men. The artist had sexual relations with both boys and women and was, as noted, convicted of sodomy. In Cellini's time masculinity, like femininity, was not so much a "role" as "the forcible citation of a norm, one whose complex historicity is indissociable from relations of discipline, regulation, punishment."[7] In his *Vita*, Cellini exposes and criticizes male gender stereotypes prized in his society. This book also utilizes the concept of self-fashioning that views the self in a double sense, as both the manipulator of culture and, at the same time, manipulated by it. Self-fashioning combines rhetorical theory, which sees the subject as able to modify cultural practices, and discourse theory, which posits that cultural discourses, in effect, speak through the subject.

In applying these critical approaches, this book attempts to understand Cellini's life and writings by examining a wide range of nonliterary texts and by relating literary texts to larger social and cultural phenomena. This study revolves around the twin poles of violation (or deviation or transgression) and innovation. Violation is the key motif of Cellini's life and work. The artist violated existing norms in three areas: sexual, literary, and artistic. As a sodomite, Cellini violated existing sexual norms and transgressed fixed gender boundaries by taking Fernando "as his wife," as the court records stated, thereby renouncing social norms. As a poet, the artist violated Petrarchan conventions. And finally, only by violating the laws of Nature was Cellini able to create, he tells us in an account replete with generative metaphors, his masterpiece the *Perseus*. His violations led, as we shall see, to surprising innovations in art, lyric, and autobiography. In the large *Gestalt* of Cellini's life and work, there is a clear pattern and overall consistency. In his language, poetic practice, and postures, there are shifts of register, tone, and lexicon in addition to a mixture of old and new, elite and popular, high and low.

This book provides a new look at this famous artist and autobiographer from the Italian Renaissance by placing Cellini in relation to a series of early modern cultural discourses and practices, including necromancy manuals, discourses of sodomy, juridical practices, and discourses of honor. It is the first biographical study of Cellini—as artist, sodomite, writer, poet—available in English, and the first to offer a comprehensive examination of his substantial body of poetry.[8] In addition, this book offers readings from his *Vita* that complement his *Rime* in the hope that we can begin to evaluate his works in prose and in verse together. I provide a new reading of the sodomy conviction that effectively ended his artistic career. Moreover, without resorting, as previous studies have done, to discussions of heroism but rather by considering contemporary standards of male honor and manliness, this book attempts to answer the vexing question of why Cellini's self-portrait is so imbued with misogyny and violence.

There are five chapters in addition to the introduction and conclusion. Chapter 1 provides a brief overview of Cellini's life and artistic career, including his major works of art and literature. Chapter 2 analyzes the sodomy trial itself, the event that, in effect, helped produce his written output. In chapter 2, I identify a legal register in Cellini's autobiography, exploring how the prosecutorial mode underlies Cellini's *Vita* and other writings. Chapter 2 addresses the renewed interest in Cellini in recent years as a symbol of gay (or queer) sensibility. The two chapters that follow concentrate on Cellini's writings, in verse (chapter 3) and in prose (chapter 4). Chapter 3 argues that the sonnet was a forum for artistic judgments in Cellini's day, and considers the stylistic features, hitherto unrecognized, of his poetry, including Petrarchan and Dantesque allusions as well as the strategies of parody, personification, caricature, and the grotesque. Sodomy reappears in Cellini's poetry. The artist often employs sodomy as his preferred mode of attack. Cellini was an innovator as a poet by taking the traditional form of the poetic *tenzone* and using it in a new way by employing it in an artistic forum. Chapter 4 considers other genres that Cellini used in his self-dramatization in the story of his life, including medieval vision narratives, ekphrastic writing, epic, romance, and theatrical comedy. Cellini's generic pastiche runs distinctly counter to the dominant later sixteenth century insistence on distinct and "pure" generic categories. Chapter 5 examines Cellini's self-presentation as a violent braggart, placing him within a larger field of masculine behavior and considers misogyny and manliness in Renaissance culture. One is not surprised, for example, that Cellini embarks on his Otherworld journey clad in a coat of mail and carrying a dagger. In exposing norms of masculine behavior, Cellini's autobiography illustrates how gender ideology restricted men as well as women in the Renaissance. In addition, by presenting a portrait of himself in the story of his life as a man who rapes, pillages, and dominates just about everyone and everything in his path, Cellini succeeded in creating a fantasy of male power. Cellini displaces martial masculinity into artistic enterprise.

This book charts the shift in the life of one Renaissance artist from self-expression through art to self-expression through writing (chapters 3 and 4) and through violence (chapter 5). A brief conclusion provides a synthesis of the artist's adventures in literary self-expression. The conclusion considers Cellini as a kind of pop icon, whose hold on the American imagination includes a Broadway play (1924), a *Classics Illustrated* comic book (1947), and an Off-Broadway play (2001). It is my hope that this book will lead to a reappraisal of Cellini as a writer and man and foster future studies of Cellini that integrate his literary corpus with his artistic creations.

CHAPTER 1

BENVENUTO CELLINI, LIFE AND WORKS

Much of what we know about Benvenuto Cellini comes from his own pen. He was born in Florence in Via Chiara on 3 November 1500 to Giovanni Cellini and Elisabetta Granacci. The Cellini family originated in Val D'Ambra, between Siena and Arezzo, but had lived in Florence since the time of Cellini's great-grandfather. His grandfather Andrea was listed as a bricklayer (*muratore*) in the Florentine tax records, known as the *Catasto*, of 1487.[1] His father, a court musician, artist, architect, and engineer, called his son Benvenuto (*Welcome*) after his wife and the midwife told him to expect another girl, a third daughter. Giovanni hoped that Benvenuto would follow in his footsteps and study music, his passion and part-time occupation. His son acquiesced to please his father but only if he could also study the art of drawing using the sketches of Leonardo and Michelangelo as models and be apprenticed to a local goldsmith. Cellini's youth was spent primarily in Florence at the shops of various goldsmiths. At the age of thirteen or fourteen, he was apprenticed at the workshop of Baccio Bandinelli's father, Michelangelo di Viviano. At fifteen he joined the shop of Antonio Giamberti, known as "Marcone." At eighteen, he worked at the shop of Francesco Salimbene; and at twenty-one, at Giovambattista Sogliani's. During these years Cellini spent some time in Siena, Pisa, and Bologna. From 1519 to 1540 the artist lived and worked in Rome and received numerous commissions from the Medici Popes Leo X (ruled 1513–21) and Clement VII (ruled 1523–34), from aristocratic Roman families, and from foreigners residing in Rome, in particular, the Spanish. He created medals, seals, coins, jewelry, and small objects such as chalices, working in bronze, silver, and gold. The artist fought valiantly at the side of the Papal Curia and pontifical army during the Sack of Rome in 1527, taking refuge in Castel Sant'Angelo.

After the siege of Rome Cellini traveled to Mantua where he created a reliquary for that city's Marquis and three seals for the house of

Gonzaga. In 1529 Pope Clement VII appointed Cellini Head of the Roman mint where he designed various coins and medals of stunning beauty and intricacy. The artist continued to spend time in Florence, and in 1531 he designed the first coin in Florentine history, the forty *soldi*, to bear the head of a sovereign (Alessandro de' Medici, ruled 1531–37) rather than the traditional symbols of Florence, the fleur-de-lis and John the Baptist, the city's patron saint, which had adorned the florin since 1252.[2] In 1539 Clement's successor Pope Paul III (Alessandro Farnese, ruled 1534–49) imprisoned Cellini in Castel Sant'Angelo on charges of stealing jewels from the papal coffers during the Sack of Rome a decade earlier. The artist escaped but was caught and incarcerated again. The Pope finally released him in 1540, thanks, in part, to the intervention of the French King Francis I.

From 1540 to 1545 Cellini worked at Francis's court. It is in this phase of his career that Cellini became internationally known and appreciated for his various artistic projects. His lifelong efforts bore dramatic financial fruit. His fame and honor spread across Europe. In 1542 Francis signed a letter of naturalization, conferring French citizenship on Cellini, and gave him a castle, the Petit-Nesle, in Paris as his residence. At Francis's court Cellini was received, in his words, "with the same hospitality that His Majesty bestowed on Leonardo da Vinci painter: seven hundred scudi a year; and in addition, he pays you for all the works you create for him; and on your arrival he gives you five hundred scudi in gold" (Bellotto, 500–01). Francis awarded Cellini innumerable grandiose commissions, including statues of the Greek gods, and both the fountain and portal for his palace at Fontainebleau. Cellini created a magnificent, intricate saltcellar in gold (1540–43) and a large statue in bronze, the *Nymph of Fontainebleau* (1542), to decorate the portal (figures 1–3). The *Nymph*, a semi-circle in half-relief, displays a nude, recumbent Diana with a Stag's head protruding from the center directly above her hips, "splitting" her body in half (figures 2 and 3).[3] This ensemble was part of a larger group of works projected by Cellini for Fontainebleau but never realized. A Satyr and two Victories were projected for the portal; the artist also made plans to create the fountain itself with other statues surrounding it. Several of Cellini's descriptions or drawings for these projects remain. We have sketches of the Jupiter, Juno, Mars, and a Satyr along with details of the plans for the fountain. Rivalries with other court artists and conflicts with Francis's mistress Madame d'Étampes (Anne d'Heilly), as well as a longing to return to his native land, forced Cellini to leave the French king's service in 1545.

Cellini returned to Florence to work at the court of Duke Cosimo I de' Medici (1519–74, ruled 1537–74) where he would remain until his death in 1571. Along with Bronzino, Cellini is listed as one of only two salaried artists at the Medici court in 1550.⁴ Like Francis, Cosimo gave Cellini a house as a gift. Upon his return, Cellini appears to have taken up residence in Via della Colonna. In 1561 he received from the Duke a house in Via della Pergola using the interior garden—entered from Via del Rosaio—as a workshop. In Florence, Cellini would make his mark as a sculptor. Along with Bronzino, Bandinelli, and Pontormo, Cellini was one of Cosimo's favored artists and was awarded numerous commissions. From 1545 to 1547 he created the large portrait bust in bronze of the Duke (figure 4) and three marble sculptures (figures 5–8), the *Ganymede* (1548–50), the group *Apollo and Hyacinth* (1546–48), and the *Narcissus* (1548–65). For nearly ten years Cellini worked on the one object that would earn him resounding acclaim and make him a "universal" artist: the large bronze *Perseus* (1545–54). Originally commissioned by Cosimo in 1545 to be placed under the arcade of the Loggia dei Lanzi in the Piazza della Signoria, it was intended as political allegory (figures 9 and 10). Cosimo wanted the *Perseus* to complement Donatello's *Judith* and Michelangelo's *David*, already displayed in the Piazza. Supporters of the Medici reinterpreted these art works as symbols of Medicean triumph over their enemies.

The *Perseus* is actually an assemblage of many objects. The larger-than-life bronze statue of the *Perseus* itself, stands on the twisted body of the headless Medusa. Both of these statues rest on an ornate marble base with grotesque ornamentation containing four freestanding bronze statues in niches of Jupiter, Minerva, Mercury, and Danae with the infant Perseus. Beneath the marble base is a bronze parapet in half-relief of *Perseus liberating Andromeda*. During these years in Florence, Cellini also created a marble bust of the Duchess Eleonora da Toledo (1545–54), presumed lost, and a bronze bust of Bindo Altoviti (ca. 1550). At his own expense, the artist carved a life-sized, white marble statue of a nude Christ on a black marble cross (1556–62) with which he intended to decorate the chapel of his own tomb. Cellini apparently worked in wood, as Donatello had; the wooden statue listed in the inventory of his household goods at his death as "Una Vergine di legnio con uno Santo Antonio"⁵ is presumed lost. Cellini's good relations with Cosimo ended after his conviction for sodomy and the arrival of Vasari's protégés at the Medici court. Cosimo shifted his preference to Bandinelli and the young sculptor Bartolomeo Ammannati (1511–92). In the 1560s Cellini tried unsuccessfully to win commissions from the

Duke: Cosimo rejected his plans for the Neptune fountain and for the half-reliefs for the chorus of the church of Santa Maria del Fiore.

In 1558 Cellini took minor orders but renounced his religious vocation two years later. During the 1560s he also produced his two major art treatises, one on goldsmithing and the other on sculpture, titled *Due Trattati, uno intorno alle otto principali arti dell'Oreficeria. L'altro in materia dell'Arte della Scultura; dove si veggono infiniti segreti nel lavorar le Figure di Marmo e nel gettarle di Bronzo.* From 1558 to 1566 Cellini wrote his *Vita*, dictating most of it to an apprentice in his workshop. In an internal reference in the *Vita*, Cellini notes that he was still writing the *Vita* in 1566 even though the events in the *Vita* recount the years only up to 1562. Toward the very end of the *Vita* the narrator surfaces and flashes forward in time, declaring to the reader that he bought a farmhouse "in the following year, in December of 1566" (Bellotto, 762–63) but then returns to recounting the events of 1562. The final pages give us a portrait of Cellini in a domestic setting. In 1562 Cellini secretly married his servant Piera di Salvatore de' Parigi; they officially married in 1567.[6] Together they had five children, but only three lived to adulthood: Andrea Simone (b. 1569), Liperata or Reparata (b. 1563), and Maddalena (b. 1566) who married the notary Noferi Maccanti. At the time of his death he owned two houses, one located in Via Benedetta (in the district of S. Pagolo) and another in Via della Colonna (in the district of S. Michele Bisdomini), which housed his workshop. In addition, Cellini owned tracts of land in the countryside outside Florence, in S. Bartolommeo a Farneto and S. Miniato a Piazzano, near Vicchio di Mugello, and a villa at Trespiano. The artist spent the last few years of his life on the periphery of Florentine court life and, it appears, in bad health. His last artwork was the large marble crucifix (figure 11). He wrote approximately eleven wills over the course of his life; in his (final) last will and testament, dated 18 December 1570, he designated Andrea Simone as his legitimate heir. It also contained provisions for his wife and two daughters. He died on 13 February 1571.

Cellini did not receive a formal education at the university, but probably learned to read and write at home or at the workshop where he was apprenticed. Literacy was relatively high in late Renaissance Florence. It is estimated that in the fifteenth century nearly thirty-three percent of Florentine boys learned to read and write.[7] Normally, young boys spent up to five years as an apprentice and two more as a journeyman. Cellini's apprenticeship at the age of fifteen to the goldsmith Antonio Giamberti guaranteed that he would learn the basic skills of writing and reading. For practical reasons, goldsmiths and other tradesmen had to know how to read and write in order to keep records, to measure amounts, and to draft bills, but this basic literacy also permitted these boys to read books written in the vernacular.

We know many details about Cellini's father, but little about his mother. Giovanni Cellini (1451–1527), a member of the prestigious ensemble of Florentine musicians known as the *pifferi*, worked at the courts of both Lorenzo and Piero de' Medici as well as of Piero Soderini, and was well-placed enough to be "one of the eleven citizens—and the only musician—chosen to decide the placement for Michelangelo's *David*" in 1504.[8] There were only four salaried civic fifers for the whole city. In the *Vita* Cellini claims that musicians in his father's day were permitted to join the greater guilds of silk and of wool (l'arte maggiori di seta et lana [Bellotto, 25]); but it seems, rather, that up until about the mid-sixteenth century, the *pifferi* could join a number of different guilds.[9] As early as the late Duecento in Florence, guild enrollment was a requirement for citizenship and office-holding privileges.[10] Cellini insisted that the Cellini clan of Florence descended from the citizen class, as evidenced by the Cellini coat-of-arms and family tree. The coat of arms, in Cellini's words, depicted "a lion rampant in gold against a field of azure, with a red lily clasped in his right paw; above there is a banner with three little golden lilies."[11] But a curious entry in the diary of Cellini's contemporary Francesco di Andrea Buonsignori (*Memorie*) claimed that Cosimo bestowed Florentine citizenship upon Cellini only in 1554 as a reward for the *Perseus*.[12]

Cellini was a reader as well as a writer. In his *Vita*, he cites three specific books that influenced to varying degrees the style and content of the stories he tells: the Bible, Dante's *Divine Comedy*, and Giovanni Villani's *Chronicle*. Cellini's familiarity with the Bible and Dante are not surprising since both books were widely read in his day.[13] The inventory of his household goods compiled at the time of his death includes the Dante manuscript as well as "18 pezzi di libri di stampa di varie sorte."[14] We know he purchased a copy of Leonardo's *Trattato della architettura*, since in his short treatise on architecture he relates to his "gentle reader" that he bought "a manuscript book, copied from one by the great Leonardo da Vinci . . . This book was full of virtue and written in a most beautiful manner, according to the marvelous genius of Leonardo (I believe there was never a greater man born to this earth than he), on the great arts of sculpture, painting, and architecture (Scarpellini, 569)."[15]

Like other Renaissance artists such as Leonardo and Michelangelo, Cellini was an author. Dario Trento has argued that Cellini's writings are "absolutely anomalous" among artists of his day for "the sheer volume of documentation."[16] Cellini composed the majority of his works—literary, poetic, artistic, and epistolary—during his years in Florence from 1545 to 1571. In addition to writing in a variety of genres, Cellini produced many texts that cross the boundaries of different genres; for instance, his seven volumes of account books (*libri di conti*) contain autobiographical entries common to diaries of the period as well as the expected accounting of debits and credits.[17]

Cellini's best-known literary work is his *Vita*, often called the earliest surviving autobiography of an artist. But it is misleading to attribute this heroic literary feat to him since autobiographical writings had actually been composed by Renaissance artists before Cellini, and include, for example, Lorenzo Ghiberti's *Commentarii* (1440s), the Florentine sculptor Maso di Bartolommeo's *Ricordi* (1447–53), and Baccio Bandinelli's brief *Memoriale* (1552–ca. 1558).[18] However, these works are fragmentary glimpses of an artist's life and artistic accomplishments and lack the comprehensiveness of Cellini's literary masterpiece. In his *Vita*, Cellini sought to provide a full account of his whole life from birth to death in a coherent narrative. Artists of Cellini's day also composed literary works—Michelangelo and Bronzino wrote poetry, too—but Cellini wrote "obsessively," as Jane Tylus has argued.[19]

This obsessiveness is evident in Cellini's account in the *Vita* of his imprisonment in Rome in 1539. In these truly fascinating and extraordinary passages Cellini narrates the remarkable and ingenious way he employs to write when confronted with the Herculean task of trying to write in prison without having either pen or paper. His jailers had refused his request for writing materials but allowed him to read two of his books, the Italian Bible and Villani's *Chronicle*. According to Cellini, suddenly "a marvelous vision in the form of a beautiful young man appeared to me in a dream, and started rebuking me" (Bellotto, 425) for losing faith in God and considering suicide. Convinced that the angel had spoken the truth, Cellini believes he is a witness to divine truth. As such, he feels compelled to record the experience in the form of a poem. But confined in his cell in complete darkness, without pen or paper, how could he write?

> [G]ittato gli ochi per la prigione, viddi un poco di mattone fracido; così lo strofinai l'uno coll'altro e feci a modo che un poco di savore; dipoi così carpone mi accostai a un taglio di quella porta della prigione e co' denti tanto feci, che io ne spiccai un poco di schegiuzza; et fatto che io ebbi questo, aspettai quella ora del lume che mi veniva alla prigione, la quale era dalle venti ore e mezzo insino alle ventuna e mezo. Allora cominciai a scrivere il meglio che io potevo in su certe carte che avanzavano innel libro della Bibbia. (Bellotto, 426)

(Glancing around the cell, I saw some pieces of musty brick; so I rubbed one piece against the other in order to make a little paste; then, still crawling on my hands and knees, I went up to the cell door and with my teeth gnawed at the edge till I bit off a small splinter; and after I had done that, I waited for the time when some light would come into the cell, which lasted from eight thirty to nine thirty. So I started to write the best that I could on some blank pages in my Bible.)

Using a brick-paste as ink and a wood splinter as pen, in the precious hour of sunlight creeping into his cell, Cellini composed poems in the pages of his Bible.

Cellini's *Vita* is generally accepted to be an unmediated reflection of the actual life lived by the artist himself. The common perception that the *Vita* is a kind of chronicle of the times is also a tribute to Cellini's success in creating his own mythology, seducing us not to doubt the veracity of his account. Cellini may or may not have killed the Constable of Bourbon, but his tale of the siege of Castel Sant'Angelo in 1527 has the tenor of an eyewitness account. This view is partially due to the fact that he dictated about two-thirds of it, thereby favoring a style that seems more closely to resemble oral discourse than formal writing. The autograph of the *Vita* in the Biblioteca Medicea Laurenziana, Florence, contains a page written in Cellini's own hand in which he states that he began to write the *Vita* himself but abandoned the project because he found it to be too time-consuming and wanted to devote himself fully to his art.[20] The lack of signs of true dictation in this manuscript, such as backtracking, restatements, or jumbled chronology, suggest that a text first dictated was subjected to later editing. Paolo Rossi has argued convincingly that the manuscript in the Laurenziana is, in fact, a clean copy prepared for the printer and that the actual first draft (or drafts) of the *Vita* was lost or destroyed.[21]

A word about manuscript history is in order. The whereabouts of the manuscript of the *Vita* from Cellini's death in 1571 to 1825 when it was bequeathed to the Laurenziana, where it remains to this day, can be traced clearly through textual evidence but with substantial lacunae. The *Vita* is not listed in the inventory of Cellini's household goods at his death.[22] In the 1630s the manuscript was in the hands of Scipione Ammirato *il Giovane* (the Younger), who compiled a two-volume set of miscellaneous accounts between 1632 and 1636 under the title *Zibaldone*.[23] In a brief section of volume 1 titled *Memorie estratte dalla Vita di Benvenuto Cellini*, Ammirato listed various episodes drawn from Cellini's *Vita* where the page numbers of events extracted from the *Vita* correspond to the page number of the folios of the Laurenziana manuscript.[24] In a 1675 letter Filippo Baldinucci claimed that the Cavalcanti family in Florence was in possession of "la *Vita* di Benvenuto Cellini scritta da sé medesimo . . . so che lo tengon caro."[25] The book turns up again in 1741 in the fourth edition of the *Vocabolario degli Accademici della Crusca*.[26] The Crusca, founded in 1583 by Anton Francesco Grazzini, Bastiano de' Rossi, and Leonardo Salviati under the protection of the Medici, devoted their energies to compiling and publishing the first important dictionary of the Italian language. While searching for texts to cite in the dictionary, Cellini's *Vita* reappeared.[27] In the entries on Cellini's contributions to their language dictionary, the academicians cite the autograph and not the printed edition of 1728, noting that the manuscript had moved from the Cavalcanti family to the collection of one of their own members, Francesco Redi: "Vita sua scritta da sé medesimo, testo a penna, che fu già di Lorenzo Maria Cavalcanti, poi tra i manoscritto di Francesco Redi."[28] From the hands of Redi, it turns up in the Library of the Scolopians in Florence who had taken over the property and patrimony of the Jesuits. As the story goes, one day a monk threw it into a box of books destined for the stall of the bookseller known only as Cecchino dal Seminario where it was bought, fortuitously, in 1805 by Luigi de Poirot. In 1825 Poirot bequeathed it to the Biblioteca Medicea Laurenziana in Florence.

The Confraternity of the Buonuomini of San Martino, founded in the fifteenth century and still active to this day, housed a number of Cellini's other writings. The last page of the printed edition of 1728 contains a note directly linking the Buonuomini to Cellini. This note states that many original documents of Cellini and his descendants were found "many years ago" at the *Compagnia di San Martino dei Buonuomini*.[29] In fact, in 1646 Cellini's son and legitimate heir, Andrea Simone named his nephew, Jacopo Maccanti, as his beneficiary. In Maccanti's last will and testament of 11 April 1655 he designated the Confraternity as his "erede universale" (i.e., beneficiary).[30] The archive of the Buonuomini contains a copy of this testament signed by the notary Ser Francesco Giuntini.[31] It seems that from 1655 to 1828 the Buonuomini's archive contained at least sixty-four original materials related to Cellini's life, including his letter of naturalization from King Francis I. This letter is a beautiful document on *cartapecora* with the king's own signature and seal.[32] On 18 July 1828 the *Buonuomo* Mattias Mazzei donated this group of documents to the Biblioteca Palatina, which later became the Biblioteca Nazionale Centrale in Florence.[33] In the book listing members of the Buonuomini, there is a certain Mattias del Cavaliere Antonio Mazzei (d. 1842).[34] The Biblioteca Palatina's director Anton Francesco Tassi listed all the documents he received from the Buonuomini on behalf of Leopold II (Peter Leopold).[35] Today this collection is known as the *Autografi Palatini Cellini*.

Cellini had difficulties publishing both his art treatises and his autobiography. At the end of his life he sent a letter to Cosimo's son, Prince Francesco I (1541–87), to whom he originally dedicated the *Two Treatises*, asking him why they had not yet been printed. In an entry on the verso of a sonnet in BRF Ricc. 2728, Cellini wondered why he has not received any news about his art treatises, lamenting that many months had passed since he sent the manuscript to Francesco: "so many months have passed since I gave my manuscript as a gift to the most Illustrious and Excellent Prince of Ours in 1567, and even though several times I asked him to print it, he had not indulged this whim of mine."[36] Cellini continues, claiming that he wanted to demonstrate his virtue to the world with words as well as with actions ("just as I still prove with my works of art, I wanted to show with my words"), but in the same breath he emphasizes that art triumphs over mere works, claiming that artistic works are "true facts and must always be shown before words" ("le opere sono i veri fatti e si debbono mostrare sempre prima che le parole").[37] This theme of saying versus doing, of words in place of actions, recurs in many of Cellini's writings from this period. When the art treatises appeared for the first time in print in 1568, Cellini had changed the dedication from Francesco to his brother, Cardinal Ferdinando I. The treatises also appeared in an expurgated form. The editor severely violated Cellini's text, downplaying its autobiographical elements to align it more clearly with the treatise genre. But censorship may also have played its part. The *Vita* would not find its way into print until 1728.

As a writer, Cellini is known primarily as an autobiographer. His larger-than-life portrait of his own life and times in the *Vita* has overshadowed his many other writings, especially his poetry. In fact, Cellini's verses are usually omitted from anthologies of Renaissance literature. A few lone voices, however, have remembered Cellini's skills as a poet even if we have forgotten them. The 1722 edition of Giulio Negri's *Istoria degli Scrittori Fiorentini* included Cellini, identifying him as a "fusore, scultore, architetto, e poeta."[38] The artist's lyric even earned him the praise of a great man of letters, himself an autobiographer. Vittorio Alfieri, too, claimed that "Benvenuto potea essere sommo poeta."[39] To this day, only a handful of modern critics have examined his lyric in any detail. In 1885 Adolfo Mabellini published the first collection of Cellini's poetry and subsequently a critical study of these verses.[40]

In 1900 Angelo Orvieto wrote a very brief piece about Cellini's poetry in a special edition of the journal *Il Marzocco* dedicated exclusively to Cellini.[41] Some fifty years passed before Bruno Maier published an important article on Cellini's poetry.[42]

The artist Cellini has fared better in critical circles. Art historians have written extensively on his art. Sir John Pope-Hennessy's masterpiece, a biography titled simply *Cellini* (1985), skillfully examines his entire artistic corpus, from his youthful medals to his mature marble sculptures. Although Pope-Hennessy's contributions to the scholarship on Cellini as artist are unparalleled, his observations on Cellini as writer or poet are less useful. At times Pope-Hennessy seems to read all of Cellini's writings through the same lens. Whether the autobiography, a letter, a sonnet, or a diary entry, he combed them all for information of a biographical nature. Pope-Hennessy's desire to show that Cellini wrote, in his words, "a careful and accurate book,"[43] has obscured a more complex view of Cellini's *Vita* as a rhetorical performance. Such transparent readings of Cellini's writings are commonplace. For Michael Cole, too, "the autobiographical element"[44] in a sonnet by Cellini takes precedence over more connotative levels of meaning. In his *Benvenuto Cellini: Opere non esposte e documenti notarili* (1984), Dario Trento published unedited notarial documents alongside his analysis of some lesser-known coins and medals now housed in the Museo Nazionale del Bargello in Florence. Trento attempted to integrate Cellini's art with his artistic writings and account books, but did not fully develop the relationship between Cellini's artistic writings and his literary texts.

The image of Cellini as social and sexual transgressor has also received wide critical attention. Drawing upon Luigi Greci's 1930 study of the court records documenting Cellini's numerous crimes, scholars such as Paolo L. Rossi and Ivan Arnaldi have examined his violent nature and criminal activities. Rossi's well-documented study of Cellini's criminal activity in his article "The Writer and the Man" (1994) and Arnaldi's thorough examination of Cellini's violent behavior, *La vita violenta di Benvenuto Cellini* (1986), help us see why critics have collapsed the distinction between the writing persona Cellini created for himself and the "historical" Cellini.[45] Rossi provides a useful study in which he enumerates the crimes the "real" Cellini committed that actually appear in his *Vita* and the crimes he omitted. But, like many scholars, Rossi implies that these omissions are calculated attempts by Cellini to cover up the "true" facts of his life. In fact, many Cellini critics appear to cling steadfastly to the notion that Cellini "lied" in his autobiography.

Scholars have tended overwhelmingly to situate the *Vita* between paradigms of unadorned truth and braggartly lying. This approach has plagued studies of Cellini's *Vita* and has limited serious analysis of the text, especially interpretations that take into account the rhetorical strategies and literary conventions of the *Vita*. To a modern reader, many events in the *Vita* appear "fictional," but by contemporary standards these fictional passages did not necessarily diminish the verisimilar nature of the work; rather, passages such as the episode of Cellini's journey to the Otherworld actually enhanced the *Vita* by connecting it to other important texts in the Italian vernacular tradition. Though the *Vita* conveys the essence of Cellini's experience, it has a more complicated relationship to truth than simply the transparent recording of "facts." Finally, this emphasis on what is missing from the *Vita* at times seems to engage scholars more than what is actually there. For instance, Patricia Rubin suggests that Vasari is more sincere than Cellini because "on the whole, the correspondence between the documentary record and Vasari's manipulation of his image through literary forms is remarkably close, unlike Cellini's, whose police file and Life diverge significantly."[46] This book is less concerned with whether the events narrated by Cellini are actually true and verifiable in historical sources, seeking instead to discover why Cellini chose to recount the stories that he did and in the way that he did.

One of the most troubling issues for Cellini critics is attempting to explain why his autobiography stands alone in its day for its utter lack of the traditional Pauline conversion. Autobiographies like Cellini's celebrating a life of violence and poems singing the joys of sexual intercourse between males are rare in European literature. In the story of his life Cellini celebrates his lawlessness, violence, and misogyny with nary a hint of remorse or apology, a shocking and puzzling fact for most modern readers. As Rudolph and Margot Wittkower first suggested, being an artist allowed Cellini a certain degree of license to misbehave and virtual immunity from prosecution. One recalls that Cellini was readily forgiven and pardoned by Pope Paul III for a series of crimes he committed in Rome, including murder. Other artists before and after Cellini, for example, Caravaggio, were also branded outlaws and troublemakers in their day, but not all were so easily let off. Caravaggio, for example, became a fugitive, behaving "like a hunted man"[47] after he killed a man in 1606, apparently after a quarrel over a game of tennis.

A second critical problem concerns Cellini's sexual identity and centers on his conviction for sodomy. Arnaldi's book devotes considerable attention to Cellini's sexual inclinations, but does not attempt to link his criminal acts with his literary practice. In the last decade, Cellini's homoerotic inclinations have been the subject of much critical debate. James M. Saslow's study of homosexuality in Renaissance art (*Ganymede in the Renaissance: Homosexuality in Art and Society*, 1986) and Leonard Barkan's examination of Renaissance homoeroticism (*Transuming Passion: Ganymede and the Erotics of Humanism*, 1991) both read Cellini's male nudes with an eye to classical ideals of masculine beauty and same-sex love. Following such theories, we find testimonies to Cellini's homoeroticism. In his writings, he celebrates male beauty; in his art, he staged the male nude; in his behavior, he had sexual encounters with boys as well as women. The *bottega* (artist's workshop) was a sexually charged and almost exclusively masculine space in the Italian Renaissance. Cellini's erotic interest in boys and his sexual activity with his assistant Fernando da Montepulciano are not disputed by scholars. What is debated is how to classify Cellini's sexuality. Chapter 2 offers an answer.

The debate surrounding Cellini's sexuality is a subtle one, centering on whether Cellini should be categorized as a sodomite, a homosexual, bisexual, gay, or, more recently, queer. Although the majority of critics argue against a historical genealogy of homoerotic experience, scholars like Pope-Hennessy have used terms such as "bisexual" to describe Cellini's sexuality.[48] If we posit a historical continuum of homoerotic experience through the centuries, as many scholars of sex and gender have been inclined to do, Cellini becomes a pivotal figure. Without taking recourse to semantics, we can still distinguish early modern homosexuality from its modern counterpart by considering the notion of identity. Michel Foucault helped us see how sexuality and identity were interrelated, and in particular, how the "discourses concerning sex" created modern subjects.[49] In the Renaissance one's sexual preference was not the linchpin of one's identity; in other words, sexuality was not the determining factor of one's identity. A male's choice of sexual partner did not necessarily condition the other choices he made or the roles he assumed in the society. Recent scholarship on court cases for sex crimes challenges us to consider whether every case of sodomy found in the archives is evidence of homosexuality, especially when we consider the broader definition of sodomy in Cellini's day. A related issue is the tendency of some critics to catalogue poets as homosexual who appear to have written no more than one or two sonnets in which the male poet speaks to a male object, as in the collection *Antologia della poesia omosessuale italiana dal tredicesimo secolo a oggi*, an established literary practice.[50] Nonetheless, Cellini's life and works are especially important because they provide evidence for tracing the contours of homoerotic desire through history.

Sodomy remained, to utilize Foucault again, a problem for both ecclesiastical and secular authorities for centuries in Italy and elsewhere throughout the early modern period.[51] In Cellini's day, prosecutions for sodomy were routine, even though convictions were less so.[52] Thousands of adult men were prosecuted; many convicted. Artists and artisans took their place alongside other men of different professions and social groups who were tried and convicted for the sex crime of sodomy. In literature, the association of artists, clerics, and men of letters with sodomy is a topos with a long history. When Dante asks his mentor Brunetto Latini to tell him "of his more famous and accomplished companions" among the sodomites, Latini responds: "In brief, know that they were all clerks and great men of letters, of great fame, all fouled with the same sin in the world."[53] In this context, Cellini's trial for this type of sex crime seems unexceptional. But several factors qualify the notion that Cellini's conviction was merely part of the normal course of judicial business in sixteenth-century Florence. He was the only major artist in the period, whose reputation as a Master had spread across France and Italy, to be convicted and imprisoned for sodomy. Cellini may merely be joining other men from various occupations convicted of sodomy in Florence during the reign of Cosimo I, but he is, without question, the most famous sodomite of all. Rumors circulated about the homoeroticism of other major artists, most notably Michelangelo, and Leonardo was formally charged twice without verdict, but no other artist of their caliber was convicted by a criminal court in Italy for these sexual acts.[54] What is exceptional about Cellini's case is precisely his artistic status at the time of the trial. By 1557 Cellini had achieved international fame throughout Europe.

Michael Rocke has suggested that sodomy was perceived as part of a "normal" manhood for Renaissance Florentines as long as it was only part of a temporary stage of life, usually during an experimental phase of youth. Prosecutions in Florence as well as Venice appear to confirm this theory. Sodomy prosecutions in these two cities tended to focus on groups of younger sodomites or on older men who continued their homoerotic activities beyond youth. Cellini was convicted not once, but twice for sodomy in Florence, first in 1523 and again in 1557. His two sodomy convictions fit both of these models. The earlier sodomy conviction fits the pattern of youthful sexual experimentation with other young males; the second, the pattern of an older man with a boy, often a pair joined through professional bonds. In chapter 2, I offer a reading of this specific case of male sexuality and desire in the context of contemporary cultural norms and consider more broadly how Cosimo used the sodomy trial to stage both his strict justice and his clemency. Scholarship in the fields of gender studies and cultural studies has stimulated reexamination of many Renaissance artists including Michelangelo, Bronzino, and Bandinelli.[55] Strangely, Cellini has remained outside this new sphere of inquiry. As noted, there exists just one monograph on Cellini the writer available in English, and not more than a handful of articles on Cellini the poet, all written in Italian. Although his *Vita* has frequently been anthologized in collections of Italian Renaissance literature, the *Vita* as a whole and its place in Cellini's literary oeuvre remains to be studied. The general scholarship on Cellini remains rather fragmented. Individual articles exist on disparate topics identified in Cellini's *Vita*. For instance, John Sturrock and Tylus have discussed the themes of fortune and labor, respectively, in the autobiography.[56] Moreover, articles on specific aspects of the *Vita* tend to view their topic in isolation. For example, Jonathan Goldberg's article on Cellini's use of earlier hagiographical models as well as Dino Cervigni's essay on Cellini's heroic disillusionment beg the question of how we reconcile the conflicting portraits of Cellini in the *Vita* as heroic martyr and Cellini the violent murderer.[57] Emphasis on the *Vita* as a spiritual autobiography and for other literary influences tends to ignore nonliterary genres as an influence on his writing.[58] Cellini's interest in other literary models besides autobiography affects not only the content of the stories he tells in the *Vita*, but also the narrative registers he selected. For Cellini, memory and tradition as well as contemporary gender norms and literary forms shaped his self-presentation in the story of his life. Furthermore, critical study integrating Cellini's artistic compositions with his literary writings is wholly lacking. For Cellini, art and literature were intimately intertwined. He viewed prose and poetry not as separate from his art but rather as other media worked by him. The artist Cellini shaped words much in the same spirit as he molded gold or bronze.

Although a few studies address the *Vita*'s rhetorical style, the literariness of the text remains marginal in Cellini scholarship.[59] Benedetto Croce was the first, perceptively, to claim that Cellini's seemingly simple prose betrayed a self-conscious literary style: "It is important to remember that simple and naive prose often requires the most effort."[60] While grounded in reality, the *Vita* is nonetheless an imaginative work by one of the Renaissance's greatest plastic artists. Analysis of Cellini's *Vita* must be linked to his written output as a whole, not only to his letters and account books but also to his art treatises and minor writings on art. Serious analysis of his poetry connects Cellini directly to a larger group of lesser-known poets—some artists, others not—who used the sonnet form as a forum for attacking court rivals as well as for expressing publicly their aesthetic judgments in contemporary debates on art. Finally, integration of texts and images, of Cellini's writings and his art, will provide the kind of comprehensive analysis necessary to understand fully the life and work of this unique Renaissance man.

Several other critical problems concerning the study of Cellini's life and works remain. His lively wordplay and double entendres, as well as his abundant use of pejoratives and diminutives are lost in available English translations. The most authoritative translation in English by George Bull—1956 and revised in 1998—is loose, often leaving out phrases at random, ignoring pejoratives and diminutives, and sanitizing much of Cellini's sexually charged language. For instance, the Parisian judge's clarification that Caterina accused Cellini of performing sexual acts "outside the canal" normally used for sexual intercourse is translated by Bull as merely "another way."[61] In addition, the now commonplace division of the *Vita* into books and chapters, found in all modern editions of his autobiography, was not done by Cellini himself. Furthermore, most modern editions of the *Vita* still mistakenly use Vasari's portrait of Ammannati rather than Cellini on their covers, as Bellotto's 1996 edition does, perhaps following Bacci's critical edition of 1901.[62] The likeness of the old, white-bearded man who is face-to-face with the figure of Bandinelli to the viewer's left in the Vasari tondo is not incompatible with the presumed portrait of Cellini in the guise of Vulcan in Vasari's painting *The Forge of Vulcan* (ca. 1565; figure 12). Both of these figures are depicted in the same profile.

Two overlooked areas indicate the possibility of a major reevaluation of Cellini's status as an uneducated artisan who merely imitated passages from the few literary works he had read. The first is Cellini's handwriting, which will be discussed in chapter 4. His hand is easy to recognize.[63] An elegant chancery italic (*italica*), it is neat and regular. For a sample of the artist's handwriting, see figure 13.[64] The artist also had the habit of using catchwords when he had many pages to write. For instance, the leaves of the Laurenziana manuscript written in Cellini's hand (fols. 464v–520r) contain catchwords, written horizontally, at the bottom verso of each page, with the exception of one folio without a catchword, fol. 480v. Because Cellini often signed documents written by an amanuensis, as in the letter to Giovanni Caccini housed in the Newberry Library,[65] autographs of his are considered rare. A second ignored issue is Cellini's innovative use of language, explored in chapter 3. In his writings, for instance, Cellini invented words, created lively puns, and used double entendres. In addition, the artist created a new alphabet using a goldsmith's tools as letters. It was a kind of secret code for members of the Academy of Design. Throughout the early modern period a foreign ambassador wrote his letters to the secretary of the chancellery in secret code. No documents survive showing that Cellini wrote in cipher.[66] As we shall see in chapter 3, Cellini invented at least one new word and used some strange words in his writings.

The notion that Cellini was a reflexive writer is not widely accepted by scholars. Yet anyone as conscious as Cellini was of his reputation and public honor in life is likely to be just as conscious of his self-presentation in literature. While it is certainly true that Cellini was not a major poet, he was highly conscious of poetic forms and conventions. He was a versatile poet. Skilled in versification, he composed madrigals, *canzoni*, and other poetic forms in addition to his more than one hundred sonnets. The artist's literary writings do reflect conscious rhetorical strategies. Cellini clearly sought to place himself within the literary tradition, using—and simultaneously abusing—the literary models that he knew, including the Bible, Dante, and Petrarch. Moreover, he experimented with a range of literary genres. Renaissance authors, even nonprofessional ones, viewed the self as both a subject of speech and writing (subjectively, in the first person) and an object of inquiry (objectively, in the third person). Autobiographies in particular, where the author creates both the narrator and the protagonist, demonstrate this doubleness.

The goal of this book is to present a multilayered study of the multifaceted Cellini: artist, writer, poet, convicted sodomite. The meticulous, almost "maniacal" attention to detail in Cellini's writings recalls the jeweler's eye for small detail.[67] The ascent in prestige of Cellini's artworks in the second half of the *Vita* works as a kind of figure of Cellini's own self-fashioning: the salt-cellar and other decorative works for Francis I, the three marble sculptures of *Ganymede, Narcissus,* and *Apollo and Hyacinth*, the casting of the *Perseus*, the marble crucifix, and "achieved" comparison with Michelangelo. Several motifs figure prominently in this book, including sex crime, imprisonment and restraint, and art and writing. Sex and violence recur as the dominant themes in Cellini's life and works, and the chapters that follow explicitly take them up. Honor ties the chapters together, since honor permeates all of Cellini's literary and artistic labors. The various roles that Cellini adopts in the story of his life are all forms of claiming status and honor as well as ways the artist negotiated his ties with the literary past.

CHAPTER 2
CRIMINAL ACTS AND
LITERARY PRACTICE

Benvenuto Cellini began composing his autobiography while under house arrest for the sex crime of sodomy. On 27 February 1557 the renowned sculptor and goldsmith, who had worked at the courts of powerful popes and kings, was convicted in Florence of sodomy (see appendix 3.A). The criminal court that passed judgment on him ruled:

> Benvenuto di Maestro Giovanni Cellini scultore, cittadino fiorentino... perchè circa di cinque anni or sono passati esso ha tenuto per suo ragazzo Fernando di Giovanni da Montepulciano, giovanetto con il quale ha usato carnalmente moltissime volte col nefando vitio di soddomia, tenendolo in letto come sua moglie... in obedienza delle leggi condannano detto Benvenuto in scudi 50 d'oro da pagarsi... et più lo confinano a stare quattro anni in le Stinche... et lo privano in perpetuo delli offitii, secondo il tenore di dette leggi.[1]

> (Benvenuto, son of Master Giovanni Cellini, sculptor and Florentine citizen... for about the last five years this Cellini had kept as his boy Fernando di Giovanni da Montepulciano, a youth who he used most frequently sexually engaging in the despicable vice of sodomy, keeping him in bed as if he was his wife... thus in accordance with the law this court condemns the said Benvenuto to pay a fine of 50 golden scudi... and to serve four years in the prison known as the Stinche... and strips him for life of holding public office, following the tenor of the said laws.)

In the wake of a formal appeal by Cellini to Duke Cosimo I de' Medici, the magistrates commuted the prison term to house arrest. Cellini's conviction for sodomy offers us a unique opportunity to examine relations between the duke, his judges, and criminals in Florence as well as between patrons and clients. It serves as a case study of Cosimo's personal involvement in legal matters in Florence and illustrates how Cosimo positioned himself strategically vis-à-vis the courts and his subjects first by enacting strict legislation and then by mitigating it with his clemency. Cosimo thus presented himself as a firm, yet compassionate ruler. The loss of ducal favor and the humiliation of imprisonment for the sex crime of sodomy in turn led the irascible artist into a scathing attack on Medicean politics.

A careful reading of Cellini's *Vita* brings out the presence of a legal register in the artist's autobiography. In telling the story of his life, the narrator informs the reader: "Io non voglio mancare che io non dica le mie ragione [*sic*] giustamente e santamente" (I don't want to fail to tell my own reasons fairly and honestly [Bellotto, 409]). The comment reveals how Cellini's autobiography is, in fact, a self-defense and how the trial metaphor is fundamental to its structure. This chapter will show how the prosecutorial mode underlies Cellini's *Vita* and his other writings. Cellini's *Vita* can be read not only as an apology or confession (traditional rationales for the writing of autobiography) but also as a judicial defense in which Cellini as author rewrites his experiences in court so that Cellini as protagonist triumphs. The *Vita* participates in a new genre of discourse, to borrow from Tzvetan Todorov's formulation, what I will call judging.[2] This discursive genre helps create "the self" in a double sense: as both an object of inquiry and a subject of speech and writing. In addition, this chapter will consider the recent resurrection of Cellini as a kind of gay icon, as attested by his appearance in numerous anthologies of gay literature.

Cellini as Paradigmatic Sodomite

In order to contextualize Cellini's trial for sodomy, it is useful to recall earlier sodomy legislation and prosecution in Florence. In contrast to the situation north of the Alps, sodomy cases appear frequently in Italian courts, particularly in Venice and Florence where sodomy fell under the jurisdiction of the civil courts. In both cities, sodomy was clearly defined in the law: it encompassed a broad range of non-procreative sexual acts perceived as disruptive of the natural social order. These acts commonly included anal intercourse, whether between men or between men and women, and intercourse with the woman on top. Sodomy was deemed to be "against Nature" because it overturned the divinely ordained purpose of sex, procreation. It was also considered dangerous to the social fabric because, for one, it violated the strict gender roles prescribed for men and women even in sexual intercourse itself. In "normal" sex, men took the active, dominant role of penetrator; women, the passive, subordinate role of being penetrated. In sodomy, the moralists argued, men were behaving like women, women like men.

Some men even forfeited marriage and offspring, they claimed, disregarding their civic duty to society: "Sodomy threatened to undermine the basic organizational units of society—family, male–female bonding, reproduction."[3] For Renaissance magistrates, sodomy constituted an act, not an identity: a person was prosecuted for doing something that was deemed sodomitical, not for being a certain type of individual. The term "sodomite" was applied to men who took the active, dominant role in sex and was understood to describe "both a man who had sex with boys and a man who engaged in the same illicit sexual acts with women."[4] In sodomy laws, Genesis 19 is the reference. Repeated violations of the sodomy law carried a symbolic penalty of death by burning.

Although sodomy could occur in heterosexual relations, most sodomy cases prosecuted by Italian courts involved sexual acts between males. In Venice, prosecution "focused on two themes: anal intercourse [between males] and its external simulation between the thighs of a passive partner."[5] In Florence, the regulation of sodomitical practices had long been a matter of official concern. As early as 1432 Florentine officials established a special magistracy solely to prosecute sodomy, the *Ufficiali di Notte* (The Night Officers). Theoretically, the Night Officers could prosecute any act that fell under the rubric of sodomy, but in practice they dealt primarily with sexual intercourse between males: "The Night Officers' main responsibility was and always remained the policing of sexual acts between males."[6] Over a twenty-four year period (1478–1502), the Night Officers prosecuted over 4,000 men for homosexual sodomy.[7] From 1432 to 1502, as many as 17,000 persons were accused of sodomy, and about 3,000 were convicted.[8] When the Night Officers disbanded in 1502, the prosecution of sodomy was passed to two other bodies, the Otto di Guardia e Balìa (Eight on Public Safety) and the Conservatori di Legge (Guardians of the Law).

At the time of Cellini's sojourn in Florence (1545–71), Duke Cosimo redefined and expanded, in at least two important ways, the role and powers of the ruler vis-à-vis the courts: first, by reforming and harshening existing sodomy laws and then by overseeing the supplication process that mitigated penalties for convicted criminals. His law of 8 July 1542, reflected "a hardening of attitudes toward sodomy and a repressive turn in measures to police it."[9] Earlier sodomy legislation had imposed mild fines on convicted sodomites, and had granted younger partners, whether active or passive, a kind of immunity.[10] In contrast, Cosimo decreed that younger, passive partners were no longer immune from prosecution. Similarly, long-term imprisonment or exile had replaced fines as the standard penalty for a first-time conviction for the active, older partner. Cosimo's innovation in sodomy legislation was to introduce a policy that temporarily removed convicted sodomites from society by imposing longer terms of imprisonment in the Stinche, the old Florentine debtors' jail.

Cosimo's new sodomy law was the one applied to Cellini. In the court records, the Otto di Guardia charged Cellini with being the older, active partner in a long-term sexual relationship with Fernando, a male youth most likely between the ages of thirteen and eighteen who worked in his goldsmith's shop, probably as an apprentice. The language used by the magistrates in the official sentence follows a pattern common to sodomy cases: using the grammatical subject and object to express the social relation between the two. In this case, Cellini is the subject of the verbs "tenere" (to keep) and "usare con" (to use with), and thereby the active, masculine partner in the sexual encounter.[11] Other archival documents from Cellini's court case show idiomatic uses of the phrase "usare con" to describe sexual relations between master and student. One such instance is a summary of the charge written in an unknown hand appearing on Cellini's letter of supplication to Cosimo: "Benvenuto Cellini per aver usato la sodomia più tempo con Fernando giovanetto suo alievo fu dal magistrato nostro Otto dì 27 detto passato condannato secondo le leggi."[12] The phrase *usare con* in this and other instances could have the feel of a middle voice in Greek: used him in his [Cellini's] own interests; or perhaps it suggests a mutual act between two people. In another archival document, to my knowledge unpublished, the magistrates referred to Cellini as "having sodomized Fernando."[13] Passive partners in sodomy denunciations were frequently feminized, referred to as whore, bitch, woman, or, as in Fernando's case, wife.[14]

Cellini was found guilty and his name was registered in the magistracy's *Book of Condemned Criminals* (Condannati) indicating that he was expected to serve a four-year prison sentence.[15] Ten days earlier, on 17 February 1557, Cellini was captured in Scarperia in an attempt to flee the area; he was arrested and remanded to Florence.[16] On 2 March 1557 Cosimo's chancellor, Ser Francesco Lapucci, notified Cellini of the court's ruling. The vote of seven black beans signified a conviction.[17] It appears that immediately thereafter, Cellini was imprisoned in the Stinche.

This was Cellini's second conviction for sodomy, and since it provides evidence that Cellini probably had a lifelong erotic interest in boys, I will briefly provide the details of the first case.[18] This first conviction for the sex crime of sodomy occurred in 1523 and also took place in Florence. The magistrates charged Cellini and a certain Giovanni di

Ser Matteo Rigoli with committing sodomy on Domenico di Ser Giuliano da Ripa. The authorities sentenced him as the adult and active partner to a fine, paid not in cash but as twelve bushels of flour.

In examining Cellini's 1557 case, previous scholars have overlooked a crucial element. Cosimo's sodomy law of 1542 contained a special provision that was used against Cellini: the right of the courts to levy harsher penalties against men convicted of having sexual relations with the same partner over a long period of time. The provision had been designed to draw "a sharper distinction between those whose involvement in sodomy was fleeting or casual and those, more culpable and subject to greater stigma, whose illicit erotic activity was more intense or habitual."[19] The court records reveal that the magistrates accused Cellini of being one of those men regarded as the most dangerous to the social order because their sexual acts with boys were not part of a temporary "stage" in life. In their eyes, Cellini fit the profile of an older (and unmarried) sodomite for whom boys were the primary erotic or affective focus. The language of the sentence is replete with terms that try to determine the quantity and quality of Cellini's sexual relations with Fernando, whom they claim the artist, "for quite some time" had sodomized "very many times."[20]

On 3 March 1557, the day following the notification of the verdict, Cellini addressed a letter of supplication to Duke Cosimo who, as we noted above, oversaw the process that mitigated sentences, particularly when they involved long-term incarceration.[21] The system of supplication involved only the writing of a letter to the duke and "amounted to a kind of negotiation between the violator and [the duke], in which the sentence was, in effect, a mutually agreed upon compromise."[22] In his letter, Cellini appeals to the duke's "most merciful and compassionate" nature and implores him to commute the prison term to house arrest, astutely using his marble crucifix as a kind of bargaining chip (see appendix 1). If Cosimo were to grant it, Cellini promised to dedicate the remainder of his life to the duke's service. Cellini's letter reveals his concerns for his public reputation and his professional career. The artist feared that this judgment would damage his reputation and cause him shame. A second letter, from the Bishop of Pavia (Girolamo de' Rossi), dated 22 March 1557, was sent to the duke on Cellini's behalf. According to Brackett, such letters, written by reliable moral authorities, and attesting to the good character of the supplicants, often led to a favorable outcome. Cosimo heard Cellini's plea and granted the request on 26 March, commuting the prison term to house arrest, thus fashioning himself as the just, clement ruler to whom Cellini had appealed. The next day, the Otto di Guardia officially commuted the sentence.

As Dario Trento has suggested, Cosimo may well have used the sodomy trial as a pretext for punishing Cellini for his bad behavior: "È difficile pensare che la carcerazione per sodomia non fosse stata manovrata strumentalmente nella corte di Cosimo I per influire in qualche modo sui comportamenti dell'artista."[23] Letters exchanged between Cosimo and Vincenzo Borghini, the superintendent of the Florentine foundling hospital for abandoned children and the duke's representative of the Accademia del Disegno, suggest that both Cosimo and Borghini felt Cellini was "boastful and dilatory."[24]

Cellini's enemies as well as friends noted that his behavior was particularly inappropriate toward his patrons. In 1539 Annibal Caro wrote from Rome to his friend Luca Martini in Florence saying that Cellini's peculiar manner of speaking brazenly to authorities made the pope fear him more for "what he can do or say in the future than what he has done or said in the past."[25] In the 1568 edition of the *Lives*, Giorgio Vasari, too, noted that Cellini behaved boldly and brashly toward his patrons, and accused him of being "a person who has been only too well able to speak for himself with Princes."[26] In a sonnet written while in prison in Florence, Cellini himself muses that he may have been incarcerated for having spoken too boldly.[27]

Unfortunately for Cellini, Duke Cosimo was not prepared to put up with detractors. By the 1540s, in fact, the duke was keen to use the law to silence opposition and consolidate his power. Cosimo's reformed sodomy law of 1542 furnished him with "an additional weapon to use against his enemies,"[28] real or perceived. A case in point might be a special decree against sodomy issued by Cosimo on 26 December 1543. When Giovanni Bandini and Pandolfo Pucci, two aristocrats close to the duke, were incarcerated in the Stinche for having committed sodomy, a number of other men of similar station and sexual orientation immediately fled the city in a panic. Cosimo's decree called for them to return to Florence to be pardoned and then noted that any further violations would be punished according to the law, that is, by decapitation.[29] Cellini's contemporary Bernardo Segni, referring to the Bandini-Pucci case, insisted that Cosimo's ultimate goal in legal matters was "the obedience of his subjects."[30]

This episode and other sodomy cases illustrate Cosimo's concern that sodomy not be (openly) practiced in Florence by any social group, including aristocrats and members of religious orders. At the same time, however, it appears that Cosimo wanted to handle these cases discreetly, especially when aristocrats were involved. Cosimo's discretion extended also to the punishment, for the duke seems to have wanted convicted sodomites removed from society, but not executed. The harshness of the decree was, therefore, mitigated by the duke's clemency. The language of the law is symbolic: Cosimo's laws are an emblem of the values and official vision of the Medici regime. In addition, a prince needed to use power in order to demonstrate that he had it. Thus, the act of making a law and subsequently granting a *grazia* was a way in which Cosimo could demonstrate to one and all that he truly exercised power and was a ruler. In this context the phrase *fare grazia* carries with it the divine connotation of bestowing grace.

The Pucci case suggests that social standing may no longer have protected the wealthy and powerful from criminal prosecution during Cosimo's reign. In 1545 Cosimo informed all state officials that "their behavior could be denounced anonymously by private citizens."[31] It will be useful to recall that Benedetto Varchi, perceived as a political dissident, ideologically at odds with the Medicean regime, was imprisoned in 1545 on what appears to be trumped-up charges of seducing a young girl. Cellini, one of only two salaried artists at the Medici court in 1550, was listed as a member of the duke's household as late as 1555, only a year, it seems, before the investigation into his sexual transgressions.[32] After his return from France in 1545, Cellini was internationally known and appreciated for his various artistic projects. His lifelong efforts bore dramatic financial fruit: his fame and honor had spread across Europe.

Cosimo's clemency went hand in hand with the influence he exerted over the law courts. First, Cosimo was, to paraphrase Cellini, "the master of the law."[33] He also accepted or denied petitions sent to the Otto di Guardia to mitigate a penalty. Cosimo was briefed daily by the secretary as to what came before the Otto. By 1556, as Giovanni Antonelli has also pointed out, Cosimo expanded his powers over the Florentine criminal magistracy by intervening directly in criminal cases, effectively limiting the autonomy of the court. Through his two appointed officers, the secretary and the chancellor of the Otto di Guardia (who often served long terms), Cosimo was able to keep a "strict surveillance" on the operations of the criminal court, in some instances interfering even before the court brought down sentences that "did not conform to his will."[34]

What Cosimo did with the criminal courts is not out of character, for he took control of a range of judicial institutions during his many years in power. For instance, he manipulated the Office of Decency (*Onestà*) by requiring prostitutes to register and pay taxes that would then go to support the convent of the Convertite, which had been set up, ironically, to house repentant prostitutes. He was responsible for policies that required prostitutes to live only in approved areas of the city and to wear a yellow veil that would distinguish them from "respectable" Florentine women.[35] Cosimo also sought control over cultural, as well as legal, bodies. As Michel Plaisance has shown, by appropriating the Accademia degli Umidi, an independent academy composed of a small group of men of letters, and transforming it the Accademia Fiorentina, an official organ of the state, Cosimo was able, in the 1540s, to eliminate those who did not adhere to the new values of the regime.[36] The drastic reform of the Accademia Fiorentina in 1547, which ejected virtually all of the artists, including Cellini, was designed to impose "silence and the control of speech, as well as the censorship of the written word."[37] This censorship of art in the secular realm paralleled the censorship of art in a religious domain begun at precisely this same time in Florence as a result of the Council of Trent.

The Forensic Quality of the *Vita*

Cellini's trial provoked a confession, albeit a literary one. At the same time in which Cellini was under house arrest for the sodomy conviction, he began writing his autobiography. This helps explain why the text is written in a defensive posture. Cellini's *Vita* transgresses the confessional mode: the textual "I" does not make the journey from error to rectitude. Unlike Augustine, Cellini does not contrast his former self and status as sinner with his present self and status as convert. Rather than using confession as a redeeming strategy for conversion, Cellini instead displays a bold shamelessness and arrogance, neither apologizing for his actions nor asking the reader for forgiveness, but rather appealing to the reader as witness, almost as juror.

Cellini's actual court appearances—not only for sodomy but for a range of different, violent crimes—gave him ample awareness of legal language and procedure, a "mode" that clearly informs certain narrative passages in his *Vita*. Critics have long noted that Cellini acts as if he is on stage, as if he is performing for an audience. If this is true, most of his stage appearances take place in courtrooms. In fact, the pattern of the lawsuit is a fundamental structural feature of the narrative. The characters Cellini meets in the story of his life primarily accuse him of crimes: they charge him with sodomy, murder, theft, counterfeiting, and speech crimes against the Medici. These moments of legal defense are some of the rare instances in the text when the split between the narrator and the protagonist is most acute. For example, when Pier Luigi Farnese exhorts his father, the pope, to punish Cellini for murdering a rival goldsmith, Cellini acts as his own counsel in the courtroom scene in Rome. In many of the *Vita*'s trial episodes, Cellini as narrator suddenly surfaces and addresses the reader directly, using the present tense, as he does here when relating the aftermath of Baccio Bandinelli's sodomy accusation: "[S]appiate, benigni lettori, che dentro mi scoppiava 'l cuore, considerato che uno . . . fussi tanto ardito, in presenza di un così gran principe, a dirmi una tanta et tale ingiuria" (You should know, gentle readers, that, inside, my heart was bursting, considering that one man . . . was so bold, in the presence of such a great prince, to say such an insult [Bellotto, 655]). The tone of the *Vita* derives in great measure from this practice of autobiography as defense. In another place, Cellini uses the rhetorical device of apostrophe to defend himself against the accusations of Cosimo's majordomo Pier Francesco Ricci: "Or senti un terribile accidente, piacevolissimo lettore" (Now let me tell you about a grave misfortune, dearest reader [Bellotto, 684]). In this context the narrator makes the astonishing claim that "Iddio amatore della verità mi difese" [Bellotto, 684]). Reading the autobiography as a trial, then, allows us to view the split between the narrator and the protagonist on another level: Cellini-narrator plays the part of the public defender who attempts to defend the actions and conduct of his client, Cellini-protagonist.

Cellini saw his own life through the lens of the trial format, and so it is not surprising that his autobiography reads like a legal transcript. In the story of his life Cellini speaks as if to an accusing tribunal. This legal mode or grid of legal structures through which Cellini viewed the contours of his own life is found in a range of texts and testimonies of his day. For example, Cellini's contemporary Francesco Guicciardini (1483–1540) wrote two works, titled the *Oratio Accusatoria* and the *Defensoria contra precedentem* (ca. 1527), in which he makes speeches posing as both prosecutor and public defender, first accusing himself of a crime and then defending himself against the charge he brought on himself.[38] In the *Accusatoria* the prosecutor (io) accuses Guicciardini (lui) of a long list of serious crimes in front of the judges (giudici) of the Florentine court of the Quarantìa: "messer Francesco Guicciardini, uomo rubatore de' danari publici, saccheggiatore del nostro contado, uomo che ha esosa la vita privata, desideroso del ritorno de' Medici, amatore della tirannide, occupatore del vostro Palazzo, inimico capitalissimo della commune libertà, e finalmente pieno di sì gravi, di sì noti e di sì odiosi peccati" (Messer Francesco Guicciardini, a man who stole public funds, sacked our countryside, corrupted private life, wanted the Medici to return, a lover of tyranny, who occupied our Palazzo [della Signoria], the deadliest enemy of communal liberty, and finally full of such grave, such well-known, and such hated sins [*Autodifesa*, 126]).

In the *Defensoria* the defendant (io), addressing the judges (voi), defends himself against his accuser (lo accusatore mio). This fragmented self is perhaps reintegrated in Guicciardini's third oration, the *Consolatoria*. Here the narrator (io) offers solace to Guicciardini (tu), using the language of honor and virtù.

Cellini strikes a similar pose in the story of his life. The artist's imagined tribunal includes his nemesis Baccio Bandinelli and his French mistress Caterina, both of whom charge him with sodomy. Imagining oneself on trial was common in Cellini's day even among those individuals not charged with a crime and actually put on trial. Tasso, for example, was so plagued by such prosecutorial thoughts that he insisted that the Inquisition interrogate him.

The new genre I have labeled judging came into being in what Todorov has called its "historically attested codification of discursive properties."[39] Several historical factors help explain the emergence of this new discursive genre in Cellini's day, including reforms of the Church and Papacy, the expansion of the definition of heresy, and an increase in prosecutions by the Inquisition after the Council of Trent. The discourse of judging was crucial to the formation of the modern subject.

The trial was a defining moment of early modern subjectivity. Paradoxically, it is the trial format itself, intended to silence the voices of social transgressors, that, in reality, produces its opposite—the words, the speech of the accused. This includes not only testimony from the accused but also testimony about the accused, producing reams of scribal transcription and infinite webs of legal documentation. The judicial procedure, in fact, produces that which it condemns, provoking the accused to then, in turn, condemn the society.

These acts of defense, which form "a special class of writing"[40] in the Renaissance, extend beyond texts identified by their authors as apologies or defenses, such as Guicciardini's humanist orations or Tasso's *Apologia in difesa della* Gerusalemme Liberata (1585), to encompass a variety of texts across a wide range of genres. This defensive mode of discourse includes autobiographies, confessional manuals, and handbooks of penance, as well as transcripts from actual trials. Cellini's autobiography forms part of a larger, legal cultural phenomenon in his day, what I have called judging. Paolo Prodi has suggested that, over the course of the High Middle Ages, the Church reorganized the administration of penance "non più come una liturgia ma in uno stile giuridico, come un processo in cui il confessore è il giudice."[41] In addition, these acts of defense represent an attitude toward the past that shapes the way one looks to the future. As Margaret Ferguson and Thomas Greene among others have suggested, this defensive stance toward the past becomes emblematic of the ambiguities of humanism itself.[42] Cellini's description of his trial, then, can be construed as an allegory about how to stage and negotiate one's relationship with one's literary predecessors.

Turning back to sodomy, although in the *Vita* the artist kept silent about his conviction for sodomy, sodomy itself appears often in his writings. Cellini clearly knew what sodomy was: in the context of Caterina's accusation analyzed below, he defined it as sexual intercourse "contra natura, cioè in soddomia" (Bellotto, 548). It involved an active and passive partner, what Cellini called an "agente" and a "paziente" (Bellotto, 551). In his autobiography Cellini tells how in 1546, in front of Cosimo and his entire court, Bandinelli, "voltomisi con quel suo bruttissimo visaccio, a un tratto mi disse: 'Oh sta' cheto, soddomitaccio!'" (Bellotto, 655). Cellini, filled with fury, responded not by denying he was a sodomite, but by feigning ignorance of, in his words, that "noble art" of the gods (*nobile arte*), and that "marvelous thing" practiced by the world's greatest emperors and kings (*mirabil cosa* [Bellotto, 655]). His defensive words here are ironic, since Bandinelli's hostile remark was triggered by Cellini's suggestion to Cosimo that he would create his *Ganymede* (figures 5 and 6) out of an incomplete antique marble statue. As such, it provides further evidence of the artist's transgressivity who challenged cultural norms by openly suggesting a homoerotic subject for the marble.

In an earlier situation in France, Cellini had responded to his model's charge of sodomy against him, understood here to be anal sex with a woman, with a lively wordplay on two sets of national practices, "il modo italiano" and "il modo franzese" (Bellotto, 551). In this episode, Cellini purposefully misunderstands the meanings attributed to these terms by the other two, a factor that provides the principle source of humor in the passage. The courtroom scene in Paris is a true comedy of errors, replete with wordplay and semantic slippage:

> Allora il ditto giudice si volse a Caterina e le disse: "Caterina, di' tutto quel che t'è occorso d'avere a fare con Benvenuto."
> La Caterina disse che io avevo usato seco al modo della Italia.
> Il giudice voltosi a me, disse: "Tu senti quel che Caterina dice, Benvenuto."
> Allora io dissi: "Se io avessi usato seco al modo italiano, l'arei fatto solo per desiderio d'avere un figliuolo, sì come fate voi altri."
> Allora il giudice replicò dicendo: "Ella vuol dire che tu hai usato seco fuora del vaso dove si fa figliuoli."
> A questo io dissi che quello non era il modo italiano; anzi che doveva essere il modo franzese, da poi che lei sapeva et io no.

(Then the said judge turned to Caterina and said to her: "Caterina, tell us everything that took place between you and Benvenuto." Caterina said that I had sex with her in the way they did in Italy. The judge turned to me and said: "You hear what Caterina says, Benvenuto." Then I said: "If I had sex with her in the Italian way, I would have done so because I want to have a son, just as you all do." Then the judge replied, saying: "She means that you had sex with her outside the canal where one makes children." To this I said that that was not the Italian way; on the contrary, it had to be the French way, since she knew about it, and I didn't. [Bellotto, 551])

In the end, Cellini does not admit his guilt, but rather disrupts the court proceedings shouting, "Burn them (Caterina and her mother)! Burn them!," thus prompting the judge to throw the case, and Cellini, out of court.

Homoerotic Desire and Homosocial Bonds in the Renaissance

The artist's *bottega* was one of many sites for male–male erotics in the Renaissance. The nature of this professional relationship meant that the master's male assistants and apprentices often slept in the workshop itself, if not in the same beds. This does not necessarily imply sexual intimacy, but the workshop itself surely provided a place/space for male sexual activity and experimentation. It also helped forge the homosocial bonds, in this case between the goldsmith and his male assistants, that structured societal organization and the very nature of male culture in the Renaissance. Master–student relations were often grounds for the charge of sodomy: "the common bed of a master and his servant might suggest something much darker."[43]

Homoerotics colors images of the *bottega* in Cellini's *Vita*. Cellini's youthful male friendships and relations with his young assistants and apprentices are fraught with homoerotic potential, if not overtly sexual potential. What Barkan identifies as the *Vita*'s many "lovingly described homoerotic sentiments"[44] includes Cellini's youthful love for Francesco Lippi: "Nel praticare insieme generò in noi un tanto amore, che mai, né dì né notte, stavamo l'uno senza l'altro" (In working together, such a great love was born between us, that never, neither day nor night, were we apart [Bellotto, 46]). In addition, instances of the homoerotic potential of male friendships are evident in many places in the *Vita*, such as the bond between Cellini and Piero Landi who "ci volevamo bene più che se fratelli fussimo stati" (we loved each other more than if we had been brothers [Bellotto, 63]), and that between the artist and a certain Albertaccio del Bene who "a me voleva bene quanto a sé medesimo" (loved me as much as himself [Bellotto, 261]).

We find expressions of Cellini's homoeroticism in the content of his art. Besides his famous *Perseus* (completed 1554), other male nudes of the artist include three marble statues of *Ganymede* (figures 5 and 6), *Apollo and Hyacinth* (figure 7), and *Narcissus* (figure 8). For Saslow, Cellini's choice of the *Ganymede* in particular was "ideally suited to embody the principal patterns of homosexuality at the time."[45] On more than one occasion, Cellini celebrates male beauty in his writings. For instance, in the *Vita* Cellini describes his model Diego, a Spanish boy involved in Cellini's famous cross-dressing prank in Rome (where he dresses up Diego as a woman and brings him/her to a party as his date) as "bello di persona, maraviglioso di color di carne; lo intaglio della sua testa era assai più bello che quello antico di Antino, e molte volte lo avevo ritratto" ([Diego was] beautiful and had a marvelous skin tone; the profile of his head was even more beautiful than the ancient one of Antinous, and many times I had drawn him [Bellotto, 107]).[46] In the *Vita* Cellini extols both male and female beauty.

In his writings, Cellini not only refused to keep silent about, but indeed celebrated, the pleasures of sodomitical sex and the joys of male love. In one of his sonnets beginning "Porca fortuna, s' tu scoprivi prima / che ancora a me piacessi 'l Ganimede!" (Maier, 900–01), for instance, Cellini celebrates his reputation as a whoremonger who unceremoniously abandons Fortune, presented in the guise of an earthly woman lover, for a male lover, his beloved Ganymede. This sonnet conforms to the model of the *accusatio* discussed earlier. The openness about male love and sexual pleasure between males evident in Cellini's poetry stands in stark contrast to the near silence and defensiveness about these subjects in the artist's autobiography. This notion that the form—the artist's choice of genre—in some sense conditions what he can or will express is strengthened by Cellini's use of the lyrical and mythological term "ganymede" in his sonnets to signify sexual intercourse between males that may include love or desire, while employing the legal term "sodomy" when referring to these same acts or desires in the *Vita*. In another sonnet ("Già tutti i Santi, ancor Saturno e Giove") the artist employs the term "ganymede" to signify homoeroticism: "chi dicie ch'io ci son per Ganimede; / altri che troppo aldacie i' ho parlato" (Maier, 900).[47] In the *Vita* there is innuendo without direct engagement on Cellini's part: the artist's reply to Bandinelli's accusation is not a denial, but it is hardly an admission. This is not surprising when we recall how the *Vita* has a forensic quality, where Cellini poses as if he were defending himself before a tribunal. Bandinelli's remarks illustrate the use of sodomy as slander. Of course, there was no firm boundary between the language of law and literature: Domenico da Prato penned a poem attacking sodomites that he titled "In opprobrium of sodomy."[48] Cellini seemed well aware of the differences in age and social status between male partners in these sexual acts. In his art, the artist staged his marble group of *Apollo with Hyacinth* (1546–48) as the adult male god with a boy.

Turning from Cellini's art to our own cultural fascination with the great artist, Cellini has, in recent years, been resurrected as a kind of gay icon. He appears, for example, in the 1995 collection titled *The Penguin Book of International Gay Writing* and more recently in *A History of Gay Literature* (1998).[49] In the Penguin anthology, Cellini's date with the cross-dresser Diego was chosen by the editor because it "illuminate[s] the experience of love between men, explore[s] the nature of homosexual identity, or investigate[s] the kinds of relationships gay men have with each other, with their friends, and with their families."[50] In *A History of Gay Literature*, Cellini is invoked on two occasions, first as a central figure in the pantheon of gay men from the past, and then again briefly in the section concerning Marcel Proust's "homo-erotic set pieces" involving Swann's dreamy vision that a young footman in the Sainte-Euverte household resembles an "'angel or sentinel' by the bisexual Benvenuto Cellini."[51] The artist also appears in a number of online lists of famous queers, for instance, in the list of "Famous or Distinguished Gays, Lesbians, and Bisexuals."[52] Whether a sodomite or bisexual, Cellini may be considered a member of a queer constituency because his sexuality was not considered "normal or sanctioned."[53]

For theorists and historians of gay history, Cellini represents a moment of resistance to the dominant cultural discourse of heterosexuality. He envisioned alternative models for male sexual experience and desire that took place alongside the enforced script of heteronormativity. Michelangelo loved within the same constraints of desire—aware that "his feelings [for Tommaso de' Cavalieri were] at odds with theological and civil morality"[54]—and the same official restrictions on male same-sex eroticism as Cellini. Unlike Cellini, however, Michelangelo did not act on his desires. In fact, Michelangelo "may never have consummated his desire (there is no evidence that he did, and good reason to believe that his own internal resistance would have prevented him)."[55] Cellini's bold declarations stand in stark contrast to Michelangelo's frequent proclamations of orthodoxy, and, as noted, life of total sexual abstinence.

All these interpretations of Cellini's sexual misdeeds raise the question of how to define gay (or queer) literature. Does gay literature comprise all those works that articulate "artistic expressions of same-sex love"[56] or that instead express what Joseph Cady has called "a language for a male homosexual orientation"?[57] Are gay texts those with homoerotic themes, or is simply transgressing any established boundary sufficient to being labeled a gay writer? Is the gay reader more important than the texts themselves, as Woods suggests when he takes refuge in "readerly" texts, claiming that he is not concerned with "whether William Shakespeare was 'gay' or 'queer' or a 'homosexual' or a 'sodomite'; or if he and the male addressee of his sonnets were 'just good friends'. . . All of this is irrelevant if any of the sonnets are amenable to being read by a gay reader *as if they were* 'gay poems.' If they work as if they were, they *are*. The reader's pleasure is paramount."[58]

Not all modern cultural artifacts about the great artist have viewed him as gay. The Hollywood film *The Affairs of Cellini* (1934) starring Fredric March as Cellini, Frank Morgan as the Duke of Florence (Alessandro de' Medici), Constance Bennett as the Duchess, and Fay Wray as Angela (a female model) portrays our hero as a hot-tempered swashbuckler and lady's man in the Errol Flynn tradition. Flynn's *Robin Hood* (*The Adventures of Robin Hood*, 1938) and March's *Cellini* are look-alikes: both dressed in a belted tunic and tights, with a sword hung diagonally across the body, and sporting a pointed goatee. The film inscribes Cellini in a purely heterosexual love story—with the Duchess, after the Duke runs off with Angela—and presents him as a composer of love lyrics to women.

A Hollywood heartthrob was born (figure 14). *The Affairs of Cellini* was nominated for four Academy Awards—Best Actor for Morgan, Best Cinematography (Charles Rosher), Best Art Direction (Richard Day), and Best Sound Recording (Thomas T. Moulton)—but failed to win any. The film, which opened on 24 August 1934, was a commercial success. It was listed in *Fame: The Box-Office Check-Up* as one of the top grossing pictures for the year 1934.[59] Directed by Gregory La Cava, *The Affairs of Cellini* is classified generically in film databases as a historical romance comedy. The romantic heterosexual love story seems to have captivated American television viewers. It was chosen by American Movie Classics to be shown on Valentine's Day in 1992 as one of three "amorous" films.

Cellini's sex appeal (presumably with women) was not lost on the writers of the 1966 Audrey Hepburn comedy, *How to Steal a Million*.

The story centers around a statue of Venus on loan to a Paris museum from the collection of Charles Bonnet (Hepburn's father in the film, played by Hugh Griffith), a legendary art collector. The small marble statue of the goddess was not sculpted by our famed Renaissance artist but was forged by Bonnet's father. Directed by William Wyler, the film stars Peter O'Toole as the burglar hired to steal the million-dollar forgery from the museum before it can be appraised as a fake. When Charles tries to persuade his daughter Nicole that the Cellini carved by her grandfather is better than any crafted by Benvenuto, he jibes: "If it was genuine, what would it be? A piece of sculpture made centuries ago by an over-sexed Italian."

Cellini's appearance in the annals of sodomy poses new challenges for scholars of the history of sexuality. What is the precise relationship between someone like Cellini, an adult man who had sex with boys, and men who have sex with men in our own (modern Western) culture?[60] As has been shown by Ruggiero and Rocke, sexual relations between men and boys in Cellini's day adhered to strict, rigid codes of behavior organized around the twin axes of power and gender.[61] This sex act between an adult man and a boy or adult woman was not perceived as a mutual exchange between social equals based on (modern) notions of respect and reciprocity. A second concern is whether we should use records of sexual crimes to speculate on the nature or existence of "masculine love"[62] in the early modern period. Sodomy records might not reveal evidence of a type of person we would call a "homosexual." But the sexual acts between Fernando and Cellini as well as between Cellini and his female models or prostitutes certainly tell us something about desire and male identity.

In Cellini's day, being a sodomite did not preclude having sexual relations with women or even being married. A sodomite was not at all a man who necessarily limited himself to same-sex relations. Indeed, the evidence strongly suggests that most contemporary sodomites did, in fact, have relations with both boys and women. Cellini certainly fit this pattern: his sexual exploits with women resulted in several illegitimate children; his marriage to his lover of several years in ca. 1562 produced numerous legitimate children afterward. Moreover, although Cellini was technically unmarried in 1557, he was likely living with his future wife at the time, suggesting that one could be both a sodomite and a husband simultaneously. In the Renaissance, then, a male's choice of sexual partner did not necessarily condition the other choices he made or roles he assumed in the society.

It is important to underscore in this regard that being a sodomite in no way detracted from Cellini's masculinity because he took the active, dominant role in sodomitical sex, whether with boys or women. The later cultural connection between homosexuality and effeminacy is simply not evident in these early modern documents. In these Renaissance discourses of sodomy masculinity was linked to penetration, irrespective of the person a man penetrated. Cellini's case further suggests that desire was fluid and dynamic rather than fixed and stable. In addition, the possibilities for desire seem more open than we might expect since, by choosing both boys and women as objects of desire, men like Cellini were successful in avoiding our own familiar homosexual/heterosexual binary.

After the Trial: The Artist's Relations with the Duke

In spite of Cellini's nonchalance with sodomy, the 1557 conviction effectively ended his artistic career. During the 1560s Cellini produced only one major work, a large marble crucifix of a naked Christ, completed in 1562 for the chapel of his own tomb (figure 11). Cosimo acquired it in 1565 for the Palazzo Pitti, but withheld half of the payment owed to Cellini until shortly before the artist's death in 1571—and then only in response to many letters from the artist imploring him to pay up. In the 1560s Cellini tried unsuccessfully to win commissions from Cosimo, in particular for the Neptune fountain and a bronze door for the Church of Santa Maria del Fiore, neither of which he obtained. In the *Trattati*, Cellini admits that he began writing his autobiography because he was "prevented from doing anything" ("da poi che m'è impedito il fare, così io mi son messo a dire" [Scarpellini, 474]). When Cellini asked Cosimo for leave to return to France, Cosimo "did not grant it, nor did he give me any more commissions: because of this I could serve neither him nor others" (Scarpellini, 473). The majority of Cellini's writings were composed between his sodomy trial in 1557 and his death in 1571. He composed his autobiography, his two art treatises on goldsmithing and sculpture, and many of his sonnets roughly between the years 1558 and 1566. Prevented from creating new works of art in the present, Cellini chose instead to write about the statues and sculptures he had produced in the past.

The original version of Cellini's art treatises reads like an autobiography. The autograph of his *Due trattati* (Two Treatises) is a technical exposition of all the art works created by its artist-hero Cellini, with digressions about the trials he has suffered.[63] But the first edition of 1568 bore little resemblance to the manuscript that Cellini gave to the editor Gherardo Spini. Spini, a member of the Florentine Academy and secretary to Cosimo's son Ferdinand to whom Cellini dedicated the treatises, removed all the autobiographical passages. Spini changed Cellini's original version, downplaying its autobiographical elements to align it more clearly with the treatise genre. But his motives were probably not wholly disinterested. Spini may have done violence to Cellini's text because the art treatises clearly put the Medici in a bad light, regardless of Cellini's assertions here and there throughout his writings that he and his forefathers were great supporters of the Medici. A recurring motif in the *Two Treatises* is the sharp contrast between the nobility of Francis I, who recognized Cellini's artistic virtù, and the inferiority of Cosimo I who neither appreciated nor fully understood Cellini's unique talents. In fact, Francis, regarded by Cellini as, "il più amator delle virtù ed il più liberale a quelle che altro uomo mai che venissi al mondo" (Scarpellini, 471), dominates the art treatises, overshadowing and minimizing the references to Cosimo.

In the *Vita*, Cellini presents the patron–client relationship with Cosimo as a master–student one. When the *Perseus* was displayed for the first time in the Piazza della Signoria, Cosimo stood, according to Cellini, "at one of the lower windows of the Palazzo, which was above the door, and in this manner, inside the window, half-hidden, heard everything that was said about the statue" ("stava a una finestra bassa del Palazzo, la quale si è sopra la porta, et così, dentro alla finestra mezzo ascoso, sentiva tutto quello che di detta opera si diceva" [Bellotto, 710]). Cosimo then ventured his judgment only after he had heard the praise of the people. Throughout the *Vita*, Cellini insists he had to teach Cosimo the basic elements of artistic appreciation and aesthetics, claiming that, for example, when he displayed his marble statue of the *Ganymede*, "So I tried, in the best way that I knew, to make his Illustrious Excellency appreciate the beauty, and the virtue of intelligence, and the rare style that it contained" ("Allora io mostrai a Sua Eccellenzia illustrissima con el meglio modo che io seppi, di farlo capace di cotal bellezza et di virtù di intelligenzia, et di rara maniera" [Bellotto, 649–50]). In Cellini's view, "Our duke really loved jewels, but unfortunately knew nothing about them" ("Il nostro Duca, che si dilettava grandemente di gioie, ma però non se ne intendeva" [Bellotto, 625]). Cellini also suggests that the duke had no appreciation for the *linea serpentinata* of the Mannerist style so beloved by the king. One recalls that Cosimo disliked Cellini's large bronze bust of him (1545–47) because it appeared alive, in motion, dynamic, so he had it removed from the Palazzo Pitti and exiled it to Elba.[64] Cosimo also banished the statue because Cellini had portrayed him "in a state of nervous belligerence,"[65] a ducal portrait at odds with Cosimo's self-fashioned image as a promoter of peace, not war. The bust was appropriate for the military fortress in Cosmopolis (the recently renamed capital of the island, formerly—and now once again—Portoferraio) but not for the princely court in Florence.

At Francis's court, too, it is Cellini who seems to form both works of art and the aesthetic judgments of the king. These master–student/patron–client relations carry all the concomitant sexual allusions entailed. Cellini's representation of his two main patrons, Cosimo and Francis, is both gendered and sexually charged. Following Aristotle, Cellini suggests that, in the act of creation, he gives a masculine form to the feminine matter (or content) of his patron's desires. For Aristotle, males provided the form and females the matter in the act of generation.[66] Thus, Cellini as the masculine artist/creator sexually dominates his feminine patrons/masters. These carnivalesque inversions resonate profoundly in all of Cellini's writings.

In his writings, Cellini may have insisted that "my ancestors had been great friends of the House of Medici, and I more than any of them loved this Duke Cosimo" ("i mia [sic] antichi erano stati molto amici della casa de' Medici, et io più che nessuno di loro amavo questo duca Cosimo" [Bellotto, 606–07]), but his depiction of Cosimo is always reduced when compared to King Francis I. In France, Cellini insists that "that marvelous King Francis gave me everything, whereas here [in Florence] I was deprived of everything" ("quel maraviglioso re Francesco, con el quale mi avanzava ogni cosa, e qui mi mancava ogni cosa" [Bellotto, 644]). Moreover, unlike Francis, Cosimo had "more the manner of a merchant than a duke" (più modo di mercatante che di duca [Bellotto, 610]), as Jane Tylus has shown.[67]

Cellini's negative judgment on Cosimo seems to have elicited tampering with, if not outright censorship of, the autograph of the *Vita*. The comment on Cosimo just cited, associating him with being a merchant, is marked by aggressive strike-outs and marginal corrections by an unknown hand.[68] Whether the individual responsible for this change was a copyist or reader is unclear, but what is clear is that the handwriting of the marginal correction on folio 444r is that of neither Cellini nor his *amanuensis*, the son of Michele di Goro.[69] These strike-outs and marginal corrections were accepted into the 1728 *editio princeps*, thus removing from Cosimo the merchant-like nature Cellini had ascribed to him and attributing to him instead "the greatest desire to perform the greatest deeds" (grandissimo desiderio di far grandissime imprese).[70] The marginal correction had only called for a "gran' desiderio di far grandissime imprese." Some modern editions of Cellini's *Vita* even retain the new phrase "gran desiderio di far grandissime imprese."[71] The anonymous editor of the first printed edition again adhered to the alterations wrought to the manuscript when, on this same page, he eliminated the second reference to Cosimo's merchant status, where Cellini had claimed that he proceeded most liberally with his Excellency "as a duke, and not as a merchant"—the phrase "not as a merchant" was struck out and removed. Two further cancellations in the autograph, and retained in the 1728 edition, again erase Cellini's derogatory portrayal of Cosimo: the first, on folio 456r, eliminates Cellini's contention that the duke "knew nothing [of jewels]"[72] (ma però non se ne intendeva [Bellotto, 625]); the second, on folio 458v, mitigates Cosimo's *sinplicità*, transforming it instead into the "semplice credenza del buon Duca."[73]

Mystery surrounds the first edition of Cellini's autobiography. Both the writer of the preface and the printer used pseudonyms. Furthermore, it is undated, contains a false place name, and is dedicated to the Englishman Richard Boyle.[74] According to Samuel Johnson, after the book's publication, it was immediately suppressed and placed on the Church's Index.[75] On close examination, it is clear that the first edition was not based on the autograph. It is missing, for example, the four verses of a burlesque poem Cellini composed attacking a rival goldsmith named Bernardo that, he tells us, he tacked up in the back of the Church of Santa Maria del Fiore in Florence (Bellotto, 705). In place of the independent poem that Cellini inserted in the manuscript, we find only "Manca il M.S."[76] These riddles lead one to wonder what really happened to those pages that Cellini claims were part of the *Vita*, pages that told the truth about Cosimo, pages that he had written about "all the years that [he] had served his lord Duke Cosimo," but that he allegedly tore up and threw in the fire (Scarpellini, 474). The autograph of the *Vita* is not listed in the inventory of Cellini's household goods at his death in 1571,[77] but suddenly, over a hundred fifty years later, it "just happened to pop up during a search for unpublished 'language texts'" sought by members of the Accademia della Crusca in the late 1720s.[78]

Ultimately, Cosimo did not silence Cellini, nor did he appear to have curbed the artist's disturbing behavior. In his autobiography, Cellini presents himself as master, inquisitor, masculine dominator. In life, he used the court as both a source and as a provocation for scandals. Cellini's trial for sodomy is productive in a literal sense: the trial procedure creates a writing persona for Cellini. Paradoxically, these writings confirm Cellini's reputation as a sodomite. They also illustrate the exposé quality typical of early modern erotic writing, found, for example, in the writings of Pietro Aretino. Sodomy may have been "unspeakable" in many cultures of early modern Europe, but Cellini and his compatriots more than made up for the silences of others.[79] After his trial, Cellini staged a continual verbal assault on his detractors, rivals, and patrons, among them Duke (then Grand Duke) Cosimo I de' Medici. In a 1560 letter to Michelangelo, Cellini's fellow artist Leone Leoni claimed that after losing the commission for the Neptune fountain, "Benvenuto balena et sputa veleno et getta fuoco per gli hocci, e brava il Duca con la lingua."[80] Rather than restraining his tongue, the trial for sodomy may have only incited Cellini to further slander.

CHAPTER 3
CELLINI'S POETICS I: THE *RIME*

In one of his sonnets Cellini celebrates his reputation as a "whoremonger" (puttaniere) who unceremoniously abandons Fortune, presented in the guise of an earthly woman lover, for a male lover, his beloved Ganymede: "Porca fortuna," he laments, "s'tu scoprivi prima / che ancora a me piacessi 'l Ganimede! / Son puttaniere ormai, com'ogni uom vede, / né avesti di me la spoglia opima" (Damn, cursed Fortune! If only you found out earlier that I also liked Ganymede. I am a whoremonger at last, as every man can see, nor did you conquer my rich spoils).[1] This satirical sonnet, filled with coarse language side-by-side Petrarchan conceits, is typical of the more than one hundred poems Cellini composed during the course of his life. In this sonnet Cellini juxtaposes two different stylistic registers, mocks Petrarch, and celebrates his own polymorphously perverse sexual nature.

Such overt references to illicit sexual practices contributed much to the opinion modern critics formed of Cellini. For Goethe, for instance, Cellini was an "unrestrained force of nature"[2] who nonetheless may have been "representative of his age and perhaps of all humanity."[3] Cellini was creative in many different areas. Skilled in working in a variety of plastic arts, he was also adept at composing literary texts in a wide range of genres. In addition to being a writer of prose, Cellini was also a lyric poet, but his verses are usually omitted from anthologies of Renaissance verse. Following the model of the Petrarchan sonnet, numerous sixteenth-century poets—male and female—sang of desire for the cruel and absent lover or the beloved companion. The burlesque sonnet was a popular form with a tradition dating back to the comic-jocose lyric of the medieval period. Francesco Berni's innovations in the sixteenth century earned him the honor of having a type of sonnet named after him, the *sonetto bernesco*. Artists such as Michelangelo and Angelo Bronzino also composed verses. In Florence in particular, sonnets covered a wide range of topics and tones and circulated freely among artists and men of letters. Active in the rich cultural milieu of Cosimean Florence, Cellini followed this trend.

In this chapter I will demonstrate that Cellini violates Petrarchan conventions in his lyric, ridiculing its language of love and celebration of female beauty, in order to align himself with the oppositional voices of his day who sought to critique contemporary family values. Like Bronzino and Pietro Aretino, Cellini chose to sing the praises of a variety of transgressive practices in his poetry, choosing sex over love, whores (or even boys) over wives, sodomy over "natural" sexual acts. Cellini thus joined a group of sixteenth-century writers who desired to expose and criticize traditional notions of love, marriage, and gender roles. But there is another reason why Cellini may have opted for textual violation in his lyric, this, too, stemming from an oppositional impulse. Cellini derides Petrarch but imitates Dante in his poetry in order to position himself oppositionally in literary history precisely at a time when Petrarch's reputation was on the rise, Dante's in decline.

While scholars and laymen alike value the splendor of Cellini's artistic contributions such as his masterpiece the *Perseus* and have vilified his personal morality as exemplified in his acts of sodomy, critical opinion largely remains silent on the merit of his *rime*. It is not surprising that Cellini's verse has garnered so little attention when we read the aesthetic judgments of his few modern critics. In 1885, Adolfo Mabellini, wrote these caustic words:

> La poesia del Cellini ... è rozza e manca del tutto di ogni grazia. La rima e il ritmo sono i più terribili nemici del Cellini; e vediamo ... che spesso ... infrange le leggi dell'una e dell'altro.[4]
>
> (Cellini's poetry ... is rough and is utterly devoid of grace. Rhyme and meter are his worst enemies; and we see ... that often ... he breaks the rules of one or the other.)

In 1900 Angiolo Orvieto wrote a very brief piece about Cellini's poetry in a special edition of *Il Marzocco* dedicated exclusively to Cellini. Entitled simply "Le Rime," Orvieto apologizes for Cellini's body of poetic work, claiming it lacks two essential qualities: "l'universalità dell'intelletto inclinato alla sintesi filosofica e la profonda delicatezza dell'anima capace di sentir fremere nella propria la coscienza di tutti gli uomini."[5] In 1952 Bruno Maier, kinder by comparison, argued that Cellini was "un mediocre verseggiatore."[6] Using terms such as "verseggiatore" and "rimatore" rather than "poeta" throughout his study, Maier suggests that he finds it difficult to classify Cellini as a poet. Both are used as derogatory terms applied to those who aspire to write poetry but never seem to get it right. For Maier, Cellini's lyric has a certain value as a historical curiosity, but contains little of literary merit. Three new articles on Cellini's lyric appeared in 2000 for the five hundredth anniversary of the artist's birth, two in Italian and the first ever in English.[7]

In this chapter I propose a reappraisal of Benvenuto Cellini's lyric, arguing that Cellini's poetry is an important and necessary component of his vast literary and artistic oeuvre. A deeper analysis of Cellini as poet can help us understand more fully the more familiar portrait we have of Cellini as artist. For this purpose, I have chosen a few sonnets that I believe are representative of broader themes in his poetic corpus, providing my own English translations. In addition, I offer readings from Cellini's *Vita* that complement his *Rime* in the hope that we can begin to evaluate his works in prose and in verse together. As we shall see, the textual violation and innovation evident in Cellini's lyric is also present in his *Vita*.

Two manuscripts in the Biblioteca Riccardiana in Florence contain the majority of Cellini's poetry. These two codices, Ricc. 2353 and 2728, contain poems written in Cellini's own hand with some insertions by friends and correspondents. Mabellini, Maier, and recently Vittorio Gatto have all edited editions of Cellini's poems, in 1891, 1968, and 2001, respectively.[8] Maier's edition largely follows Mabellini's, but corrects a series of false attributions. Mabellini attributed six sonnets in Ricc. 2353 to Cellini that are actually by Annibal Caro. Since Maier's edition is considered the most complete and authoritative, and since Gatto's edition draws its texts of the sonnets from the Maier edition, while adding more commentary, I have utilized Maier's edition. Occasionally, however, I have added commentary based on my study of the autographs where I felt that Maier's transcriptions sacrificed the unique flavor of the original. I have also done so because Maier does not always incorporate corrections made by Cellini. For example, Cellini's correction in the margin of the sonnet beginning "Fermate il pianto, ché l'è al ciel beata" (Maier, 906–07), replacing the word "poggiando" for "salita" in line 2, does not appear in the Maier edition.[9] Another instance is the artist's sonnet captioned *Sulla gotta* and beginning "Sol immortal, Signior, sol Dio del tutto," where Cellini's change in verse 1, clearly in his hand, of "sol Dio" to "Padre" is likewise not incorporated by Maier (BRF, Ricc. 2353 fol. 103r; Maier, 918–19; Gatto, 71). A few other sonnets by Cellini are preserved in scattered anthologies, but they are not autographs. These poems, alongside the lyric of contemporaries like Michelangelo, Benedetto Varchi, and Anton Francesco Grazzini, appear in verse anthologies that were assembled in later centuries. However, these collections present no new poems by Cellini; rather, they duplicate poems found in the two Riccardiana manuscripts.

No collection of Cellini's verse was published in his lifetime. This was not unusual for lesser-known poets of the day: Michelangelo's verse was also not published in his lifetime. Although Michelangelo did intend to publish an edition of his poetry, he abandoned the project for reasons that remain obscure.[10] When the first collection of Michelangelo's *rime* was printed in 1623, the sonnets addressed to a male beloved were changed to a female object or eliminated completely by Michelangelo the Younger, his grandnephew.[11] Even Pietro Bembo—the champion of imitating Petrarchan verse—published his own *Canzoniere* in 1530, after it had circulated in manuscript form. In fact, throughout the sixteenth century in Italy it was not uncommon for literary works, including poems and letters, to circulate in manuscript form before they found their way to the printing press.[12] Cellini may not be among the great poets of the Renaissance, but he was a versatile one. The artist composed a considerable number of poems, exchanged verses with better-known poets of the day, including Varchi and Laura Battiferra degli Ammannati, and experimented with other poetic forms besides the sonnet, including the madrigal, *canzone*, and *capitolo*. Several of Cellini's sonnets were published during his lifetime or shortly after his death.[13]

Turning to quantity, Cellini produced a sizable corpus of poems on widely varied topics: one hundred and sixteen appear in Maier's edition (all taken from the two Riccardiana codices), including the sonnet with which Cellini opens his *Vita*. Two additional sonnets inserted in the *Vita* bring the number to one hundred and eighteen. Two newly discovered sonnets, discovered by chance in a Florentine library, and never before published, would bring the total number of sonnets to one hundred and twenty (see appendix 2 and figure 15).[14] Cellini also wrote poems of various meters—one *capitolo* in *terza rima*, one *canzone* stanza, and a dialogue in verse, all of which appear in the story of his life—as well as uncompleted compositions (i.e., fragments). Since Cellini wrote the poems on separate sheets of paper and circulated some of them to his friends and fellow artists, a common practice in the period, it is impossible to establish a fixed number for his poetic compositions. Occasionally, Cellini re-used the paper on which he had written a poem for other purposes (or vice-versa). A few folios used for sonnets also contain, for instance, financial entries concerning payments for his art and various drawings.[15] On a large astrology chart bound in manuscript Ricc. 2353, "Lunario dell'anno 1570" by a certain Marcantonio Villani *veronese*, Cellini wrote two fragments and four sonnets. The chart, numbered folio 131, containing horoscopes and phases of the moon, predicts "la morte...di grande homo" during the calendar year beginning

25 March. Did Villani prophesize the death of our own maestro who departed this world on 13 February 1571?

Considering content, Mabellini, Maier, and Gatto all artificially divide Cellini's corpus into four general thematic categories: poems about the dispute between painting and sculpture, poems written in prison, spiritual compositions, and finally poems of "various arguments."[16] In his sonnets, Cellini both attacked his enemies and rivals and included deeply religious verses. I believe it much more useful to examine Cellini's poetic oeuvre in the broadest terms possible, identifying general trends in his poetic corpus, since many of his poems cross over into more than one rubric. For example, poems categorized as being about the painting and sculpture debate are really parodies of his fellow artists; likewise, sonnets written in prison are similar in language, tone, and imagery to his so-called spiritual sonnets. Such readings diminish Cellini's use of the language of Petrarch and Dante and his innovations in the use of the poetic *tenzone*. Furthermore, I will show that Cellini's poetic output is not only imitative of his poetic predecessors, but also fashionably innovative. The artist's poetic corpus includes parody, personification, caricature, and the grotesque.

Cellini's verses take up the themes of self-assertion and artistic rivalry, the debate over the relative virtues of sculpture and painting (called the *paragone*), and art and writing. Together with Michelangelo, Cellini played an active role in changing the social perception of sculpture. In his poetry, Cellini casts himself both within and against the literary tradition: he parodies Petrarch and imitates Dante. Cellini mocks Petrarch by taking the sonnet form and inserting coarse and quotidian language in it. He emulates Dante by becoming Dante-pilgrim in his verse as well as his prose. Cellini does this consciously and strategically for two reasons, to satirize his contemporaries and to aggrandize the status of sculpture. At the root of many of these poetic innovations lies Cellini's own need to assert and maintain his personal honor among his contemporaries.

An Artist's Use of the Poetic Tenzone

Cellini wrote sonnets of necessity because they were the primary form for debate in his day. Sonnets could be used, for instance, as love poetry to praise the beloved, but they could also serve as a public forum for debate. For artists in particular, the sonnet was a forum for aesthetic judgments in artistic matters in Florence. When Cellini's *Perseus* was unveiled in 1554, artists and men of letters attached encomiastic sonnets to its base, celebrating Cellini's artistic virtue. These verses were collected and printed as an appendix to his *Due trattati* published by the Panizzi and Peri firm in 1568 and titled "Poesie toscane et latine sopra il Perseo statua di bronzo, e il Crocifisso statua di marmo fatte da messer Benvenuto Cellini." Over fifty artists and men of letters, including Michelangelo, Bronzino, and Varchi, contributed Latin epigrams or Italian sonnets to the printed edition of Cellini's art treatises. Similarly, verses praising Giambologna's marble group of the abduction of the Sabine women were printed in another volume in Florence in 1583, attesting to the sonnet as a public, social form.[17] The sonnet was a forum not only for praise, but also for censure. When Bandinelli's marble group of *Hercules and Cacus* was displayed, numerous artists and writers heaped vituperative abuse upon Bandinelli.[18] This Florentine practice recalls the Roman tradition of posting poems in public onto the Pasquino statue.

Cellini used the polemical sonnet in a new way. The poetic *tenzone* was a well-established practice of poetic exchange in which the first poet proposed the theme and established rhyme scheme (*proposta*) and the second poet replied in kind (*risposta*).[19] Cellini took the *tenzone* and used it to engage other artists and men of letters in the debate concerning the relative virtues of painting and sculpture. This heated and often acrimonious debate raged in Florence over a twenty-year period, from 1545 to the mid-1560s. Begun in the fifteenth century, this controversy reached a fever pitch after Michelangelo's death in 1564.[20] A few years later, in 1568, Vincenzo Borghini would remind Vasari that Florence in particular had "una lingua pungente e maligna."[21]

Cellini wrote over a dozen sonnets that take up this theme of the *paragone delle arti* directly. The following poem is exemplary of many of the sonnets Cellini composed about the painting versus sculpture debate.

Quel immortale Iddio della natura,
che fecie i cieli e 'l mondo, e noi fé degni
delle sue mani, senza far disegni,
come quel che ogni arte aveva sicura,
    di terra fecie la prima scultura,
e la mostrò agli angel de' suoi regni:
per qual ne nacque quei crudei sdegni,
cagion d'inferno, e morte acerba e dura.
    Cadde nel fuoco colle sue brigate
quel ch' ubbidir non volse 'l suo maggiore,
che aveva tante gran cose create.
    Questo fu 'l primo che si fé pittore,
che con tal ombre ha l'anime ingannate,
qual non può far nessun buono scultore. (Maier, 893–94)

(That immortal God of Nature who made the heavens and the earth, and made us worthy of his hands, without [depending] on designs, as one expert in every art, made the first sculpture out of the ground, and He showed it to the angels of his kingdom: from which those cruel afflictions were born, which caused the creation of Hell, and of bitter and harsh death. He who did not want to obey his master, who had created so many beautiful things, fell in the fire with his companions. This one was the first to be a painter, who with such shadows has deceived souls as no good sculptor can.)[22]

This text illustrates that Cellini participated fully in ongoing artistic debates and clearly sided with those who favored sculpture. Cellini aggrandizes the status of the sculptor by identifying God as a sculptor. This association had been made by other sixteenth-century artists; for example, Giorgio Vasari and Anton Francesco Doni also used this image of God as the first sculptor.[23] Pontormo (Jacopo Carucci)'s letter to Benedetto Varchi about the greater nobility of sculpture likewise argued from divine authority: "Quando Dio creò l'uomo, lo fece di rilievo, come cosa più facile a farlo vivo"[24] (When God created man, he made him in relief, as an easier way to give him life). Pontormo wrote his letter in response to a specific query by Varchi who had asked eight of the leading artists of the day to argue whether painting or sculpture was the nobler art. The artists he invited to contribute were Cellini, Michelangelo, Vasari, Pontormo, Bronzino, Battista Tasso, Tribolo, and Francesco da Sangallo. Their epistolary responses were collected and printed in an edition published by the Torrentino firm in Florence in 1549.

Cellini's letter to Varchi, dated 28 January 1547, contains many of the themes found throughout the sonnets dedicated to the *paragone* of painting and sculpture. His sonnets attempt to elevate the status of sculpture in the artistic hierarchy of the day that privileged painting. In a poem in praise of sculpture (Maier, 893), Cellini defends sculpture by arguing from another authority, not divine but classical. According to the poet, Socrates first practiced the art of sculpture before abandoning it to devote himself to philosophy (verse 9: "Socrate ti lasciò quand'io ti presi"). According to Cellini, Socrates became one of the greatest thinkers in history precisely because he was first trained as a sculptor. In his response to Varchi, as in his sonnet "Quel immortale Iddio della natura," Cellini defends sculpture over painting by aligning sculpture with divine forces and painting with demonic powers:

[L]a scultura è madre di tutte l'arte [*sic*] dove s'interviene disegno . . . La pittura non è altro che o arbero o uomo o altra cosa che si specchi in un fonte. La differenza che è dalla scultura alla pittura è tanta quanto è dalla ombra e la cosa che fa l'ombra.[25]

(Sculpture is the mother of all the other arts where design plays a part . . . Painting is nothing more than a tree or a man or anything else that mirrors itself in a fountain. The difference between sculpture and painting is as great as that between a shadow and the object that casts it.)

This image of painters as deceivers did not originate with Cellini. A fifteenth-century *novella* by Franco Sacchetti (CXCI) portrays the painter Buonamico as a trickster who fools his master Taso into believing that the cockroaches he has attached candles to are really demons.[26] Another notable example is chapter 50 of book 1 of *Il Libro del Cortigiano* where the participants debate the relative virtues of painting and sculpture. The interlocutor Ioanni Cristoforo argues that both arts are an artificial imitation of nature, but that paintings in particular deceive the viewer by tricking the eyes: "Ed a me par bene, che l'una e l'altra sia una artificiosa imitazion di natura . . . in una tavola, nella qual non si vede altro che la superficie e que' colori che ingannano gli occhi."[27]

The majority of Cellini's sonnets addressing the painting versus sculpture polemic date from the 1560s. By this time, his reputation as a sculptor was firmly established. Two of his three marble works—the *Ganymede* and the group *Apollo with Hyacinth*—date from the late 1540s. Cellini had demonstrated *virtù* as a sculptor by sculpting life-size or larger than life-size marble figures in the round. The anonymous *Catologo dei fiorentini famosi in scienze ed arti* listed the artist's accomplishments as a sculptor: "Fiorentini famosi nella scultura: Benvenuto Cellini, fece in spagna un istupendissimo crocifisso di marmo et in firenze quel bel perseo che è [nel] le logge de' tedeschi."[28] One recalls that the printed edition of his two art treatises of 1568 also identified him as a *scultore fiorentino*. Such a characterization clearly came as a surprise to some of Cellini's contemporaries. According to Vasari, Bandinelli was stupefied that Cellini "should have thus changed in a moment from a goldsmith into a sculptor, nor was he able to grasp in his mind how a man who was used to making medals and little things, could now execute colossal figures and giants."[29] Only after achieving acclaim as a sculptor could Cellini successfully defend sculpture as an art form in his poetry. Cellini seems to have found his poetic voice only after making his mark as a sculptor.

Cellini's contemporaries perceived him as the most vocal and articulate proponent of the superiority of sculpture. But by those who favored painting, he was viewed as a disruptive force. Cellini's polemical sonnets praising sculpture circulated in Florence after he refused to attend the ceremony honoring Michelangelo in 1564.[30] Varchi was charged with delivering the funeral oration at the obsequies, a speech titled, *Orazione funerale di M. Benedetto Varchi, fatta e recitata da lui pubblicamente nell'essequie di Michelagnolo Buonarroti in Firenze, nella Chiesa di San Lorenzo. Indiritta al molto Mag. et Reverendo Monsignore M. Vincenzio Borghini, priore degli Innocenti,* and later published (Giunti, 1564).

Cellini was outraged that Vincenzo Borghini, cofounder of the Confraternity and Academy of Design and organizer of the ceremony, dishonored sculpture by placing it on the left side of the catafalque while painting was placed on the right, in the place of honor. Borghini (1515–80), an early proto-philologist and historian, was a member of the Benedictine order, a prominent figure at the Medici court, and a powerful ally of Vasari.[31] He was appointed by his patron Cosimo I as superintendent of the Florentine foundling hospital for abandoned children, the *Ospedale degli Innocenti,* and, later, as *luogotenente* (the Duke's representative) of the Academy of Design. Borghini and Vasari had founded the *Compagnia e Accademia del Disegno* in 1562, which the Medici officially incorporated the following year. Originally configured as both a lay confraternity and a school, it was envisioned as "a homogeneous body of practitioners whose productivity would serve the publicity of the court."[32]

Borghini had elected four artists to help plan the obsequies for Michelangelo: Cellini and Ammannati were chosen as sculptors, Bronzino and Vasari as painters. Cellini clearly disliked many of Borghini's ideas for the ceremony and took the offensive immediately. In a letter to Borghini, Cellini calls for a small ceremony that would glorify Michelangelo the great sculptor. This view was clearly at odds with the wishes of Borghini and Vasari who had in mind an elaborate, grandiose display that celebrated the divine Michelangelo as painter. Borghini wrote to Vasari that Cellini had already begun "to stir up trouble" (*intorbidare*) shortly after the formation of their committee. The relationship between Cellini and Borghini quickly deteriorated and name-calling ensued. Borghini referred to Cellini as "that hopeless lunatic."[33] The event, scheduled for 28 June, actually took place on 14 July 1564.[34] Not surprisingly, Cellini was nowhere to be found, having felt, according to Vasari, "somewhat indisposed from the beginning" (2: 755). This is an understatement. The public seemed troubled by Cellini's conspicuous absence. A champion of Michelangelo, he was also reputed throughout Italy and France as a sculptor, goldsmith, and jeweler. Officially, Cellini's absence was explained as a result of ill health, but it did not take long for Cellini to discredit that version.

Cellini showed his contempt for Borghini, Vasari, and Giovan Maria Tarsia in a group of sonnets he composed both before and after the ceremony. He sought to disparage them by enlisting other artists in a poetic attack on Borghini and Vasari who, in his view, had dishonored Michelangelo with their pompous display and elaborate ceremony. Maier has categorized these sonnets as pertaining to the debate over painting and sculpture, but this rubric only tells half the story. These verses disparage Borghini and Vasari for their mockery of a ceremony that was intended to honor the divine Michelangelo and instead had caused him, in Cellini's opinion, great dishonor. In certain lines from one of these sonnets (Maier, 890), Cellini mocks them by claiming that the friar and the painter prefer painting because they are not sculptors themselves: "Lodan più 'l frate e Giorgio la pittura, / perché lo sculpir eglino non sanno" (verses 5–6). Tarsia was also subjected to attack by Cellini. Although Tarsia's speech delivered on Michelangelo's death seems merely to hint at the superiority of painting, in Cellini's mind Tarsia had clearly and blatantly sided with the painters and against the sculptors. Cellini wrote three sonnets and a madrigal attacking Tarsia as a foolish *pedante*. One of these (Maier, 886) expresses concern that Michelangelo will be ruined in death by Tarsia's funeral speech as if "stretto dentro una tarsia," a pun on Tarsia, his name, and *tarsia* (an inlaid work in wood or stone, most likely to Cellini), a coffin.

Throughout these years Borghini viewed Cellini as a disruptive force who violated all rules of decorum. In the months following the ceremony, Borghini wrote various letters to Vasari assailing Cellini for causing dissension from the beginning. In his letters, Borghini expresses concern that Cellini had incited the public against him, believing that people were criticizing how he (Borghini) handled the event. In a letter dated 19 August 1564, Borghini tries to assure Vasari that he has the upper hand over that "asinine beast" (*bestia asinina*).[35] In many of his other writings Borghini attacked Cellini and his defense of sculpture. For instance, in his long discourse entitled "Selva di notizie," Borghini expanded his criticism of Cellini's explanation of why painting was inferior to sculpture, dissecting the artist's argument in detail, and sparing no venom.[36]

Petrarch and the Poetics of Parody

Cellini's sonnets about the painting versus sculpture debate were one group of sonnets he composed during the course of his life. He wrote another sizable number of sonnets parodying Petrarch. These verses link him to a larger group of sixteenth-century writers of anti-Petrarchan verse. Cellini's poetics includes parody, the grotesque, and caricature. Cellini's knowledge of Petrarch and sixteenth-century Petrarchism was derived from a personal acquaintance with Pietro Bembo and from the cultural milieu of mid–sixteenth-century Florence. Cellini met Bembo in Rome in the 1530s and designed a medal of him in 1539.[37] Bembo's *Prose della volgar lingua* (1525) defended the Petrarchan norm as the model for lyric poetry. According to Bembo, poets should imitate Petrarch; poetic language should be lofty and harmonious; poetic themes should include love, interiority, and spirituality. Through this treatise, Bembo set out to "authorize" Petrarch by "encourag[ing] widespread acceptance of a Florentine patrimony."[38] The second influence on Cellini's poetic practice was the Florentine Academy. He was admitted on 23 April 1545, upon successful submission of a sonnet, and was a member from 1545 to 1547. Founded in 1540 as the *Accademia degli Humidi*, the *Accademia Fiorentina* was a kind of literary salon where artists and writers met to practice their oratorical and rhetorical skills. The Academy boasted among its other members the artists Michelangelo and Bronzino as well as Varchi and Luca Martini. The purpose of the academy, as stated in its annals, was to read Petrarch and to compose sonnets.[39]

Yet despite the preponderance of Petrarchan sonnets in the sixteenth century, other poets like Francesco Berni and Grazzini savaged the model with their burlesque, anti-Petrarchan verses. Berni, in particular, was celebrated for his sonnets that satirized the Petrarchan topos of the *donna crudel* (the cruel lady). In a Berni caudate sonnet probably dated 1518, the male speaker laments the impossible financial and psychological demands being made on him by his lady:

Un dirmi ch'io gli presti e ch'io gli dia
Or la veste, or l'anello, or la catena,
E per averla conosciuta a pena,
volermi tutta tôr la robba mia;
   un voler ch'io gli facci compagnia,
che nell'inferno non è maggior pena,
Un dargli desinar, albergo, e cena.
Come se l'uom facesse l'osteria;
   Un sospetto crudel del mal franzese,
un tôr danari o drappi ad interesso,
per darli verbigrazia, un tanto al mese;
   un dirmi ch'io vi torno troppo spesso,
un eccellenza del signor marchese.

(Telling me to lend her and to give her first a dress, then a ring, then a necklace, and for hardly knowing her, she wants to take everything I have. Wanting me to keep her company and in Hell there isn't a greater punishment than this. Giving her meals, lodging, and dinner, as if this man were an innkeeper. A cruel suspicion of the French disease, taking money or fine cloth from the moneylenders, in order to give them, for example, so much every month. Telling me that I come back too often, Her Excellency Madame Menstruation.)

To the reader's surprise the cruel lady, rather than being the absent lover, is a prostitute:

Eterno onor del puttanesco sesso;
   un morbo, un puzzo, un cesso,
un toglier a pigion ogni palazzo
son le cagioni ch'io mi meni il cazzo.[40]

(Eternal honor of the whorish sex. A plague, a stench, a cesspool, renting every palazzo are the reasons I'll jerk off instead.)

Whereas Berni had parodied Petrarchan topoi, Cellini, on the other hand, went one step further and violated both Petrarchan content and language. Cellini used the sonnet, a form associated with Petrarch, and within that structure parodied him by celebrating a variety of transgressive themes. For example, this male speaker sings defiantly, "I am a whoremonger" (verse 3), and proudly affirms sex between men:

Porca fortuna, s'tu scoprivi prima
che ancora a me piacessi 'l Ganimede!
Son puttaniere ormai com'ogni uom vede,
né avesti di me la spoglia opima.
   Dinanzi ai tuo' bei crin così si stima;
né chi 'l merta gli dai, né chi te i chiede;
gli porgi a tal che non gli cerca o vede.
Cieca, di te ormai non fo più stima.
   Che val con arme, lettere o scultura
affaticarsi in questa parte o 'n quella,
poi che tu se' sì porca, impia figura?
   Venga 'l canchero a te, tue ruote e stella;
t'hai vendicata quella prima ingiuria:
che nol facevi nell'età novella. (Maier, 900–01)

(Damn, cursed Fortune! If only you found out earlier that I also liked Ganimede. I am a whoremonger at last, as every man can see, nor did you conquer my rich spoils. Before your beautiful locks, we are judged as follows: You don't bestow your favors on those who merit them; Nor on

those who ask you for them. You give them out to those who neither
seek them nor see them; Blind woman, I no longer am putting my faith
in you. What use is it to tire oneself out with warfare, literature, or
sculpture, in this realm or that, Since you are such an impious bitch?
Pox on you, your wheel and star! You vindicated that first injury in
my youth.)[41]

Here Fortune appears in the guise of an earthly woman lover whom the
male speaker will neither depend on nor woo, but abandons for a male
lover. Cellini's sonnet violates linguistic conventions. Rather than using
the accepted lofty, elevated diction appropriate to love poetry, the poet
uses not merely ordinary, quotidian language, but language that is
downright coarse and vulgar. Cellini's anti-Petrarchan lexicon includes
the word "porca" (damn, bitch) that appears twice, then "puttaniere"
(whoremonger), and finally "canchero" (cancer, pox). These specific
lexical items can also be found in the poetry of Berni, who, significantly,
also hurled the epithet "porca" at Fortune ("porca de la Fortuna a' buon'
ribella") and in the writings of Aretino, who deployed "puttaniere."[42]
Like Cellini, Berni and Aretino employed "canchero" as a malediction.[43]
In terms of content, unlike Petrarchan poems, this sonnet celebrates sex,
not the idealized spiritual love of the *Canzoniere*. Here the male interlocutor is defiant: "I'm a whoremonger as every man can see," he boasts.
Furthermore, the sonnet celebrates sexual acts between males: "Porca
fortuna," he laments, "if only you found out earlier that I also liked
Ganymede!"

Cellini attacks Petrarch by emptying the sonnet of its lofty language
and its celebration of love and filling it instead with coarse words and a
celebration of sex between men. According to Jean Toscan, the theme of
sodomy was a recurring one in the burlesque poetry of sixteenth-century
Italy: "La poésie burlesque de caractère érotique réserve à la sodomie une
place de choix."[44] Cellini's poem is more than a parody of Petrarch: it is
a direct assault on Petrarch. Cellini is a true terrorist of his sources. He
begins a verse using lyrical Petrarchan language, then suddenly under-
cuts it. Verses 9–10 of "Porca fortuna" cited above demonstrate Cellini's
violation of Petrarchan norms. It begins in a high register, celebrating
the noble themes of arms and letters:[45]

Che val con arme, lettere o scultura
affaticarsi in questa parte o 'n quella

(what use is it to tire oneself out with warfare,
literature or sculpture, in this realm or that) (BRF, Ricc. 2353, fol. 8r)

After this bow to convention—surely we expect something about the ravages of time, the higher realms of contemplation, the inexpressibility of beauty—Cellini surprises the reader by attacking Fortune as "an impious bitch" in verse 11: "poi che tu se' sì porca impia figura." The male speaker invokes the Petrarchan topos of female beauty ("i biondi capelli," "be' occhi" of Petrarch's sonnet 11) by alluding to the beautiful locks of Fortune (the "bei crin," verse 5) only to undermine it by turning the poem into a curse ("pox on you!").[46] This feature of Cellini's poetics resembles Bertold Brecht's notion of *étrangement*, the juxtaposition of incongruous elements designed to shock the reader.

Lewd sexual themes are also evident in the writings of many of Cellini's contemporaries, most notably Bronzino (1503–72) and Aretino (1492–1556). Bronzino, whose poems contain a "ludic spirit and mocking attitude,"[47] is best remembered for his burlesque *capitoli* that are literally about fruits and vegetables, metaphorically about sex. They belong to the tradition of lyric that developed out of the carnival songs (*canti carnascialeschi*) invented in Florence in the preceding century. Carnival songs accompanied the public festivities of processions, races, and tournaments performed during the period of Carnival in Italian cities. Books of carnival songs circulated in manuscript and print form in the Renaissance. Following the lead of Berni, poets like Bronzino used the *capitolo* in *terza rima* to celebrate vice, to attack rivals, or to sing the praises of a seemingly insignificant topic. For example, in Bronzino's "Capitolo del ravanello" the speaker sings the virtues of the *ravanello* (radish), a metaphor for the penis:

> [Le donne] mangiano il ravanel molle e asciutto,
> E innanzi e dietro al pasto, ed a merenda;
> E senza romper l'inghiottiscon tutto. (Toscan, 1: 409)
>
> ([Women] eat the radish flaccid/wet and hard/dry,
> Before and after a meal, and at snacktime
> And, without breaking it, they swallow it whole.)

According to Toscan, the metaphorical level of meaning includes the act of sodomy: women consume the radish both according to nature (vaginally) and contrary to nature (anally), from in front and from behind.[48] Whereas Cellini's sonnets celebrate sodomy as a sexual act between men, here Bronzino's *canti* sing the praises of sodomy as an "unnatural" heterosexual practice.

Aretino's famous *Sonetti lussuriosi* contain no such euphemistic subtleties. He composed them in Rome in 1524–25 to accompany the erotic woodcuts of Marcantonio Raimondi, based on drawings by Giulio Romano. They later became known as the "Sedici modi" (the sixteen pleasures, literally positions, of sexual intercourse).[49] Dubbed the "Scourge of Princes" by Ariosto (OF XLVI 14.3), Aretino composed the *Sei giornate*, published in two installments as the *Ragionamento* (1534) and the *Dialogo* (1536), dialogues about the benefits and disadvantages of the three main professions for women in society (nun, wife, prostitute), ultimately concluding that the prostitute's life was the only honorable one for women.[50] Aretino's verses contain explicit sexual language not found in the comic-burlesque poetry of the Florentine tradition. Sexually explicit terms such as "fottere" (to fuck), "cazzo" (cock), and "culo" (ass) recur throughout the *sonetti lussuriosi*. In 1558 many of Aretino's works were placed on the Church's Index of Prohibited Books. A complex, contradictory figure like Cellini, Aretino produced works of literature in a variety of genres, some of which are highly misogynistic, in addition to composing deeply religious works. Although direct contact between Aretino and Cellini was limited, Aretino did refer to Cellini in several of his letters to other artists. In a 1537 letter to the Florentine sculptor and architect Niccolò Tribolo, Aretino places Cellini and Tribolo in the Tiziano painting, *San Pietro Martire*, as the two angels observing from above the martyrdom of Saint Peter.[51]

Since Petrarchan verses are centered so much around desire, is one justified in looking for this thematic among Cellini's lyrics? Where is the cruel lady, where is the absent lover? Looking for Love in Cellini's poetry, we find one such sonnet where the poet directly invokes Love. The first quatrain contains the conventional image of the wounded poet-lover:

> L'arco et lo strale, Amor, per cui già 'l petto
> portai squarciato, et lacrimoso il volto,
> e quel legame da chi io fui avvolto
> tra mille nodi fuor d'ogni diletto, (Maier, 968)
>
> (The bow and arrow, Love, which caused me to bear my chest ripped
> open and my face covered in tears, and that tie that bound me, tied in
> a thousand knots, deprived of all pleasure,)

Petrarch's sonnet 109 contains precisely this image of the injured and bound poet-lover:

> Lasso, quante fiate Amor m'assale,
> (che fra la notte e 'l dì son più di mille)
> torno dov'arder vidi le faville
> che 'l foco del mio cor fanno immortale.

(Alas, whenever Love assails me (which between night and day is more than a thousand times), I return where I saw those sparks burning that make immortal the fire of my heart. [Trans. Durling, 216])

As we should expect, Cellini violates his model by introducing coarse language in the very first line of the second quatrain:

> càcciati omai nel cul per più dispetto,
> ch'io son, come già fui, libero e sciolto,
> né temo il foco, il foco tuo che tolto
> m'aveva al primo mio vero intelletto.
> Adopra pur ver me quant'hai valore,
> ché non ti stimo; avventa pur de' strali,
> ch'armate ho contra te le luci e 'l core.
> Fuggite, o ciechi e miseri mortali,
> fuggite meco oggi il crudel signore,
> ch'altro non porge mai ch'oltraggi e mali. (Maier, 968)

(Get it through your ass, with [my] disrespect, that I am as I was before free and unbound. Nor do I fear the fire, your fire that took from me my intellect. Go on! Use towards me whatever's in your arsenal! Because I don't put my faith in you; Go ahead! Fling some arrows! Since I have armed myself against you with my eyes and my heart. Run, oh you blind and miserable mortals! Flee from the cruel lord like me today who offers nothing but insults and evils!)

What is surprising when comparing Cellini's poetry to Michelangelo's is the virtual lack of a substantial number of poems about love in Cellini's poetic oeuvre. In addition, the language of love is found primarily in Cellini's poems about God.[52]

Cellini deviated from Petrarchan poetic norms in various ways but conformed to Petrarchan conventions in several of his encomiastic sonnets. Not surprisingly, perhaps, two of these encomiastic sonnets found their way into print. A representative example is the sonnet he wrote in praise of Laura Battiferra, wife of sculptor and architect Bartolommeo Ammannati, a poet in her own right, as Victoria Kirkham has argued.[53] Here the speaker sings of Battiferra's beauty and grace, comparing her to Petrarch and Orpheus and identifying her with Petrarch's own Laura (verses 9–11): "Lassù v'alzò il Petrarca, e dietro poi / ne venne a rivedervi in Paradiso, / sete scesi in un corpo ora ambidoi."[54] This sonnet by Cellini was printed in 1560 in Battiferra's first volume of poetry, *Il primo libro dell'opere toscane di Madonna Laura Battiferra degli Ammannati*, along with her reply (*risposta*) in kind.[55] Her *canzoniere* contained one hundred and eighty-seven poems, one hundred and forty-six by Battiferra herself and forty-one by contemporary artists and men of letters, including Annibal Caro, Varchi, and Bronzino. Another sonnet written by Cellini in praise of Battiferra ("Quella più ch'altra gloriosa e bella" [Maier, 932]) likewise conflates her with Petrarch himself. One of Cellini's sonnets praising Benedetto Varchi, beginning "BENEDETTO quel dì che l'alma varchi" and punning on his name, was printed postumously in Florence in Varchi's *Sonetti spirituali* (Giunti, 1573).[56] This appears to be the "moral sonnet" referred to by Battiferra in her 9 June 1557 letter to Varchi.[57] These two published encomiastic sonnets to Battiferra and Varchi demonstrate that Cellini was able to alternate between adopting and violating poetic models, in this case, Petrarchism. As a poet, then, Cellini was capable of polished Petrarchan verses. Other sonnets of his resonate with Petrarch's voice. For instance, verse 11 of the sonnet that opens the *Vita*, "nostri fragil pensier sen porta 'l vento" (Bellotto, 4), is a faithful echo of verse 8 of Petrarch's sonnet 329: "quante speranze se ne porta il vento!"[58]

Cellini composed numerous encomiastic sonnets that went unpublished. They include sonnets to patrons Cosimo I ("Quel clemente, immortal, celeste Iddio" [Maier, 922–23]) and Francis I of France ("O monarca immortale, io pur ti chiamo" [Maier, 921–22]), friends Francesco Maria Molza ("Molza, che mentre avrà possanza il sole" [Maier, 941]) and Sforza Almeni ("Gentil messer Sforza, se amore" [Maier, 928]), and fellow artists Bronzino ("Scendi, Giove, dal ciel tra nube e pioggia" [Maier, 943]) and Michelangelo ("Solo una fronda della tua corona" [Maier, 934–35]). Cellini's sonnet to Bronzino is his reply to Bronzino's sonnet praising the *Perseus* as a divine artwork ("Ardea Venere bella, e lui ch'in pioggia") and published in Cellini's *Due trattati* of 1568.[59] Cellini's sonnet to Michelangelo shows a deep respect and almost reverence for the artist who served throughout his life as both master and emulative model for Cellini.

Returning to Cellini's use of sex and satire, we find Bandinelli and Vasari to be other targets of Cellini's satirical techniques. Baccio Bandinelli (1488–1560) was Cellini's arch-rival at the court of Duke Cosimo I de' Medici during his sojourn in Florence. It is not without irony that Vasari depicted Bandinelli, whom Cellini referred to in a letter as "il maggiore nimico ch'io avessi al mondo," face-to-face with Cellini in his tondo of Cosimo I and his artists in the Salone dei Cinquecento.[60] Bandinelli did, in fact, try to thwart Cellini at every turn. He prevented Cellini from using a stone cutter who was employed by the Opera di Santa Maria del Fiore on a project overseen by Bandinelli and from having a marble block that eventually became the *Apollo and Hyacinth*. In both cases, Cosimo had to intervene personally on Cellini' s behalf.[61] Cellini's caudate sonnet, beginning "Veduto Giove poi sciolto il furore" (Maier, 979–80), starts out in a classical manner, with no hint of satirical rancor:

> Veduto Giove poi sciolto 'l furore,
> che i voti eran già 'l tempio della Pacie,
> non volse più soffrir: l'ardente facie
> strinse; poi comandò come signiore
> Iunon, Pluto e Nettunno, ch'ogniun fore
> sortissin con lor forze più voracie:
> soffiate, venti, aquilon fiero aldacie,
> esca Piton, Pandora, escha 'l terrore.
> Disfarete, lor disse, ormai la terra,
> poi che ciascun s'è fatto mio ribello
> con falsi inganni, latroncini e guerra.
> Dove porrèn 'l gran Mondo, già sì bello?
> Signior, ché in te pietà pur s'apre e serra, (Maier, 979–80)

(Jove [having seen] the fury unleashed, [and that] the offerings were already made at the temple of Peace, did not want to suffer any longer: he held the burning thunderbolt tightly, then he commanded like a lord that Juno, Pluto, and Neptune each come out with their most powerful forces: Blow you winds, come out Python, like a fierce and courageous kite, come out Pandora, like a terror. You will destroy the earth! he told them, since everyone has become my rebel, with false tricks, larceny, and war. Where will we put the great Earth, so beautiful? Lord, since pity resides in you,)

Thus far, the poem retells a mythological tale, when suddenly it shifts to a sexually graphic attack on Bandinelli and Vasari:

> ogni cosa entri in culo al Bandinello;
>   e se non ha cervello,
> per l'uno e l'altro polo io vi prometto
> ch'ogni cosa enterrà 'n culo a Giorgietto.
>   S'e' non ha più diletto,
> sel torrà in culo la sua pulita moglie,
> che può cavarsi tutte le sue voglie.
>   Son poeta da coglie,
> perch'ho 'l pel bianco e già l'avevo nero:
> basta così ridendo dirvi il vero. (Maier, 980)

(Let everything go up Bandinelli's ass, and if he has no brain, in one way or another, I promise you that everything will go up Giorgetto's ass.

If he no longer enjoys it, his pure wife will take it in the ass and fulfill all her desires. I'm a foolish old poet, because I have white hair that used to be black: I'm satisfied, laughing, to tell you the truth.)

In this poem, Cellini employs sodomy as his preferred mode of attack. Cellini's satirical caudate sonnet depicts both Bandinelli (spelled Bandinello) and Vasari (identified as "Giorgietto" rather than "Giorgio") as sodomites. Cellini's use of the caudate sonnet links him to a larger group of poets who used this genre to express a kind of vernacular political satire.[62] Cellini wrote two other sonnets directly attacking Bandinelli (Maier, 932–34). In the first addressed "Al cavalier Bandinello" (Maier, 932–33), Cellini teases Bandinelli for not being able to respond to him in kind, since he is not a poet. Although in the *Memoriale* attributed to Bandinelli, the author insists that he wrote sonnets during the course of his life, no poems have been found to corroborate his claim.[63] The poet then recalls their verbal sparring in front of Cosimo I about the Hercules and Cacus statue when Cellini made everyone laugh at court at Bandinelli's "dua [sic] figure . . . mal fatte et tutte rattoppate" (Bellotto, 734). In verses 9–10 the speaker continues his attack on Bandinelli who "splintered and destroyed many rocks" whereas Cellini "brought them back to life" (De' vivi ho percosso io: voi molti sassi / fracassati e distrutti [Maier, 933]).

Vasari reappears in Cellini's *Vita*, it, too, marked by a parodic quality. Cellini often relies on the grotesque to achieve parody. For instance, he uses grotesque imagery to paint a verbal portrait of Vasari. In his prose Cellini presents Vasari as a sodomite who constantly scratches his dry skin with his long, sharp fingernails.

> Giorgetto Vassellario, aretino, dipintore . . . gli aveva una sua lebbrolina secca, la quale gli aveva usato le mane [sic] a grattar sempre, e dormendo con un buon garzone che io avevo, che si domandava Manno, pensando di grattar sé, gli aveva scorticato una gamba al detto Manno con certe sue sporche manine, le quale [sic] non si tagliava mai l'ugna. (Bellotto, 312)
> (Little Giorgio Vasari, the maker of vases, the aretine, painter . . . had a dry-skin disease which he used to scratch with his hands constantly, and when sleeping with a good apprentice I had, who was named Manno, thinking that he was scratching himself, he flayed Manno's whole leg with those dirty little hands of his, whose nails he never cut.)

Cellini refers to Vasari as "giorgino" or "giorgetto" throughout the *Vita*, as he has done in his poetry. These diminutives of his name, coupled with the other words ending in *-ina* or *-ine* found in this passage ("lebbrolina," "manine"), diminish his status and ridicule him. They are also meant to feminize and demean him. Furthermore, the term "vassellario" is a clever pun. Cellini's characterization of Vasari as "vassellario" demeans him by suggesting that he is an artisan, one who makes *vasselli*, vessels or vases. These techniques apply to another rival whom Cellini meets in the story of his life. In the *canzone* stanza he tacks up in the Church of San Giovanni, Cellini attacks the rival goldsmith Bernardo Baldini, head of the Florentine mint, by ridiculing him as "Bernardone" (Big Bernie) and his son Baccio as "Buaccio" (ugly ox):

> Qui giace Bernardone, asin, porcaccio,
> spia, ladro, sensale, in cui pose
> Pandora i maggior mali, e poi traspose
> di lui quel pecoron mastro Buaccio. (Bellotto, 705).

> (Here slops Big Bernie, ass, dirty pig,
> spy, thief, broker, in whom
> Pandora placed the greatest evils, and then she transferred them
> from him to that big sheep, the ugly ox, master Baccio.)[64]

In his use of the scathing four-verse stanza, Cellini may be imitating Grazzini who was notorious for his series of four-line stanzas attacking his enemies that he began "Qui giace."[65] This short stanza in the *Vita* plays on the pun of hooved livestock. The -accio suffix is a deliberate mocking and misspelling of names. Like the use of diminutives, use of pejoratives (the *-accio* ending of "porcaccio" and "Buaccio"), often left out of English translations, is another element of Cellini's violation of Petrarchan conventions.

Cellini's poetic attacks on his artistic rivals could also include his friends. In a sonnet with the provocative rubric, "Perseo che si maraviglia di questa innusata e favorita braveria grifona," Perseus himself is the speaker (Maier, 929–30). This sonnet, addressed to Ammannati, does not quite fit the theme of *statue parlanti* because Hercules does not actually reply. Perseus recalls the fierce competition among Florentine artists to win the commission for the Neptune fountain ultimately won by Ammannati. In the poem, Perseus addresses Neptune using the affectionate "tu" form, lamenting that the great god, saved from Bandinelli's ineptitude, is nonetheless "ruined" (*guasti*, literally *broken*, verse 6) because he will be created by the "beastly" Ammannati: "Guarti pur, gran Nettunno; io non son tale: / ché se ben ti scampai dal Bandinello, / quest'è più bestial forza d'animale" (verses 9–11). In a similar passage in the *Vita* the narrator, too, expresses sympathy for Neptune. Two of Cellini's voices collapse in this one utterance: the narrator and poet join together in unison to express sympathy for that "poor, unfortunate marble" ("povero mal fortunato marmo," Bellotto, 731) intended for Neptune's birth. In this way Cellini made it clear to his friends that they could easily become the objects of his derision.

Turning back to the elements of Cellini's poetics, in addition to the grotesque, the artist's poetics also includes caricature. Cellini caricatures powerful women in the story of his life. For instance, he portrays King Francis's mistress as a kind of Harpy. For Cellini, Madame d'Étampes was "nata . . . quasi per la rovina del mondo" (Bellotto, 586). In another passage, the Duchess of Florence (Eleonora da Toledo) resembles one of the Furies. Cellini describes an encounter with her in this way: " . . . subito si scrucciava con tanto arrabiato furore meco, che io mi spaventavo" (Bellotto, 700). Nor do the ancients escape from his parodic treatment. Classical allusions abound in the *Vita*, and are frequently used for satirical, not humanistic, purposes. Faustina, the wife of Marcus Aurelius, in Cellini's hands, becomes a Bolognese prostitute (Bellotto, 100). Likewise, Cellini transforms Ovid's Penthesilea, the noble queen of the Amazons, into yet another prostitute he meets in the story of his life (Bellotto, 120–27). In using both the grotesque and caricature, Cellini could display his expertise in ancient history and at the same time savagely attack his contemporary rivals and enemies. Moreover, by attacking powerful female rulers such as Cosimo's wife in his verse, the artist sought to demonstrate his domination over them.

Dante and the Poetics of Personification

Cellini used the sonnet form for satirical purposes, to parody both his contemporaries and historical figures. His sonnets violate Petrarchan conventions by incorporating high and low stylistic registers in a single poem. Cellini's use of Dante, on the other hand, his other poetic predecessor, is quite different from his abuse of Petrarch. Cellini invokes Dante in two specific places in his literary works, when he is in prison and when he is in court.

The prison thematic in the *Vita* has been the focus of much critical attention perhaps because Cellini alludes to Dante. Cellini narrates his imprisonment in Rome at the hands of Pope Paul III for charges of stealing jewels from the papal coffers during the Sack of Rome. In prison, Cellini plays the role of the Christian martyr. But he also imitates Dante, becoming Dante-pilgrim. He journeys to the Otherworld with a boy-angel as his guide, first to Hell where he sees an infinite number of suffering souls, and then to Heaven, where he envisions the Godhead in the form of a sun and cross. Cellini, like Dante, was a witness to divine justice (Hell) and love (Heaven). His final vision is that of the Virgin Mary sitting enthroned with the infant Jesus.

Jonathan Goldberg, among others, has interpreted this scene as a Dantesque tale of martyrdom and conversion, as indeed it is.[66] But we must not fall into performing a synecdochic sleight-of-hand: critics have been mistaking the part for the whole. Goldberg is not alone in arguing that Cellini's *Vita*, although containing elements of the romance and picaresque genres, is really a spiritual autobiography in which the textual "I" narrates a journey of self-recognition and conversion, as does Dante's *Comedy*. But the narrative of the autobiography as a whole is not a conversion narrative.[67] Cellini does not contrast his former self and status as sinner with his present self and status as convert. Instead, Cellini displays a bold shamelessness and arrogance, neither apologizing for his actions nor asking the reader for forgiveness. Rather, the *Vita* transgresses the confessional mode.

Cellini used Dante because Dante provided him with the language of pilgrims and prayers. Dante also offered Cellini a form for poetic expression. In the *Vita Nuova*, Dante-poet narrates a dream-vision, writes a poem encapsulating the dream-vision, and then interprets it. Like Dante, Cellini performed exegeses of his own two "dreams:" each of Cellini's dream-sonnets (Maier, 949–61) is followed by a prose declaration (*dichiarazione*). Cellini composed "due 'sogni' tradotti in poesia dapprima e poi spiegati da un commento in prosa, ambedue con un travestimento metaforico giocoso."[68] In the first dream the poet laments how the art of painting is in serious decline, and that this decline is now affecting the arts of sculpture and architecture. To remedy this situation, Michelangelo and Cellini ask Hercules for help. Hercules responds that his aid was sought once before by a certain sculptor named Bandinelli, *in marmorea figura*, but Bandinelli treated him so badly that he vowed he would return only if called by a certain goldsmith who created his half-brother, Perseus. Hercules concludes that since the goldsmith no longer invoked his assistance, he did not return, thus hinting at Cellini's loss of favor and status at the Medici court and, in turn, his lack of commissions. According to Dario Trento, the second dream is modeled on lectures Varchi delivered at the Accademia Fiorentina.[69] Both dreams conclude with a kind of longing, with the speaker lamenting how has not been able to practice actively as an artist because his patron no longer awards him commissions. Thus, Cellini is compelled to work on his (non-commissioned) marble crucifix (he called 'l mio bel Cristo), intended for the chapel of his own tomb.[70]

Other Dantesque influences on Cellini's verses are evident in several of the artist's spiritual compositions. For instance, the first verse of a sonnet that the artist wrote while imprisoned in Castel Sant'Angelo, and inserted in the *Vita*, beginning "S'i' potessi, Signor, mostrarvi il vero" (Bellotto, 440–41) recalls the verse "S'io posso mostrarti un vero" of *Paradiso* (Par. 8, 94–95). Another short spiritual composition, a dialogue in verse, was inserted into the narrative of the *Vita* by Cellini. The poem ("Afflitti spirti miei" [Bellotto, 426]), a dialogue between the artist's body and soul ("intellectual spirits"), which took place after his failed suicide attempt in prison, may have drawn its inspiration, as Maier had first suggested, from the *Vita Nuova*. Echoes of the *Inferno* in particular are evident in a few of Cellini's sonnets.[71] Where we do find Dante in Cellini's writings, however, is in the artist's prose rather than his poetry.

In his prose, too, Cellini is Dantesque but in a much more innovative way than critics have thus far noted. The *Vita*'s Dantesque journey to the Otherworld is really quite conventional. However, Cellini's use of Dante in the courtroom scene in Paris is more innovative. In 1543 Cellini was charged with wrongful eviction. In his account of the courtroom scene, the judge utters Dante's words, a verse from the seventh canto of *Inferno*. One recalls that *Inferno* 7 begins with Pluto's exclamation,

> *"Pape Satàn, pape Satàn aleppe!"*
> cominciò Pluto con la voce chioccia;
> e quel savio gentil, che tutto seppe.[72] (Inf. 7, 1–3)

In his account Cellini likens the judge to Dante's Pluto, not surprisingly, and ascribes to him the Dantesque motto, "Sta' cheto sta' cheto, Satanasso, levati di costì, e sta' cheto" (Bellotto, 542). Cellini elaborates on the judge's words: "Queste parole innella lingua franzese suonano in questo modo: 'Phe phe Satan phe phe alè phe.'" Allen Mandelbaum among others has interpreted these words in Dante's poem as an invocation to Satan, but admits that many other interpretations are possible.[73] Cellini deploys this Dantesque rhetoric to illustrate the infernal nature of judicial spaces, and in this particular instance, of court proceedings in France. Cellini equates Parisian courtrooms with Hell itself, insisting to the reader, "in Parigi dove per le ditte cause si può dire quel luogo dove si litiga essere uno Inferno" (Bellotto, 542). One recalls that *Inferno* 7 is the Circle of the Grasping Avaricious, and is therefore particularly well-suited to Cellini's perception of the "devilish" nature of French judicial practices in his day and was no doubt part of his joke.

In the courtroom scene, as in the prison scene, Cellini reenacts Dante: he becomes Dante-pilgrim, witness and judge. A sixteenth-century reader of Jacopo della Lana's *Commento all'Inferno* (1324) recalled Cellini when he read the commentary of *Inferno 7*. Jacopo della Lana (1290–1365) wrote one of the earliest commentaries of the *Comedy*. At the top of the third page of manuscript Ricc. 1009 in the Biblioteca Riccardiana, the reader wrote a long passage about Cellini's use of Dante. But the anonymous reader also added a few observations of his own: he praises Cellini, whom he calls "uomo acutissimo," for "correcting" Dante's text by citing the verse in French. He then claims to have asked Cellini himself to explain to him why the Devil spoke French rather than some other language:

> Benvenuto Cellini quand era in parigi si abbattè ad un giudice . . . e ricordatosi di questo luogo di Dante . . . volesse raccontar il romore che per l'ordinario i diavoli fanno, e dicesse loro quelle parole in lingua franzese. e così corriggeva benvenuto uomo acutissimo questo testo. Domandatogli io perchè parlasse Pluto a suoi diavoli più in franzese che in altro linguaggio, rispose che diavolo lo sa.[74]

> (Benvenuto Cellini when he was in Paris met a judge . . . and he recalled these lines from Dante . . . he wanted to recount the sound that devils ordinarily make, and he told them those words in French, and so Benvenuto, a very sharp man, corrected this text. I asked him why Pluto spoke to his devils in French rather than another language, and he replied that the devil knows [why].)

What is so striking about this Dantesque scene in the *Vita* is that Cellini has not merely become Dante-pilgrim, he has become a Dante commentator. The exact meaning of these words, "Pape Satàn, pape Satàn, aleppe!" has perplexed many a Dante commentator. But not, or so it seems, Cellini. According to Cellini, "questi comentatori gli fanno dir cose le quale [*sic*] lui non pensò mai" (Bellotto, 543). Cellini actually owned a manuscript of a text by Dante: the inventory of his household goods at his death lists "uno Dante in penna."[75] Cellini claims that he is similar to Dante in yet another way. Like Dante, Cellini had traveled to Paris and spoke excellent French:[76]

> Io che benissimo avevo inparata la lingua franzese, sentendo questo motto, mi venne in memoria quel che Dante volse dire quando lui entrò con Vergilio suo maestro drento alle porte dello Inferno. Perché Dante a tempo di Giotto dipintore furno insieme in Francia e maggiormente in Parigi . . . però ancora Dante intendendo bene la lingua franzese, si servì di quel motto. (Bellotto, 542–43)

(I, who had learned French very well, when hearing this phrase, remembered what Dante meant when he entered the gates of Hell with his master Virgil. Because Dante and the painter Giotto were both in France and especially in Paris . . . since Dante also knew French well, he utilized this phrase.)

Cellini as a Dante-interpreter is also strengthened in the episode itself, that is, that the episode is an instance of Cellini affirming he is "right" where the other commentators are "wrong": "m'è parso gran cosa che mai non sia stato inteso per tale" (Bellotto, 543). Cellini may also have quoted Dante because being Dantesque was, by definition, not being Petrarchan. Bernard Weinberg among others has argued that Dante was not as fashionable as Petrarch in sixteenth-century Italy.[77] Debates raged over whether the *Comedy* could be characterized as an epic since critics accused Dante of violating decorum by mixing high and low registers. Bembo himself criticized Dante for his low, mixed diction: he attacked Dante for employing "Latin and foreign words, Tuscan words altered and deformed, low or hard-sounding ones."[78] However, in Venice, writers of the Venier salon preferred the *capitolo* written in Dantesque *terza rima* to the Petrarchan sonnet.[79] Michel Plaisance has argued that in the sixteenth century Dante was often more popular than Petrarch because Dante was considered to contain all scientific knowledge, and his *Comedy* was read as if it could teach astronomy and geometry.[80] Cellini, too, composed a long *capitolo* in Dantesque tercets, addressed to Luca Martini, and inserted it into his *Vita* (Bellotto, 453–63). Cellini thus chose Dante over Petrarch in order to align himself with the oppositional elements in his culture. In this way, the artist positioned himself oppositionally in literary history precisely at a time when Petrarch's reputation was rising and Dante's declining.

Through the centuries scholars have viewed Cellini in a variety of different ways—as artist, courtier, and proud sodomite—based on knowledge of his *Vita* only. A closer examination of his lyric is valuable in demonstrating what a disruptive character he really was. Cellini's violation of existing Petrarchan norms in his poetry links him to a larger group of sixteenth-century *anti-Petrarchisti*. His conventional use of the sonnet for encomiastic or polemical purposes connects him to an even larger group of minor poets consisting predominantly of artists like Cellini and women poets such as Tullia d'Aragona. However, Cellini's poetic activity is endemic of broader cultural phenomena. Wider literacy, the spread of education beyond the narrow confines of the university or monastery, the burgeoning book culture, and the new printing presses all combined to create a new group of poets who composed, exchanged, and printed their compositions. In his poetry Cellini uses a variety of registers, juxtaposing high (elite) and low (popular) elements. He used the sonnet form to engage other artists in artistic debates, to attack his rivals, and to express a wide range of sentiments. In his verse, Cellini played with language and deployed the poetic *tenzone* in an innovative way. He also invented words. In a sonnet beginning "Glorioso Signiore, poi che a Dio" (Maier, 899), for example, Cellini coined a new verb, "ducare." Salvatore Battaglia has described this as a "verbo attivo inventato, per quanto pare, dal Cellini per esprimere lo insignire della dignità ducale."[81] The Accademia della Crusca immortalized one instance of the artist's strange vocabulary; for instance, for their fourth edition they chose Cellini as their model for the bizarre term "ingannacontadini." The word, used by the artist in his 1547 letter to Varchi, signified a kind of fool's gold.[82] Moreover, the artist also regularly employed artistic terms such as *figura*, *rilievo*, and *disegno* in his verse. And finally, Cellini's words appear at least a dozen times in the *Grande Dizionario della Lingua Italiana*, and for three particular words, *bordellerie, broccardo*, and *sodomitaccio*, Cellini's usage is the only entry.[83]

In short, the stylistic features of Cellini's poetry—Petrarchan and Dantesque allusions, the strategies of parody, personification, caricature, and the grotesque—are more sophisticated and polished than hitherto believed. The artist was a versatile poet who displayed his ability at writing in different registers. In a sonnet ("Se la mia boschereccia poesia / non dicie le parole belle e rare" [Maier, 966]), which serves as Cellini's poetic manifesto, he defended his right to compose verses, even if others found them to be rough and inelegant. Cellini may have insisted he was merely a humble writer of verse, evoking Leonardo's claim that he was just an "omo sanza lettere,"[84] yet he was a fine poet in his own right.

CHAPTER 4
CELLINI'S POETICS II: THE *VITA*

The *Vita* continues to invite speculation about the texts that influenced Cellini when he was composing the story of his life. The majority of scholars writing about the *Vita* underscore the influence of autobiography or biography, especially those of earlier or contemporary artists. Dino Cervigni remains the expert in this area, arguing for the importance of earlier autobiographical writings of artists; Jonathan Goldberg has noted the importance of spiritual autobiography. More recently, Victoria Gardner has asserted that Cellini's *Vita* was modeled explicitly on Giorgio Vasari's biography of Michelangelo in his *Lives of the Artists*.[1] What is missing from these accounts is serious consideration of other literary models that may have influenced Cellini besides autobiography and biography. As we have seen in Cellini's poetry, Dante and Petrarch figure prominently. His imitation of Dante is evident in his prose as well as in his poetry. In this chapter, I consider other literary genres that Cellini used in his self-dramatization, including medieval vision narratives, ekphrastic writing, epic, romance, and theatrical comedy. In his *Vita* Cellini plays the roles of Dantesque pilgrim, chivalric hero, and *magus* (magician). Moreover, not all the influences on Cellini were textual.

Many critics have written about the allusions in Cellini's *Vita* to a particular author or specific genre without discussing whether it was possible that Cellini even knew these authors or books. Numerous studies show the similarities between the *Vita* and another text without providing solid evidence of a direct link between the two; for example, Cervigni has compared Cellini's *Vita* to Spanish picaresque novels of the day without actually claiming that Cellini had read any of them. Ettore Allodoli has suggested that a passage in the *Vita* evokes a letter written by Pietro Aretino.[2] Cellini could read Italian and French, but not, it seems, Latin, although he recites prayers and sings in Latin while imprisoned in Rome. Cellini does not tell us much about his reading practices; thus, it is difficult to know with certainty whether he knew a work in an original version or through oral transmission. The problem of direct influences is complex when studying Cellini. What were the titles of those eighteen books listed in the inventory of his household goods at his death?[3]

It will be useful to begin by considering textual evidence for the books that he had read or knew. He cites Dante and Vitruvius by name and the Bible and Giovanni Villani's *Chronicle* by title. Cellini claims that Girolamo Savonarola's sermons were read to him during his imprisonment in Castel Sant'Angelo. He owned a copy of Leonardo da Vinci's art treatises and probably some version of Dante's *Comedy*. Cellini's copy of Dante as well as the Bible help explain his role as Dantesque pilgrim and his journey to the Otherworld. Leonardo's art treatises along with the treatise on goldsmithing and sculpture that Cellini wrote on his own easily demonstrate his knowledge of technical writing. To gauge Cellini's familiarity with texts in other genres, we can compare the content and lexicon of the *Vita* with important texts in the Italian tradition. Narrative affinities in the *Vita* suggest an awareness of Ariosto's *Orlando Furioso* if not of earlier medieval chivalric narratives. Cellini's "theatrical" self-presentation seems to demonstrate an acquaintance with drama; undoubtedly, he knew the popular Florentine dramatic form called the *sacra rappresentazione*. In Maier's view, several episodes in the *Vita* are reminiscent of Boccaccio's *Decameron*.[4] Detailed passages in the *Vita* about conjuring demons suggest an awareness of contemporary books of necromancy. Cellini used classical material, notably figures from Greek mythology, as inspiration for his art works. Popular knowledge of classical mythology may have been derived from sixteenth-century vernacular translations of classical texts. As Carlo Ginzburg has shown, Titian's knowledge of classical myths was drawn not directly from Ovid, since he could not read Latin, but from a popular vernacular translation.[5]

For indirect influences, we can recall Cellini's personal acquaintances with artists and men of letters of his day, including Annibal Caro and Benedetto Varchi. Cellini may have heard lectures on Dante by Giambattista Gelli at the Florentine Academy. Appointed official *lettore di Dante*, Gelli delivered public lectures on Dante during the 1540s. At the *Studio Fiorentino*, there were also private lectures on Petrarch. The cities in which Cellini resided during his lifetime can also provide important clues about his training. Ferrara, Naples, and Venice were all important cultural centers in his day. In this chapter, I would like to suggest some cultural models that Cellini incorporated in the story of his life without precluding the possibility that some of these intertextualities may be analogues that might have occurred to a contemporary reader. Not every stylistic character, image, or figure in the *Vita* necessarily had some outside inspiration. It will be useful to recall earlier biographies and autobiographies. When composing his *Vita*, Cellini had the model of sacred biographies. During the Italian Renaissance, saints' lives rivaled chivalric romances in popularity.[6] Anton Francesco Doni's bibliography of sixteenth-century vernacular works, *La libraria* (1550), lists *Vita de' santi* as well as numerous *Vite* of the holy fathers, Christ, and little-known figures such as the *beata Osanna da Mantova*.[7] As noted, the theatrical form of the *sacre rappresentazioni* drew subject matter from a wide range of sacred material, including saints' lives and hagiography. Sacred biographies typically recounted a saint's religious devotion and interior life. What is unusual about Cellini's autobiography when compared to saints' lives of his day is the complete absence of a definitive conversion. The autobiographer does not express remorse for his violent acts of assault and murder, nor does he ask for forgiveness from the reader. Cellini may have derived his use of the Otherworld journey from earlier or contemporary saints' lives since this topos also belongs to this genre. The similarities between Cellini's *Vita* and Teresa of Ávila's *Libro de la Vida*, composed at the behest of her confessor between 1561 and 1565, have been noted by Mirollo, but it seems likely that contemporary accounts of religious lives, such as Aretino's *Vita di Maria Vergine* (1539) or *Vita di San Tomaso signore d'Aquino* (1543), played just as important a role in Cellini's self-conscious self-fashioning. Finally, turning to secular lives, there were lay biographies such as Giovan Battista Pigna's biography of Ariosto, printed in 1554 and reprinted in 1556 in Venice by the Valgrisi firm, and, as some scholars have claimed, the model of Petrarch's *Secretum*.[8] But the question of the influence will remain problematic primarily because Cellini was silent on the subject.

Turning from biographies to autobiographies, Cellini had a wide range of texts at his disposal. Earlier autobiographical writings, particularly those of other artists, clearly influenced Cellini's portrait of himself in the story of his life. Peter Burke has provided a concise overview of these autobiographies and biographies circulating in Renaissance Italy, following the lead of Julius Schlosser.[9] For fifteenth-century Florence one must consider Lorenzo Ghiberti's *I Commentarii* (ca. 1450) and Antonio Manetti's *Vita di Filippo di ser Brunellescho* (1480s). Cellini's *Vita* resembles Ghiberti's *Commentarii* but differs from Manetti's biography of Brunelleschi. Like Cellini's *Vita*, Ghiberti's *Commentaries* on art is a work "tecnica e storica ad un tempo" that combines "biografia e trattatistica."[10] They contain an autobiographical section in which Ghiberti proudly recounts the numerous commissions he won throughout his lifetime. He tells the reader that the works of art that he created as a sculptor and goldsmith earned him honor and glory, precisely as Cellini does when he emphasizes how the metalworks he created in Rome were sure to bring him honor and profit ("onore . . . utile" [Bellotto, 69]). Like Ghiberti, Cellini paraphrases Vitruvius.[11] Ghiberti apologizes to the reader for digressing from his commentaries in order to elaborate on his own works of art, immodestly insisting that "poche cose si sono fatte d'inportanza nella *sua* terra non sieno state disegnate et ordinate di *sua* mano."[12] On the contrary, Cellini apologizes to the reader for digressing from his own art to recount events of a more historical nature, stressing that he was an artist, not a historian. With his biography of Brunelleschi, Manetti attempted to place Brunelleschi above Leon Battista Alberti in the Florentine artistic pantheon of the day. Like Cellini's narrative, Manetti's relates "a series of encounters with ignorant and malicious opponents from which the protagonist emerges victorious."[13] However, while Brunelleschi employs "geniality and wit" to triumph over his adversaries, Cellini often takes recourse to violence.[14] Both Manetti and Cellini employ a polemical posture throughout.

Cellini's *Vita* lends itself for comparison with the *Memorie* (1405–25) of Oderigo di Andrea di Credi as well as the autobiography of the Florentine goldsmith Raffaello Sinibaldi da Montelupo (ca. 1504–66). However, Cellini's *Vita* is different in both style and in content from earlier artists' autobiographical writing. Earlier writing by artists was brief and incomplete, concentrating primarily on the life of an artist: his training, patrons, and works of art. Fifteenth-century books by artists often contained events of an autobiographical nature from an artist's life, such as rivalries with other artists, but they are not, strictly speaking, autobiographies. For instance, Oderigo di Credi's *Memorie* is almost exclusively a *libro di conti*, an account book listing debits and credits, occasionally recounting events in his life, but rarely narrating his thoughts or actions. The majority of artists' writings from the fifteenth century follow this pattern. Maier has compared Cellini's *Vita* to the autobiographical fragment of Raffaello da Montelupo, concluding that Cellini's *Vita* is a literary masterpiece, lyrical at the same time it is mythic, while Raffaello's "si esaurisce in una piatta enumerazione cronologico di avvenimenti e di vicende."[15] Like Cellini, Credi was trained at the workshop of Baccio's father, Michelangelo del Bandinelli. He began writing the story of his life in 1564. His autobiography begins with his birth but ends abruptly in 1527, thus covering his life only up to age twenty-three.

In contrast to these artists' autobiographies, Cellini's *Vita* recounts the life of an artist, narrating the life of a man and his exploits, while simultaneously being a kind of chronicle of his times. It was Goethe who articulated most clearly this doubleness when he insisted that Cellini was "a representative Renaissance figure—at once exceptional and typical, unique and problematic, robustly conscious of his individual virtù while summarily reflecting all the incongruities of his age."[16] Unlike earlier writings by artists, Cellini's *Vita* generally conforms to Phillippe Lejeune's definition of an autobiography as a narrative encompassing an individual's whole life from birth to death but without focusing exclusively on personality. Much like fifteenth-century artists, Florentine merchants expanded their account books to include entries about events in their family life such as births, marriages, and deaths.[17] This type of writing is autobiographical in nature, but these account books are not properly autobiographies. They do not seek to recount a full and complete life history, as T.C. Price Zimmerman has observed: "What distinguishes [autobiography] from memoirs, diaries, journals, recollections, and other forms of 'autobiographical' writing is the author's viewing of his past life in an effort to construe it as a whole."[18] Typically, the *Ricordi* or *Memorie* by artists utilize the style of a diary, as Bandinelli's alleged *Memoriale* will demonstrate, rather than the "uninterrupted" narrative prose style of historical writing found not only in autobiographies but also in medieval chronicles and "histories." In the *Memoriale* (composed 1552–ca. 1558), Bandinelli structures his book by citing the number of the *memoria* (from 1–12) and then follows with a brief autobiographical event.[19] Although the episodes appear in chronological order, they are not linked together in the text. One "memory" ends; another begins. The various memories that Bandinelli recounts are separated thematically as well as spatially. Each account stands apart separately from the others. No attempt is made to link the disparate events together by addressing the reader directly, making explicit the course of the narrative, or apologizing for a lengthy digression, as Cellini commonly does. In fact, in a practice viewed as standard in modern novels, Cellini often addresses the reader as "dear reader" or "gentle readers." Unlike Bandinelli, Cellini consciously sought to fashion his autobiography into a smooth, logically flowing narrative. Cellini began his *Vita* in 1558; Bandinelli on 18 May 1552. Cellini's *Vita* covers the years from his prodigious birth to age sixty-two in 1,036 folios; Bandinelli's *Memoriale* spans the years from his rather unceremonious birth in 1488 to ca. 1558 in 48 folios. Cellini dictated his *Vita* to an apprentice; Bandinelli, to his son Cesare. Cellini's intended audience is posterity;

Bandinelli's ideal readers are his sons, whom he addresses throughout as "figlioli miei." Bandinelli's *Memoriale* reads like a last will and testament, detailing the inventory of his household goods alongside instructions to his kin for his burial. These features of Bandinelli's *Memoriale* were common to another early modern genre, the Jewish "ethical will," which "had sometimes included, along with the disposition of the inheritance and the prescriptions for burial, pages of moral injunctions and rules for the children."[20]

Cellini was an innovator in autobiography; thus, a word about the genre's general form is in order. The definition Philippe Lejeune has proposed of autobiography as "[a] retrospective prose narrative written by a real person concerning his own life, where the focus is his individual life, *in particular the story of his personality*" is a useful general definition of the genre.[21] Cellini's *Vita* adheres to Lejeune's conventional definition of the genre—the story of his own life, from birth to old age, written by himself—but Cellini emphasizes not so much his personality as his actions and accomplishments, in artistic and other spheres. His ideal audience may have included his contemporaries but his intended public was posterity, the future generations.

Cellini did something new with the genre of autobiography that he had inherited. He wrote an account of his life full of incident. Earlier artists' autobiographies lack the comprehensiveness, the unity, the myth-making of Cellini's *Vita*. In his autobiography Cellini used a variety of tones and registers, amply employed rhetorical devices, and made allusions to medieval and Renaissance Italian literary sources. He attempted to write an autobiography that would encompass the entire arc of his long life. His *Vita* recalls the great book of Augustine's *Confessions* in which the textual "I" cries out to the reader, narrating an extraordinary individual's full life of passion, joy, despair. Cellini, though primarily a visual artist, was keenly aware of literary forms and poetic conventions.

Mixing genres was a common literary practice in Renaissance Italy. Lodovico Ariosto (1474–1533), like many sixteenth-century writers, mixed components from romance and epic when he composed the *Orlando Furioso*, a poem in octaves about the exploits of Roland, the warrior hero from medieval French chivalric texts. Genre-mixing was also a topic of intense debate. Years after Cellini's death Battista Guarini (1538–1612) would defend the practice of mixing elements from tragedy and comedy to create a new dramatic genre, the tragicomedy, in his *Compendio della poesia tragicomica* (1601).[22]

Cellini comes at a pivotal moment in the contemporary debate about genre-mixing, between defenders and detractors of Ariosto and Tasso.

A key figure in this debate and a practitioner of genre-mixing was Giovanni Battista Giraldi Cinzio (1504–73). Born in Ferrara, Cinzio was a tragicomic dramatist who wrote novellas, tragedies, and a number of discourses on general poetics. Cinzio introduced widely varying materials into his tragedies and defended himself against purists in his discourse, *Tragedie a lieto fine* (ca. 1541). He wrote extensively about romance as a new genre, a genre different from the epic, and was one of Ariosto's earliest defenders. Tasso, in his *Apologia in difesa della Gerusalemme Liberata* (1585), defended himself against attacks by the Accademia della Crusca by insisting his own poem was not a blending of epic and romance elements but rather adhered to Aristotelian principles of epic.[23] By playing with genres, Cellini assaults the burgeoning conventions of autobiography.[24] His *Vita* mixes essential components of romance and epic, narrating the story of an errant knight in search of personal glory and recounting the tale of a crusader battling barbarians during the Sack of Rome while defending the faith. The *Vita* contains a technique common to sixteenth-century *commedia erudita*: cross-dressing. As an author, Cellini innovated by appropriating several of the genres circulating in sixteenth-century Italian culture (the art treatise, romance and epic, and regular comedy) and figuratively hurling them at contemporary critics who chastised writers for violating decorum by mixing genres. Cellini enacts his violence and rage on people as well as texts and their rules.

The *Vita* as Art Treatise

It will be useful to examine the notion of genre transgression by comparing Cellini's *Vita* to his *Treatise on Goldsmithing*. An episode from the autobiography in dialogue form narrates how pleased Cosimo was when Cellini showed him a small model of the *Perseus*. Cosimo commissioned the *Perseus* (figures 9 and 10) from Cellini in 1545 for the Loggia dei Lanzi in the Piazza della Signoria, the central civic square in Florence. Cellini did not complete the statue until 1554, most likely because the entire composition consisted of the larger-than-lifesize *Perseus*, the *Medusa* writhing below *Perseus* at the top of the base, the ornate, grotesque base itself containing four freestanding bronze sculptures of Jupiter, Minerva, Mercury, and Danae, as well as the large low-relief bronze of Perseus liberating Andromeda. Cosimo wanted Cellini's work to complement the great works of art already on display in the piazza, Donatello's *Judith* and Michelangelo's *David*. Cellini elaborates on his encounter with the Duke, inserting dialogue into the episode:

> Da poi che l'ebbe considerato assai, crescendogli grandemente di piacere, disse queste parole: "Se tu conducessi, Benvenuto mio, così in opera grande questo piccol modellino, questa sarebbe la più bella opera in piazza." Allora io dissi: "Eccellentissimo mio Signore, in piazza sono l'opere del gran Donatello e del maraviglioso Michelagnolo, qual sono istati dua li maggior uomini dagli antichi in qua. Per tanto Vostra Eccellenzia illustrissima dà un grand'animo al mio modello, perché a me basta la vista di far meglio l'opera, che il modello, più di tre volte." (Bellotto, 608–09)

> (After he had studied it for a while, becoming more and more pleased, he said these words: "My dear Benvenuto, if you produce a large work just like this little model, it will be the most beautiful work in the piazza." Then I replied: "My Lord and Excellency, there are works in the piazza by the great Donatello, and by the marvelous Michelangelo, who are the greatest artists since the time of the ancients. Since your most Illustrious Excellency is inspired by my model, let me say that I will produce a statue that is three times better than the model.")

The account of this same event in the *Trattato dell'Oreficeria* is nearly identical:

> E fatto ch'io ebbi, io lo portai a sua eccellenza illustrissima, la quale maravigliatasi disse: "Benvenuto, se e' ti dessi il cuore di fare quest'opera grande di questa eccellenzia che tu l'ài fatta piccola, io ti dico certissimo che questa sarebbe la più bella opera che fussi in piazza." . . . io dissi al duca: "Considerate bene, eccellentissimo mio signore, che è in quella piazza quella di Donatello e quella di Michelagnolo Buonarroti, qual sono e' maggior uomini del mondo, forse che fussi mai; ma quanto al mio modellino, a me basta la vista di far l'opera mia che sarà meglio tre volte del modello che voi vedete." (Scarpellini, 472–73)

> (And when I had finished [the model of a Perseus], I took it to his Illustrious Excellency who marveled at it and said: "Benvenuto, if you had the courage to do a large work of this skill as you have it in a small scale, I tell you with certainty that it would be the most beautiful work in the piazza" . . . I said to Duke: "My Lord and Excellency, you well know that in that piazza are works by Donatello and by Michelangelo Buonarroti, who are the greatest men in the world, perhaps that ever lived, as for my own little model, I will undertake to make a statue that will be three times more beautiful than the model that you see here.")

Cellini's *Vita* is ekphrastic, and his original version of the *Treatises*, autobiographical. Ekphrasis is commonly defined as the rhetorical device of describing an art object in detail within a narrative. For Cellini and his contemporaries, ekphrasis signified a detailed description in writing of a work of art, creating a verbal representation of a visual object. The autograph of his *Two Treatises on Goldsmithing and Sculpture* contains many autobiographical passages exactly like the one quoted above. Another example is when Cellini recounts how to cast figures in bronze in the third chapter of the treatise on sculpture. In this chapter he narrates his Herculean feat of fusing the *Perseus*, although hindered by ill health and incompetent workers:

> When I was casting my Perseus, calling to aid some of those fellows, I found them so absolutely devoid of sense that in their stupidity they, disheartened, all swore that my mold was ruined... there as I lay prostrate on my bed with a high fever, one of them in whom I had a little more confidence than the rest came to me, and speaking very gently, said: "Benvenuto, resign yourself to the worst, the furnace has been ill prepared, a cake has formed on the metal." (Scarpellini, 535–36)

The comparable passage in the *Vita* recounts the same events—illness, anger at his workers, the curdling of the metal—in virtually the same words: "Struggling against these perverse accidents for many hours... I was suddenly attacked by a fever... and was forced to throw myself on my bed... In the midst of these immeasurable tribulations I caught sight of a man making his way into my room... Poor Benvenuto! Your work is all ruined—there's no hope left!... I went at once to inspect the furnace, and found that the metal had all curdled, had caked as they say" (Bellotto, 667–71).

When the *Two Treatises* were printed for the first time in 1568, four years before Cellini's death, all the autobiographical passages were gone. The *editio princeps* of the art treatises contains none of the digressions of an autobiographical nature. The editor, Gherardo Spini, removed them all.[25] Chapter 2 argued that Spini, a member of the Florentine Academy, changed Cellini's original version of the *Two Treatises*, downplaying its autobiographical elements to align it more clearly with the treatise genre. It was the editor's responsibility to improve a book's readability, but Spini may also have done violence to Cellini's text because the *Vita* clearly puts the Medici and especially Cosimo in a bad light. Cosimo acted like a merchant rather than a duke for failing to protect Cellini from the competitive marketplace that had begun to replace "a symbolic economy of nourishment and gift-giving."[26] Not surprisingly, Cosimo, offspring of a powerful banking family, chose to place a "vulgar, monetary value" on Cellini's priceless talent and works of art unlike the

French king who sought to confer "upon his equal Cellini a similarly immeasurable value."[27]

The art treatises in Cellini's original version are a highly technical, didactic work with digressions about the adversities, triumphs, and injustices suffered by its hero-artist Cellini. This is precisely what the autobiography is: the life of an artist. His autobiography is a kind of technical treatise. It is an exposition, often in technical language, of all the art works created by its artist-hero Cellini, with digressions about the adversities, triumphs, and injustices he suffers. Autobiographical accounts abound in the art treatises; technical passages in the autobiography. Two more passages from the *Vita* and the *Two Treatises* demonstrate that the *Two Treatises* are autobiographical and the *Vita*, ekphrastic. In the twelfth chapter of the *Treatise on Goldsmithing* concerned with casting tiny, intricate objects, Cellini describes the saltcellar (figure 1) he created for King Francis I of France in minute detail.

[I]o feci. . . una saliera d'oro, in forma ovata, di lunghezza di dua terzi di braccio in circa. . . con molti richissimi ornamenti. Di poi avevo compartito in piacevole e bel modo. . . Il Mare e la Terra. . . Questo era figurato per Nettuno dio del mare; e lo avevo posto a sedere in su una conchiglia, cioè un nicchio marittimo, fatto in forma di trionfo, con i sua quattro cavagli marittimi. . . e al detto Nettuno inella mano dritta avevo posto il suo tridente. . . A rincontro al detto Nettuno io avevo fatto una figura femmina, della medesima grandezza del mastio. . . e mi ero accomodato che le gambe del mastio e della femmina con bellissima grazia d'arte entravano l'una nell'altra. . . Ed in mano alla detta figura avevo accomodato un tempietto riccamente lavorato, di ordine ionico. . . Di poi avevo fatto nella grossezza del detto ovato un partimento di otto zane, nelle quale avevo figurato la Primavera, la State, lo Autunno, ed il Verno; nelle altre quattro si era figurato l'Aurora, il Giorno, Crepusco, e la Notte. (Scarpellini, 479–80)

(I made a saltcellar in gold, oval in shape, and about two-thirds of a cubit high. . . very richly ornamented. And I divided it up in a pleasing and pretty manner. . . one part I made as the Sea and the other as Land. . . The Sea was personified by Neptune, god of the Sea, and I made him in a shell, a kind of nautical triumphal car to which were yoked four seahorses. . . In Neptune's right hand I put a trident. . . on the opposite side of Neptune I placed a female figure, of the same size as the male, and I devised it that the legs of the male and the female were entwined most gracefully one with the other. . . By the side of the female figure I put a little Ionic temple, very carefully crafted. . . in the oval body of the oval for the salt I had planned out eight niches, in each one of which was figured Spring, Summer, Autumn, and Winter on one side, and Dawn, Day, Twilight, and Night on the other.)

Again, the autobiographical passage is nearly identical to the passage in the *Trattato dell'Oreficeria*:

[L]a ditta saliera . . . era in forma ovata et era di grandezza di dua terzi di braccio incirca, tutta d'oro . . . avevo figurato il Mare e la Terra, a ssedere l'uno e l'altro, e s'intramettevano le gambe . . . così propriamente avevo dato loro quella grazia. A il Mare avevo posto in mano un tridente innella destra; et innella sinistra avevo posto una barca sottilmente lavorata, innella quale si metteva la salina. Era sotto a questa detta figura i sua quattro cavalli marittimi . . . Per la Terra avevo figurato una bellissima donna, con il corno della sua dovizia in mano . . . nell'altra sua sinistra mana [*sic*] avevo fatto un tempietto di ordine ionico, sottilissimamente lavorato . . . in una basa d'ebano nero . . . innella quale io avevo compartito quattro figure d'oro, fatte di più che mezo rilievo: questi si erano figurato la Notte, il Giorno, il Graprusco, e l'Aurora. Ancora v'era quattro altre figure della medesima grandezza. (Bellotto, 565–66)

(The said saltcellar . . . was oval in shape and about two-thirds of a cubit high, all gold . . . I represented the Sea and the Land, both seated, with their legs entwined . . . in this way I gave them their necessary grace. I had placed a trident in the right hand of the Sea; and in his left hand, I had put a delicately worked ship to hold the salt. Below the figure were his four sea-horses . . . The Land I had represented by a very beautiful woman, holding her horn of plenty in her hand . . . In her left hand I had made a very delicately worked Ionic temple . . . in the base of black ebony . . . I had a small bevel on which I had set four gold figures, executed in more than half relief, representing Night, Day, Twilight, and Dawn. Besides that there were four other figures of the same size.)

Cellini may have written his art treatises because that technical genre was extremely popular in Cellini's day. Many were intended primarily for professional artists; others were written to assist in the appreciation of art. Before Cellini's time, there are the treatises on painting by Cennino Cennini, Leon Battista Alberti, and Leonardo. Cennini's *Il libro dell'arte o trattato della pittura di Cennino Cennini* was written about 1390; Alberti's art treatise appeared first in Latin as *De pictura* (1435) and subsequently in the vernacular as *Della pittura* (1436); Leonardo's writings on the art of design, composed ca. 1490–92 and ca. 1513–14, circulated in manuscript form in the Renaissance. Contemporary with Cellini's is the treatise by Vincenzio Danti titled, *Il primo libro del trattato delle perfette proporzioni di tutte le cose che imitare e ritrarre si possono con l'arte del disegno di Vincenzio Danti* (Florence, 1567). The treatise as a genre had widespread appeal because the new, literate public was capable of buying affordable printed books and was eager to teach itself new skills. Humanism helped produce the revival of the treatise as a form.

The discovery of a new manuscript of Vitruvius' *De architectura* by Poggio Bracciolini contributed to the increased interest in ancient architecture, which ultimately reached our own Benvenuto.

When Ettore Camerasca compared Cennino Cennini's art treatise to Cellini's treatises on goldsmithing and sculpture, he was struck that Cellini's "*Trattati* are much closer in spirit to the 'recipe book' of C. Cennini than they are to the celebrated *Vite* of his rival [Vasari]."[28] With its insistence on technical recipes such as the step-by-step instructions in metallurgy necessary to fuse the *Perseus*, Cellini's art treatises, like his *Vita*, are a book of secrets. In William Eamon's view, the sixteenth century "was an age of 'how-to': secrets were spelled out; calculation began to take the place of cunning."[29] The enormous popularity of how-to manuals may explain in part why Cellini was able to print his art treatises. Technical books were widely read in the sixteenth century; they constituted the largest category of books found in Florentine households in the second half of the sixteenth century.[30] Vernacular books of secrets were how-to manuals that "published scores of artisanal recipes from a broad range of crafts, from metallurgy and 'practical alchemy' to dyeing textiles and preparing drugs."[31] Recipe books in the Renaissance were often magical or alchemical in nature. Alchemy was a science based on "a secret [doctrine] reserved for only a few privileged adepts possessing the intellectual and moral qualities requisite for obtaining it."[32] The sixteenth-century binding of Leonardo's *Codex Atlanticus* ties his work to the esoteric arts: the cover reads, "Disegni di machine et delle arti secreti et altre cose di Leonardo da Vinci racolti da Pompeo Leoni."[33] The long title of Cellini's art treatises reveals its claim that it, too, is a book of secrets: *Due Trattati, uno intorno alle otto principali arti dell'Oreficeria, l'altro in materia dell'Arte della Scultura; dove si veggono* infiniti segreti *nel lavorare le Figure di Marmo e nel gettarle in bronzo* (emphasis added). Tylus has suggested that Cellini's art treatises were intended to transmit secret knowledge to a small group of initiates: "But the *Trattati* also...seek to define the artist, not as an alienated individual, but as the member of the community whose knowledge of *il fare* and ability to pass that knowledge on to others might make it, if not self-sufficient, at least the possessor of secret 'wisdom.' "[34]

The Mixture of Genres: Autobiography as Epic, Romance, and Comedy

In his *Vita* Cellini conflates two types of chivalric hero, the crusader drawn from epic and the knight errant taken from romance. He portrays himself as a crusader battling barbarians during the siege of Rome in 1527, but also as a wandering knight who falls in love while restlessly searching for a lord to serve. By Cellini's day, the Arthurian romance and the medieval *chanson de geste*, songs of chivalric deeds, were completely conflated. Written in the eleventh century, the Old French epic the *Chanson de Roland* (Song of Roland) recounts the individual adventures of brave knights serving King Charlemagne and narrates the collective story of their devastating defeat in battle in 778 by the Saracens. Its hero is Roland (*Orlando*). The slaughter of the rearguard of Charlemagne's army under Roland at Roncevaux provided material for the French heroic epic. Retellings of the *Song of Roland* circulated widely in manuscript and print forms in medieval and Renaissance Italy. From the thirteenth to the sixteenth centuries minstrels, troubadours, and *cantatori* sang of the adventures of chivalric heroes such as Roland in piazzas throughout Italy. Medieval authors of chivalric epic romances mixed the Carolingian cycle of epics—known as the Matter of France, inspired by stories of Charlemagne and his soldiers—and other cycles. The Carolingian cycle material was dynastic and warlike; the Bretonic cycle material—known as the Matter of Britain, based on the adventures of King Arthur's knights—amorous and magical.[35] By the fifteenth century in Italy the two cycles were fused. Scholars of medieval literature employ the terms "epic romance" (to emphasize the predominance of elements from the epic register such as battles, warfare) and "romance epic" (to underscore the centrality of features from the mode of romance, including amours, emotions) to classify chivalric texts.[36]

Earlier medieval chivalric stories about Roland were continued by Pulci, Matteo Maria Boiardo, and Ariosto. Pulci's *Morgante* appeared in two parts in 1478 and 1483; Boiardo's *Orlando Innamorato* was published as three books, one posthumously, and ultimately left unfinished at his death (1483 for the first two, 1495 for the third); Ariosto's *Orlando Furioso* was printed in three versions, in 1516, 1521, and 1532. All three writers adapted the material they inherited from medieval chivalric texts, producing new adventures for Roland. Pulci narrates the exploits of Orlando and Rinaldo alongside the comic adventures of the giant, Morgante, and the half-giant, Margutte. Pulci helped popularize the Orlando stories by developing more fully the character of Morgante from earlier Orlando *cantari* of the fourteenth century. In his *Orlando Innamorato* Boiardo retold the story of Orlando and his fellow knights, adding new adventures for the hero. Ariosto expanded Boiardo's story by making the hero Orlando not merely *innamorato* (in love) but *furioso* (madly in love, that is, insane through the effects of love). Ariosto's

Ovidian use of irony was perceived as one of his many innovations with the Orlando material.

Scholars of the *Orlando Furioso* have long noted that Ariosto's conflation of epic and romance is evident in the very first verse of his poem. The poet tells the reader that he sings of, "ladies, knights, arms, love" (le donne, i cavallier, l'arme, gli amori [OF I, 1]). Here Virgil provides the epic features of knights and arms; romance provides the themes of ladies and love.[37] Ariosto's text harmoniously mixes features from both epic and romance: "from one perspective, [the *Orlando Furioso*] resembles a classical work, while from another it resembles a medieval romance."[38] Albert Russell Ascoli and David Quint likewise have shown that Ariosto uniquely and skillfully integrated components of the two genres. They also emphasized that unlike the majority of medieval writers of chivalric texts, Ariosto's use of classical sources is derived from the classics themselves, directly from his readings of Ovid and Virgil, rather than indirectly from a medieval or contemporary text based on classical material. Ariosto's grafting together of two genres, the classical epic and the chivalric romance, may have enraged literary purists of the later sixteenth century, but contemporary readers did not perceive this mingling in a negative light at all; on the contrary, readers of Ariosto's day made the *Orlando Furioso* one of the most widely read books in sixteenth-century Italy.[39] By the end of the sixteenth century the *Orlando Furioso* had appeared in print one hundred and eighty-three times, rivaling only the works of Petrarch in popularity with Renaissance readers.[40] Like Ariosto, Cellini participated in the Renaissance practice of genre-mixing. From Virgilian epic, Cellini employs a genealogy and accounts of military exploits. From both epic and romance, he derives the element of casting himself as a hero by stressing his marvelous or miraculous origins. From the romance genre, Cellini appropriates his use of magic.

Cellini may have appropriated his use of a genealogy from the epic. Epics trace a genealogy linking the hero to a noble, often divinely ordained past. Medieval heroic epics commonly link the hero to a lineage from classical antiquity. Cellini narrates how one of his ancestors, a certain Fiorino da Cellini, was a courageous captain in Julius Caesar's army:

> Aveva Iulio Cesare un suo primo e valoroso capitano, il quali [*sic*] si domandava Fiorino da Cellino, che è un castello il quali [*sic*] è presso Monte Fiasconi a dua miglia. (Bellotto, 11)
>
> (Julius Caesar had a first-ranking and brave captain named Fiorino who came from Cellini, a village about two miles away from Monte Fiasconi.)

Cellini's imagined ancestor Fiorino was a virtuous and loyal soldier of Caesar whose very name christened the city of Florence. According to Cellini, Caesar himself named the city of Florence "Fiorenze" to capture the essence of the city filled with flowers as well as to honor his brave captain "Fiorino:"

> Avendo questo Fiorino fatti i sua alloggiamenti sotto Fiesole, dove è ora Fiorenze . . . tutti quelli soldati et altri, che avevano a ffare del ditto capitano, dicevano: "Andiamo a Fiorenze" . . . così . . . Iulio Cesare . . . questo nome di Fiorenze pose nome alla ditta città; et ancora per fare un tal favore al suo valoroso capitano, et tanto meglio gli voleva, per averlo tratto di luogo molto umile, et per essere un tal virtuoso fatto da llui.
> (Bellotto, 11–12)

> (This Fiorino decided to have his quarters under the hill of Fiesole, where Florence is today . . . All the soldiers and other people connected with this captain acquired the habit of saying when they went to pay him a visit: "Let's go to Fiorenze" . . . so . . . Julius Caesar . . . decided to call the city Florence as it was a very beautiful name and very apposite, and it seemed, with the suggestion of flowers, to make a good omen; and besides that he wanted to show what a high regard he had for his courageous captain.)

In this episode about his lineage, Cellini underscores his noble ancestor's fundamental place in Florentine history and in the Tuscan language. He also aggrandizes his family tree by linking his personal family history to the history of Rome during the reign of Caesar. Epics commonly employed genealogies to affirm the noble origins of the hero and his right to rule. In the *Aeneid* Virgil linked Roman history to Greek epic in the figure of Aeneas, a Trojan, founder of Rome. Linking the lineages of heroes to antiquity was a common feature of fifteenth-century chivalric epics and Renaissance epic-romances.[41] Medieval chroniclers typically employed genealogies to structure their historical narratives.[42] In the sixteenth century, too, Ariosto portrayed his patron Alfonso I d'Este in the *Furioso* as the descendant of the hero Ruggiero, crowned the first Count of the House of Este by Charlemagne.

The fabulous origins of Florence was a topos of both "real" and legendary historiography. Cellini may have derived his use of this narrative motif from Villani's *Chronicle*. In chapter 7 of book 1 Villani narrated the legendary origins of Fiesole, musing on the etymology of Fiesole as "*Fia sola*, cioè prima sanza altra città abitata nella detta parte."[43] A similar topos is found in Boccaccio's *Ameto*.[44] In Cellini's day, Vasari's frescoes on the founding of Florence, in the Salone dei Cinquecento in the

Palazzo Vecchio, also take up this theme.[45] Cellini's use of Dante, like his request to read Villani's *Chronicle* while imprisoned in Castel Sant'Angelo, is quintessentially Florentine. Heroes of epics as well as romances commonly have early adventures. Cellini recounts two such memories from his childhood. The first centers on a scorpion, the second around a salamander. In his *Vita* Cellini narrates how, as an infant, he picked up a scorpion, proudly showing it to all the members of his family. When his horrified parents and grandfather tried to persuade him to put it down, the little Benvenuto refused, tenaciously holding onto it:

Ancora viveva Andrea Cellini mio avo, che io avevo già l'età di tre anni incirca, e lui passava li cento anni. Avevano un giorno mutato un certo cannone d'uno acquaio, et del detto n'era uscito un grande scarpione, il quali loro non l'avevano veduto, et era dello acquaio sceso in terra, e itosene sotto una panca: io lo vidi, e corso a llui, gli missi le mani a dosso. Il detto era sì grande, che avendolo innella picciola mano, da uno degl'illati avanzava fuori la coda, et da l'altro avanzava tutt'a dua le bocche. Dicono che con gran festa io corsi al mio avo, dicendo: "Vedi, nonno mio, il mio bel granchiolino!" Conosciuto il ditto che gli era uno scarpione, per il grande spavento e per la gelosia di me, fu per cader morto; et me lo chiedeva con gran carezze: io tanto più lo strignevo piagnendo, ché non lo volevo dare a persona. (Bellotto, 20–21)

(My grandfather Andrea Cellini was still alive when I was about three years old, and he was well over a hundred. One day they had replaced a cistern water pipe when a large scorpion crawled out of it, which they hadn't seen, and had slipped to the ground, and scuttled under a bench: I saw it, and ran over to it, and scooped it up. It was so big that when I had it in my tiny hand, its tail hung out at one end and both its claws at the other. They told me that, laughing happily, I ran over to my grandfather and said: "Look, grandpa, look at my beautiful little crab!" He recognized at once that it was a scorpion and almost dropped dead from shock and anxiety for my safety; then he tried to coax me into giving it to him: but the more he did so, the more I tightened my grip on it tearfully, refusing to give it to anyone.)

Finally, his terror-stricken father entices him into letting him "snip off the scorpion's tail and claws" (Bellotto, 21). The Cellini family regards this incident involving the scorpion as "a good omen." Cellini's playing with the scorpion could also be a variation on Hercules strangling snakes in his cradle, or on hagiographic narratives in which infant saints remain unharmed in the midst of mortal dangers.[46] As we have seen in Cellini's poetry, Hercules is an important interlocutor for Cellini, whom he addresses in a familial tone in his dream-visions. In the scorpion episode Cellini presents himself as a bold and courageous child, prefiguring qualities he would exhibit throughout the course of his life. The scorpion was an important motif for Cellini since, he is quick to tell the reader, he was born under the sign of the scorpion, on 3 November 1500.[47]

The second childhood memory recounts how Cellini's father showed the five-year-old boy a salamander "running around in the very hottest part of the flames" in their fireplace (Bellotto, 21). His father takes the sight of the salamander as a unique and auspicious occasion, telling the toddler that it "has never, as far as we know, been seen by anyone before" (Bellotto, 22). The salamander story is a tale of marvel: salamanders were believed to be signs of good fortune in the Renaissance and were often used as tropes for good luck in literature. This second story functions to illustrate how Cellini was predestined to greatness. The salamander in the fire was also a personal device of Francis I, perhaps in allusion to his devotion as a lover.

The romance-epics of the Italian Renaissance narrate tales of warrior knights who prove physical valor in arms and who participate in large-scale battles or wars. The arts of warfare are typical of epics. The wars between the Christians and the Saracens were the backdrop for the Old French epics. In the poems of Boiardo and Ariosto the individual acts of warrior knights fighting for personal glory are as prominent as the collective action of an army fighting for a Christian victory. In the *Orlando Furioso* Ariosto's knights fully engage in heroic defenses of cities (for instance, Rinaldo in Paris); similarly, there is the figure of Albracca in Boiardo's *Orlando Innamorato*. The protagonist of the *Vita* is portrayed as a brave soldier, warrior, and leader of a band of men. Likewise, the autobiography recounts the heroic deeds that the warrior knight Cellini performs "in the service of the Church" during the Sack of Rome in 1527 by the troops of Emperor Charles V (Bellotto, 142). In his *Vita* Cellini claims to be a kind of epic crusader, defending the Church and his lord, the Pope, during the Sack, much like the Christian warrior knights of medieval epics who battle the Saracens during the Crusades or who participate in long military campaigns. These passages from the *Vita* about the siege in 1527 are filled with elements belonging to the epic register. The autobiography recounts the story of a pious and patriotic Cellini loading cannons and firing guns, slaughtering "a great number of the enemy" to prevent them from entering Rome, resting a short time, and then returning to "que' furori delle artiglierie" (Bellotto, 135). In the *Vita* we find descriptions of new Renaissance technologies that changed the face of war including guns, cannons, and gunpowder. We can add Cellini to Michael Murrin's list of writers of epic who took up the theme of "the new technology of firepower."[48] Cellini tells us he "made his own gunpowder, discovering the most wonderful secrets that are still unknown to anyone else" (Bellotto, 94). Here secrets refer to technique. In his autobiography Cellini portrays himself as a brave knight who was admired for his "military character and bearing" (Bellotto, 125). In this episode Cellini tells the reader that he was a better soldier than artist, insisting that he was actually "more inclined to [soldiering] than to [his] real profession, and as a result [he] made a better job of it than [he] did of being a goldsmith" (Bellotto, 133).

This tale of the Sack of Rome is punctuated throughout by Cellini's commonplace rhetorical technique of *self-accumulatio*. Cellini claims to have singlehandedly saved the Church during the siege, and, to outdo himself, he seriously injured the Prince of Orange, striking him in the chest, exactly dead-center. The Prince of Orange, Philippe de Châlons (ca. 1500–30), was commander of the imperial army after the death of the Constable of Bourbon. In these passages the figure of Cellini bears some resemblance to Dante's warrior spirits, Christian defenders of the faith, such as William of Orange and Roland, in Canto XVIII of *Paradiso* in the *Comedy*. Like Roland, William was a hero of medieval French epic; the character was based on an actual military leader. The presence of two men of Orange, Philip and William, in both Dante and Cellini, may not be coincidental.

Chivalric romances were "tales of adventure in which battles, villanies, vengeances, escapes, journeys, chance encounters, duels, tournaments, loves, births, and deaths carried the story."[49] This definition fits Cellini's autobiography as much as it does Ariosto's *Furioso*. The protagonist of the *Vita* is a kind of knight errant in search of adventures. In his autobiography Cellini casts himself as the chivalric hero of romance by falling "madly" in love. The autobiographer Cellini and the poet Ariosto position themselves as mad lovers in their texts. As emblematic romance hero, Cellini depicts himself as rendered insane by love: "I had fallen in love with a very beautiful Sicilian girl...I did all sorts of crazy things in order to find her again" ("m'ero innamorato d'una fanciulletta siciliana... e feci pazzie inistimabile [*sic*] per ritrovarla" [Bellotto, 231]). The poet of the *Furioso* is "mad" (*furioso*) because love is a kind of madness. He confesses to the reader that although he is writing during a *lucido intervallo* (a lucid moment), he, like the hero Orlando, has become mad through love. One recalls that Hercules, an important figure for Ariosto and for Cellini, was also struck by Cupid's arrow, falling in love with

Althaea. The poet of the Ariostan romance invokes Apollo to inspire in him *quel profetico lume* (OF III, 2.7). Poets and prophets could also derive inspiration from the melancholic influence of the planet Saturn. The power of melancholy "made some men divine, foretelling things to come; and some men poets."[50] The narrator of the *Vita*, likewise, claims that he was melancholic, telling the reader that he was melancholy by nature. And finally, Cellini's insistence that he would "defend the ladies" whom he meets one night at an inn in Naples from those who would do them harm is a play on the conventional chivalric gesture of defending the weak (Bellotto, 251–56).[51]

Cellini's self-presentation in the *Vita* draws on other texts and traditions, including theatrical comedy. In the story of his life Cellini acts as if he were performing for an audience by using characters to drive action. William Howarth has classified this theatrical view of Cellini's *Vita* as exemplary of "dramatic autobiography," a strategy employed by the autobiographer to present life as a staged performance.[52] In Howarth's view, Cellini's *Vita* moves dramatically from episode to episode with little character development, stressing spectacle and blurring the distinction between the narrator and protagonist. In the autobiography, as in *sacre rappresentazioni*, encounters between characters take on a dramatic form. Maria Galetta has asserted that Cellini's low style renders the *Vita* close in spirit to comedy and popular tales: "[L]'autobiografia celliniana . . . grazie soprattutto agli abbassamenti di stile, si avvicina di più alla commedia o alle novelle popolari."[53] The influence of drama on other forms, including autobiography, were many. Cellini's personal acquaintance with the Florentine dramatists Annibal Caro and Anton Francesco Grazzini help explain the influence of drama on his autobiography. The comedies of Caro and Grazzini were regularly performed in Florence during the period 1540–66.[54] Moreover, contemporary models for "oral performance" included theatrical as well as confraternal activities.[55] And finally, there is a hint of the Miles Gloriosus of roman comedy, a prototype for the Renaissance figure of the Braggart Captain, in the protagonist's violent boasting.

In the *Vita* Cellini uses a comic technique commonly found in sixteenth-century comedies, cross-dressing.[56] For instance, Pietro Aretino's *Il Marescalco* (The Stablemaster) dramatizes the joke [*burla*] played by the Duke of Mantova on the stablemaster.[57] Written in 1527, the *Marescalco* was published in 1533. In the play the Duke plans a marriage between the stablemaster, who prefers young boys, and a young girl. In theatrical cross-dressing, the boy in disguise (whether on or off stage) causes friction between the person who believes the boy to be a woman and the audience, aware all along that the disguise is part of an elaborate trick. In the comedy the girl-bride turns out to be Carlo the page, not surprisingly, to the delight of the stablemaster. Often the trick is revealed and the true identity of the boy exposed when the unwitting party gropes his genitals, as the stablemaster did, triumphantly exclaiming, "Wow! This is fantastic!" (Act V, scene x). Cellini's *Vita* recounts a similar episode of cross-dressing during a party in Rome. Cellini dresses up Diego as a woman and takes him as his date. Diego was a boy of sixteen, the son of a Spanish metalsmith who lived nearby, whom Cellini occasionally used as an unpaid model. At the party, the other women quickly become envious of Diego because the men at the party proclaim Cellini's companion, "Pomona," the most beautiful woman there. The women ask "Pomona" questions and are told that she is pregnant. When one of the incredulous women feels her stomach to gauge how far along she is, she unwittingly handles Diego's genitals instead. All the party guests, including the painter Giulio Romano, roar with laughter, proclaiming Cellini the life of the party:

> Subito le due donne, che in mezo l'avevano, mossosi a pietà di Pomona, mettendogli le mane [*sic*] al corpo, trovorno che l'era mastio. Tirando presto le mani a loro con ingiuriose parole, quali si usano dire ai belli giovanetti, levatosi da tavola, subito le grida spartesi et con gran risa e con gran maraviglia, il fiero Michelagnolo chiese licenzia da tutti di poter darmi una penitenzia a suo modo. Avuto il sì, con grandissime gride mi levò di peso, dicendo: "Viva il Signore! viva il Signore!" (Bellotto, 111)

> (Immediately, the two women who were on each side of Pomona, moved by pity for her, start touching her body, and discovered that she was a he. They drew their hands away quickly, shot up from the table, and began insulting him, in words usually reserved for pretty young men; immediately everyone started shouting and laughing uproariously in great amazement, then the proud stern Michelagnolo [da Siena, a sculptor] asked permission from the others to give me the penance he thought proper. Getting their approval, with loud shouting from everyone, he lifted me up and shouted: "Long live Benvenuto! long live Benvenuto!")

Bruno Maier has suggested that the comic episode involving Diego drew inspiration from Boccaccio's novelle.[58] During the Renaissance, there appeared more editions of Boccaccio than of Petrarch or Dante, attesting to the influence of Boccaccio on Renaissance writers.[59] In Maier's view, Cellini's company of artists resembles Boccaccio's *lieta brigata* who joined together to flee the plague in Rome. Like Boccaccio's merry band, Cellini's guests end their pleasurable evening with singing and music. Lexical items such as "piacevole" and "carnale" as well as descriptions of characters recall the vocabulary of the *Decameron*. The language and gestures of Michelangelo, who falls to his knees and recites a prayer when greeting Diego, as well as Diego himself, who in turn responds by giving him a "papal" blessing, evoke the Boccaccian parody of religious language for comic effect that we find, for instance, in the tale of Rustico and Alibech (III, 10). Maier has claimed that Cellini's insistence on invoking San Giuliano in his speech to Paolo Micceri in Paris recalls Rinaldo d'Asti's devotion to San Giuliano (II, 2).[60]

Other textual evidence supports the theory that Cellini may have derived some of the humor found in the *Vita* from Boccaccio, or perhaps from Sacchetti. One recalls the narrator's sudden claims, startling to the reader, that he "left Naples at night with [his] money on [his] person, so he would not be attacked and murdered, as is the Neapolitan custom" (Bellotto, 251–52) or that the deluded castellan, imprisoned with Cellini in Castel Sant'Angelo, insisted that "he was an oil-jar; another time he thought he was a frog, and jumped around like a frog; another time he thought he was dead, and they had to bury him: every year one of these various delusions (*umori*) seized him. This time he began to imagine that he was a bat, and so every once in a while he would let out a deafening shriek like bats do; at other times he would flap his hands and body as if he wanted to fly" (Bellotto, 387–88). There is a possible analogue here with Boccaccio's tale of Andreuccio da Perugia, but on the whole Boccaccio is much less visible a presence in Cellini's writings than Petrarch and Dante.

Cellini as Dante

Thus, in his *Vita*, Cellini borrowed elements from the art treatise, epic, romance, and comedy. The hero's journey to the Otherworld is another feature common to both medieval romance and classical epic.[61] In Cellini's day, authors of chivalric romance included these supernatural voyages in their narratives. For example, in the *Furioso* Astolfo travels to Hell and then to Paradise to fetch Orlando's wits. His trip is really a mock-epic journey in part because he ventures only to the first circle of Hell and the first sphere of Paradise, the Moon. Astolfo's actions are in deliberate parodic imitation of Dante's. Throughout the Ariostan romance Ariosto abbreviates or amplifies narrative features from Virgilian epic to produce a new effect. In addition to playing the role of epic crusader and chivalric hero, Cellini casts himself as a Dantesque pilgrim.

Cellini's account of his journey to the Otherworld during his imprisonment in Rome in 1539 is an imitation of Dante's pilgrimage. These passages are centered in the prison scenes in Castel Sant'Angelo, which are the midway point of the *Vita*. Structurally, the prison scenes in Rome, not the fusion of the *Perseus*, are precisely at the center of the narrative. Cellini joins a small select group of men, including St. Paul and Dante, chosen by God to travel to Hell and Heaven. After enduring many physical and emotional hardships while in prison, Cellini tells us that he decides to end his own life. He rearranges the wooden beams in his cell in such a way that when he strikes one with his arm, they will all tumble down on top of him, crushing him beneath. When the moment arrives and Cellini reaches up to knock out the beam, an "invisible hand" casts aside his hand and hurls him across the room. The angel reappears several days later and acts as Cellini's guide in his Otherworld journey. The angel in the form of a young boy leads Cellini to Hell where he sees an infinite number of suffering souls:

> Dette queste parole, da quello Invisibile a modo che un vento io fui preso e portato via, e fui menato in una stanza dove quel mio Invisibile allora visibilmente mi si mostrava in forma umana, in modo d'un giovane di prima barba; con faccia maravigliosissima, bella, ma austera, non lasciva; et mi mostrava innella ditta stanza, dicendomi: "Quelli tanti uomini che tu vedi, sono tutti quei che insino a qui son nati e poi son morti." Il perch'io lo domandavo per che causa lui mi menava quivi: il qual mi disse: "Vieni innanzi meco e presto lo vedrai." Mi trovavo in mano un pugnaletto et indosso un giaco di maglia; e così mi menava per quella grande stanza, mostrandomi coloro che a infinite migliaia or per un verso or per un altro camminavano. (Bellotto, 435–36)

> (Having said these words, I was taken and carried away as if by a wind by that Invisible force, I was led to a room where that Invisible companion of mine became visible and appeared in human form as a young man with his first beard; his face so marvelous, beautiful, but austere not lascivious, and as he showed me into the room he said: "These men that you see, they are all those who have ever been born and then suffered death." I asked him why he had brought me there: and he replied, "Come with me, and you will soon understand." I found myself with a dagger in my hand and dressed in a coat of mail; and he led me like this through that great hall, showing me all those people wandering here and there in their infinite thousands.)

Cellini had a number of sources for this episode. He may have derived his dagger and mail from Virgil. The Sybil tells Aeneas to raise his sword just after he enters Hell: "vaginaque eripe ferrum" (*Aeneid*, 6.260).[62] Ariosto does not mention Astolfo's armor in Hell but tells us that

Astolfo carries a sword (OF XXXIV, 8.6). Cellini's image of "infinite migliaia" could echo "più di mille anime distrutte" in Dantesque or Virgilian epic. Cellini's insistence that his guide is a beautiful but austere boy is perhaps a Michelangelesque touch.

After his appearance Cellini's supernatural helper leads him to another place where he is suddenly "unarmed and dressed in a white garment, with [his] head uncovered" (Bellotto, 436). Cellini, "filled with wonder" at the blazing sunlight, asks "My friend, what must I do to ascend so high that I can see the sphere of the sun itself?" (Bellotto, 436–37). The angel-boy shows Cellini a staircase and replies, "Go there by yourself" (Bellotto, 437). Here the angel leaves him, as Virgil left Dante, and so Cellini, alone, ascends "those great stairs . . . I quickened my step; and went up and up, until I discovered the whole sphere of the sun" (Bellotto, 437). The sun burns brighter and brighter, blinding Cellini, who at first closes his eyes, then, realizing his "error," stares fixedly at it, and cries out, "The sun—the sun that I have so much desired! I never want to see anything else again, even if your rays blind me!" (Bellotto, 437). This experience convinces Cellini that God has bestowed divine grace upon him.

Cellini's divine vision of the sun appears to him as "a bath of the purest liquid gold" (un bagno di purissimo oro istrutto [Bellotto, 438]), a metaphor that is a stylistic illustration of the congruence of genre with the life of an artist. The sun/divinity then changes its shape, transforming itself spontaneously into "a Christ on the Cross, made out of the very stuff of the sun; and He was of such entrancing beauty and so gracious in His appearance that the human mind cannot imagine even a thousandth part of what I saw" (Bellotto, 438). Then the sun changes form again, and "took the shape of a most beautiful Madonna, seated on high with her Son in her arms, full of grace and appearing to smile; on either side were two angels of such great beauty that it is beyond imagining" (Bellotto, 438). Cellini's mystical vision uniquely connects art to life: his visions of Madonnas are themselves works of art. Moreover, these scenes read like the artist's descriptions of his sculptures.

Cellini's journey to the Otherworld is clearly an imitation of Dante. Like Dante, Cellini was witness to a beatific vision in Paradise, insisting "all these things I saw were true, clear, and vivid" (Bellotto, 439). Both men saw God, in the form of a blazing sun, and the Virgin Mary. For Dante, God appeared as three circles of light:

> . . . tre giri
> di tre colori e d'una contenenza;
> e l'un da l'altro come iri da iri

parea reflesso, e 'l terzo parea foco
che quinci e quindi igualmente si spiri. (Par. 33, 116–20)

Cellini does not recount traveling to Purgatory in his *Vita* probably because here he equates Purgatory with prison. When he was contemplating suicide, Cellini laments that he "had become used to that purgatory" ("la mia buona conplessione si fu accomodata a quel *purgatorio*" [Bellotto, 423, emphasis added]).

But Cellini's vision is also very similar in content and tone to medieval vision narratives in which the protagonist, like Cellini, travels only to Hell and Heaven. Typically, early medieval visions do not include journeys to Purgatory because the notion of Purgatory did not exist prior to the twelfth century: "In the mid-twelfth century the concept of purgatory as a separate and distinct place was formalized... the visions written before the *Divine Comedy* of Dante concern themselves with only heaven and hell."[63] The concept of Purgatory as an intermediary realm of the Otherworld where an individual soul purges itself of sin, ultimately ascending to Heaven and attaining salvation, was firmly established in the late Middle Ages. According to Jacques Le Goff, this "new region of the other world took shape in two phases, first in theological-spiritual literature between 1170 and 1180 at the prompting of Parisian masters and Cistercian monks, and then in visionary literature stemming from the 1180–1215 period."[64] Cellini's vision of Heaven and Hell contains the essential elements of early medieval vision narratives: a journey to heaven and hell with a guide who acts as a protector. What is unusual about Cellini's vision is that he actually envisions God, a characteristic uncommon in medieval vision narratives but a feature of Dante's vision in the *Divine Comedy*. This component of envisioning God renders Cellini's experience, like Dante's, a mystical vision.[65] In Eileen Gardiner's view, most medieval visions "offer the visionary purgation and some degree of illumination, but definitely stop before divine union."[66] Cellini's dream-vision of receiving writing across his forehead evokes how Dante, while in Purgatory, received seven P (for *Peccatum*, "sin" in Latin, representing the seven cardinal sins) across his forehead: "Ancora innel tempo che io ero in carcere, in un terribil sogno mi fu fatto, modo che con un calamo iscrittomi innella fronte parole di grandissima importanza . . . Quando io mi svegliai, mi senti' la fronte contaminata" (Bellotto, 452).

Critics have focused much attention on this religious episode because the saintly behavior exhibited by Cellini is so Dantesque in its content and language, and, as such, so uncharacteristic. Pointing to this section,

James Mirollo has suggested that his *Vita* presents a portrait of the artist as heroic martyr.[67] By his own account, Cellini's saintliness was evidenced by the golden halo encircling his head that was, in his words, clearly visible to a few of his friends. This tale of martyrdom and unjust imprisonment is striking not only for its demonstration of spiritual piety, but also because it depicts some new spiritual practices. Cellini's activities in prison can be linked to the programmatic diffusion of techniques of lay piety under the Counter-Reformation. In sixteenth-century Italy religion was a contested realm of experience. Reformers stressed an individual's personal, even intimate relationship to God, one unmediated by the clergy. In these episodes Cellini's spiritual practices demonstrate just such a direct connection with the divinity. In prison, Cellini sings, prays, and even talks with God: "I began to sing a *De profundis clamavit*, a *Miserere*, and *In te Domine speravi* . . . I repeated many of my prayers in a loud voice; then I said a *Qui habitat in aiutorium*; and then I conversed with God for a while" (Bellotto, 432–33).[68] While a prisoner in Castel Sant'Angelo, Cellini continues creating works of art: he composes his only *capitolo*, also a Dantesque form, praising the prison ("I want to transcribe the *capitolo* I wrote in prison and in praise of this prison" [Bellotto, 453]) and draws a figure of the Risen Christ in Triumph in charcoal on the cell wall.

Cellini's attachment to his Bible seems a bit unusual for a Catholic in this period. Reading the Bible was a point of contention in the sixteenth century for Protestant and Catholic reformers alike. Catholic reformers of Cellini's day did advocate reading the Bible both in the vernacular and in Latin, but traditionalists did not. Orthodox reformers wished to limit Bible reading either to the Latin or to specific vernacular translations, that is, in approved psalters. They were hostile to the circulation of scripture in the vernacular but encouraged familiarity with the psalter in Latin of the sort that Cellini shows. While in prison, Cellini recounts how he reads and meditates on the Bible: "I began the Bible from the beginning, and devoutly I was reading and was meditating on it" (Bellotto, 424). In the climate of the Counter-Reformation, the Church became increasingly more concerned with what people were reading, issuing two lists of prohibited books, Pope Paul IV's Index of 1559 and the Tridentine Index of 1564. Included in these lists were some editions of the vernacular Bible.[69]

By his own account, in prison Cellini had heard sermons written by the controversial Florentine preacher Girolamo Savonarola (1452–98), read to him by a preacher who was accused of being a Lutheran. One recalls that Cellini had spent time in Naples around 1534 or 1535, during the time when the fiery preacher Bernardino Ochino (1487–1563) and the Spanish reformer Juan de Valdés were active. In 1538 Ochino spoke in Florence. Accused of Protestantism, Ochino fled to Geneva where he met Calvin. As Michel Plaisance has shown, the teachings of Ochino influenced several members of the Florentine Academy, including Anton Francesco Grazzini.[70] When we recall Cellini's bold, outspoken nature, it is perhaps not surprising that Cellini recounts these unorthodox spiritual practices while he is a prisoner of the Pope, in the Pope's own prison, but it is still a controversial and daring move on his part.

The Artist as Necromancer

There is some sharp social satire in another place in Cellini's *Vita*. In his account of conjuring demons in Rome he portrays a priest as a necromancer. In this same episode Cellini casts himself as a *magus*. These passages also reveal Cellini's Counter-Reformation interest in witchcraft. In his autobiography Cellini represents goldsmithing as necromancy.

In the *Vita* Cellini is a kind of wandering knight who encounters a demonic rather than magical realm. Cellini recounts conjuring demons in the Coliseum in Rome with a Sicilian priest who was "extremely intelligent and had a very good knowledge of Latin and Greek" (Bellotto, 232). When Cellini expresses interest in learning about the art of necromancy, the priest invites him to his secret ceremony. Together with a friend of his and a young apprentice, Cellini went to the Coliseum where

[I]l prete a uso di negromante, si misse a disegnare i circuli in terra con le più belle cirimonie che inmaginar si possa al mondo; e ci aveva fatto portare profummi preziosi e fuoco, ancora profummi cattivi. Come e' fu in ordine, fece la porta al circulo; e presoci per mano, a uno a uno ci messe drento al circulo; dipoi conpartì gli ufizii: dette il pintàculo in mano a quel altro suo compagno negromante, agli altri dette la cura del fuoco per e' profummi; poi messe mano agli scongiuri. Durò questa cosa più d'una ora e mezo; comparse parechi legione, di modo che il Culiseo era tutto pieno. (Bellotto, 232–33)

(The priest dressed himself up the way that necromancers do, and then with the most beautiful ceremonies you can imagine he began drawing circles on the ground; he made us bring along precious perfumes and fire, and some evil-smelling stuff as well. When everything was ready he stepped in the circle, and taking us by the hand, brought us in one by one with him; then he assigned us our duties: he gave the pentacle to his necromancer friend to hold, and he put the rest of us in charge of the fire for the perfumes. And then he began his incantations. All this lasted over an hour and a half; several legions appeared till the Coliseum was filled with them.)

Cellini's account is far more detailed than the magical encounters found in medieval and Renaissance Italian romances. In romances such as Pulci's *Morgante*, Boiardo's *Orlando Innamorato*, and Ariosto's *Furioso* (with the exception, perhaps, of OF, III) descriptions of actual magical practices are typically very general. For example, when a magician gives a knight a love potion, the poet does not specify to the reader what ingredients were used to make it. Similarly, if a sorceress casts a spell on an errant knight, the poet does not tell the reader what particular words she uttered. In contrast, Cellini details movements, specifying precisely where individual bodies are positioned, whether inside the circle, outside the circle, or under the pentacle. His account is replete with detail. Cellini later identifies the "evil-smelling perfume" as *asafetida*, a powder commonly used in conjuring demons, found in necromancy manuals of the period. He also specifies the particular languages in which the incantations were uttered when he tells us that the priest conjured the demons through incantations spoken "in Hebrew, as well as in Latin and Greek" (Bellotto, 234), languages that were commonly employed in necromantic practices of his day. Latin and Greek were also the languages of Neo-Platonism. Ariosto's *Negromante*, Bibbiena's *Calandria*, and Bruno's *Candelaio* are other sixteenth-century examples of texts concerned with magic, sorcery, and necromancy.

Cellini's passage about necromancy conforms to the letter to necromantic handbooks of the period as well as to actual practices found in court cases tried by the Inquisition. According to Ruth Martin who studied the Venetian Inquisition's prosecution of witchcraft from 1550 to 1650, necromancy was "a sophisticated form of magic involving a fairly high level of literacy and considerable financial outlay."[71] The Florentine philosopher Marsilio Ficino (1433–99) distinguished between black and white magic. In his *De triplici vita* (On the Threefold Life, 1489), he argued that white (or natural) magic tapped into the natural forces of the universe, while black (or ritual) magic used unnatural powers such as demons. In this opposition, necromancy was considered a form of ritual magic. The key book of necromancy, the *Clavicula Salomonis* (The Key of Solomon the King), recounted how God sent an angel to take Solomon a magic ring giving him power over demons.[72] Magical books such as the *Clavicula Salomonis* circulated widely in early modern Italy. All of the elements in Cellini's account are found in the court cases studied by Martin in which necromancers were prosecuted: drawing circles on the ground, standing inside pentacles, invoking demons in Hebrew, dressing in priestly garb, and burning incense.[73] Because of their knowledge of classical languages, priests were paradigmatic necromancers. Sections of the *Clavicula Salomonis* provided specific instructions on how to consecrate a book to the demons in order to find buried treasure or love. After their second adventure in the Coliseum, Cellini tells us that the necromancer tried to persuade him to return with him yet again so that they could consecrate a book to the demons and find abundant treasures ("mi persuadeva che io fussi contento di volere esser seco a consacrare un libro: da il quale trarremmo infinita richeza" [Bellotto, 238]). But Cellini returns to the business at hand, finishing Pope Clement's medals.

Cellini's adventure continues when they all return to the Coliseum a few days later. As requested by the priest, Cellini brings with him a young virgin boy. According to Martin, "The potency of virginity featured prominently in numerous [necromantic] experiments throughout the period . . . "[74] On this occasion the necromancer performs even more elaborate rituals, leads them all into the circle, and then begins burning the perfumes. Cellini tells us that the priest "handed me the pentacle, telling me to turn it in the directions he showed me; then I placed my little apprentice boy under the pentacle . . . The result was that in a short span of time the Coliseum was filled with a hundred times more demons than there had been on the previous occasion" (Bellotto, 234–35). Their encounter with demons concludes when Cellini asks his friend Agnolo Gaddi, who "si era tanto ispaventato che le luce degli ochi avea fuor del punto et era più che mezo morto" (Bellotto, 237), to throw some asafetida on the fire. Instead, Agnolo "fece una strombazzata di coreggie con tanta abundanzia di merda, la qual potette molto più che la zaffetica," sending the demons running "a gran furia" (Bellotto, 237) from the tremendous stench. This recourse to scatology was a comic technique commonly found in romances such as Pulci's *Morgante* as well as the popular comic writings of Rabelais. Moreover, there is something eerily pre-Tassian about Cellini's assembly of demons in the Coliseum when compared to Goffredo's vision of the heavenly host when assaulting the walls of Jerusalem in the *Gerusalemme Liberata*. Cellini mixes high and low elements in his magical account: he harmoniously juxtaposes elite, learned necromancy with popular, body magic. According to John Tedeschi, the "magical arts" constituted the largest category of cases under the rubric of heresy tried by the Inquisition in early modern Italy. From the sixteenth to the eighteenth centuries, for example, nearly one-third of the convictions by the

Inquisitions in Venice and Naples were for offenses such as necromancy, love magic, and casting spells.[75] Turning from Cellini's use of magic to the problem of magic among genre theorists, it is useful to recall that magic was an important marker of genre debates of Cellini's day. Genre theorists sought to impose a strict boundary between the epic and the romance genres. Sixteenth-century commentators often distinguished epic from romance precisely on the basis of some examples of poets' use of magic. In epic, magic is peripheral; in romance, it is central. The medieval *Roman de Tristan* (Romance of Tristan and Iseult) narrates a tale of tragic love set in motion when Tristan accidentally drinks a love potion destined not for him but for King Mark. According to C.P. Brand, writers of romance preferred multiplicity of action and digressions to unity of action and plot.[76] Pigna criticized Ariosto because "his frequent use of magic and the supernatural violate[d] contemporary usage."[77] Although Pigna defended the *Orlando Furioso* in some of its generic mixings, he accused Ariosto of creating a poem that was disorderly, contained too many digressions, and had multiple stories. Many of Pigna's criticisms of the *Furioso* could be applied to Cellini's *Vita*, particularly concerning the use of magic and digressions. Ariosto's innovation in genre manipulation leads to Cellini.

If for Cellini necromancy was a crucial mode of self-exploration, for Ariosto, magic shared the linguistic and performative properties of poetry. In the *Orlando Furioso* Atlante, Ruggiero's surrogate parent, is a necromancer, constantly conjuring demons to create castles to hold his foster son, and also an astrologer-prophet who foresees Ruggiero's early, untimely death. David Quint has argued that Atlante is "a surrogate figure for Boiardo"; for Ascoli, Merlin is a poet-figure for Ariosto.[78] Atlante conjures the demons that he needs to build his first steel-girt castle "in the burning of incense and in magical incantations" (*suffumigi* and *sacri carmi* [OF II, 42.6]). In the *Furioso* magical books of spells function to promote chaos, impeding the actions of knights, while anti-magical books "promote the orderly advancement of the plot."[79] Magical incantations were often predicated upon words. Cornelius Agrippa, a contemporary of Ariosto, compiled a popular system of magic in three books entitled *De occulta philosophia* (1533). He devoted separate chapters to the study of words, speech, writing, and alphabets. A chapter of one of Ficino's books, too, was dedicated to showing how words effect change in the universe.[80] Contemporary practitioners of magic seem to prefigure the distinctions made by twentieth-century semioticians between the graphic elements of writing and the sound elements of speech.[81] For a magus, words are not merely elements in formulas; rather, words *do* things. For instance, to curse someone is not to state that you have cursed someone but to perform the action of cursing.[82] It is the words themselves, when disposed in special ways, that produce magical effects: "in conjuration it was the words used that were of primary importance."[83] Ariosto stages magic by foregrounding where magical objects are placed and by stressing the forms, colors, and textures of those objects rather than the landscape of which they are part. At Alcina's palace Melissa finds the following magical objects: "figurines to burn, seals to remove, knots, magic squares, and whorls to disarrange" ("imagini abbrucciar, suggelli torre, e nodi e rombi e turbini disciorre" [OF VIII, 14.7–8]). The narrator stresses the precision with which the objects are placed when he tells us that Melissa hoped to find *ogni cosa a sua posta*, as indeed she does. These objects are drawn from a broad range of contemporary magical practices, found in both theoretical texts by philosopher-magicians as well as in court records of the Inquisition describing actual practices of alleged witches. The "images to burn" belong to the category of conjuration involving tying knots in a rope while reciting chants to cause impotence.[84] Mathematical figures like "squares" and "whorls" were used by magicians applying geometric principles to conjure demons.[85] Ariosto's specificity and precision suggests that he had a sophisticated knowledge of contemporary magic that he probably could not have derived solely from his literary sources. Ariosto took up the subject of necromancy explicitly in his comedy *Il Negromante* (The Necromancer), performed in Ferrara in 1528. But Ariosto's tone in this text is clearly satirical as he presents the necromancer as a trickster. The necromancer is a charlatan not unlike the artist, as he tells us in the prologue.

Like Ariosto, Grazzini also portrayed the necromancer as a charlatan in his short story, "A Trick Played by the Scheggia on Gian Simone Berrettaio."[86] This tale was part of his collection of *novelle* begun in 1549, and entitled *Le Cene*, or *Dinner Parties*. Two friends, Masaccio's brother Scheggia and Piluca, play a trick on Gian Simone so that they can acquire his money when he tells them he has fallen in love with a beautiful widow. Scheggia and Piluca tell Gian Simone that they will enlist the help of their friend, the necromancer Zoroastro. Zoroastro tells Gian Simone that for twenty-five florins, he promises "to arrange it so that his lady wouldn't be able to live without him."[87] When Gian Simone arrives, Zoroastro "pretended to read great and profound things. He knelt down and kissed the ground from time to time, and sometimes gazed up at the sky. He put on the strangest show in the world for a quarter of an hour."[88] Some Renaissance artists clearly viewed magic as fraud. In his so-called Prophecies (or satirical riddles), Leonardo expressed hostility toward magi and satirized artists of his day for seeing themselves in this guise. In E.H. Gombrich's view, the Prophecies allowed Leonardo to attack "the claims and absurd pretensions of charlatans," specifically necromancers and alchemists.[89]

For Cellini, artistic creation was similar to necromancy. This metaphor of the artist as necromancer was new in Cellini's day, distinguishing the writings of sixteenth-century goldsmiths and sculptors from earlier artists' writings, which stressed the affinities between artistic creation and prophecy. Poliziano's Latin epigram on Giotto's tomb invokes the image of the artist bringing the dead art of the past to life, but not the present work of art being created by the artist. In the *Furioso* Astolfo journeys to the Moon to retrieve Orlando's wits. On the moon St. John tells him that poets raise their patrons from the dead: "oltre che del sepolcro uscirian vivi" ("They would otherwise emerge living from the grave" [OF XXXV 24.5]). Ariosto inserts St. John's observation in a lengthy discourse about the powers of poetry: the poet recounts the story of the old man dropping name plates in the river of Lethe to illustrate how swans, like rare poets, preserve only a small fraction of the names of patrons. Scholars have interpreted this tale as an allegory of Time or as a trope exalting poets who preserve their patrons' lives from oblivion, but in light of the prevalence of magical writings in this period, it may be aligned with the notion of the magical properties of words. Contemporary demonologists defined necromancy as "summoning of and speech with the dead."[90]

In their own writings Cellini and Michelangelo cast themselves as necromancers. Cellini used this metaphor of the goldsmith as necromancer when he narrates the fusing of the *Perseus*: after overcoming a life-threatening fever and the curdling of the metal, he tells us triumphantly that he "had brought a corpse back to life" ("Or veduto di avere risucitato un morto" [Bellotto, 672]). Michelangelo, too, links artistic creation to necromancy. In a letter written to his brother in 1518 he wrote that as a sculptor he "had taken to resuscitating the dead" ("Io ò tolto a risuscitar morti a voler domestichar questi monti e a mecter l'arte in questo paese").[91] For Cellini, artistic creation could be demonic. There is something proto-Frankenstein in Cellini's creation of the *Perseus*, as if the *Perseus* were a "living" being created by a man. In presenting "la materia come cosa viva," Cellini becomes an alchemist, as Margherita Orsino has shown.[92] This link between goldsmithing with the arts of alchemy, metallurgy, and necromancy is visually represented in a painting by Vasari, "The Forge of Vulcan" (figure 12). Here Vasari stages a nude Cellini in the guise of Vulcan amidst naked men and boys.[93] Vasari's presumed portrayal of Cellini as Vulcan, a muscular old man with a white beard forging a shield in a vaulted workshop writhing with the bodies of nude male figures, captures the essence of the artist and man: goldsmith and sodomite, godlike, but at the same time diabolic. There is a struggle between heaven and hell, a tension between the divine and the demonic in all of Cellini's writings about artistic creation. In Renaissance Italy artistic creation may be perceived as a "struggle" or a "liberation" of something living from lifeless matter, but the image of the artist "breathing life" into a statue may hold deeper secrets about Renaissance culture. These accounts by artists of Cellini's day partake of the language of resurrection, evoking New Testament miracles. In his biography of Michelangelo, Vasari marvels that with the *David* Michelangelo had "restored to life a thing that was dead." The *gonfalonier* Piero Soderini agrees, telling Michelangelo, "You have given it life."[94] By Cellini's day the artist had become a kind of necromancer.

Cellini as Michelangelo

Contemporary books on necromancy account for Cellini's interest in presenting himself as a *magus*. Books of Cellini's day from a variety of genres influenced his portrait of himself in the story of his life. Allusions to earlier and contemporary texts in the Italian tradition abound. However, more than books were involved in Cellini's self-dramatization. Cellini modeled the story of his life on the "real" and imaginative life of Michelangelo.

In all of his writings Cellini is, in a sense, always comparing himself to Michelangelo. The *Vita*, in particular, is based on an exemplar, but the exemplar beyond reach for Cellini is not a saint or Christ: it is the divine Michelangelo Buonarroti. Vasari's biography of Michelangelo influenced Cellini's self-construction in his imaginative life, as Victoria Gardner has argued: "Cellini's self-presentation depends on the reader's identifying him with Michelangelo . . ."[95] Vasari's "model life" can only have been the life of Michelangelo whom he presents as a figure of rare genius. Through his biography of Michelangelo, the only living, active artist to appear in the first edition of the *Lives* in 1550, Vasari succeeded in creating an image of Michelangelo as celestial, perfect, and divine, an immortal among mortals. Any one could have learned the details of Michelangelo's life from the funerary pamphlet published in Florence in 1564 following the obsequies for Michelangelo that had been celebrated in the Church of San Lorenzo. In addition, Vasari incorporated details from the funeral booklet of 1564 into his revised biography of Michelangelo that appeared in the second edition of the *Lives* (1568).[96] The actual psychological and sexual lives of Michelangelo and Cellini are similar. Michelangelo and Cellini both worked in a variety of media, wrote for self-expression, and composed sonnets that take up homoerotic themes. Vasari's biography and Cellini's autobiography both narrate similar accounts of clashes with patrons, of religious experiences, and of creating unparalleled works of art.[97] However, few scholars have noted the remarkable similarities between Cellini's written autobiography and Michelangelo's biography by Vasari. The *Vita di Benvenuto Cellini* parallels Vasari's *Vita di Michelangelo* in uncanny ways. Cellini directly modeled episodes in his *Vita* on accounts that Vasari relates in his *Vita di Michelagnolo Buonarroti*. Several of the stories Cellini chooses to tell about himself in his autobiography are similar to tales that Vasari recounts about Michelangelo's life. For example, Cellini's unfinished *Perseus*, when displayed prematurely by Cosimo I, nonetheless earns him great praise, as did Michelangelo's incomplete cycle of Sistine Chapel frescoes when unveiled at the insistence of Pope Julius II. In another passage Vasari recounts that Michelangelo had secretly traveled to Venice where he met Tiziano. According to Vasari, on his way to Venice Michelangelo had stopped in Ferrara. Likewise, Cellini narrates how he secretly fled Florence for Venice, stopping in Ferrara. Michelangelo's biography by Vasari and Cellini's autobiography are populated by some of the same patrons, clients, and fellow artists: Pope Clement VII, Titian, and various members of the Medici family, to name but a few.

It will be useful to compare the handwriting of both artists. Cellini composed the majority of his written corpus, including his *Vita*, *Rime*, and letters, in chancery italic. The paleographer Armando Petrucci has described Cellini's handwriting as "una bella italica inclinata e sicura."[98] By the sixteenth century, chancery italic was the new humanistic script, the hand of the cultured, literate classes. In contrast, Michelangelo wrote in chancery italic only later in his life. Michelangelo composed most of his earlier works in the mercantile script called *mercantesca*. Leonardo also wrote (right to left, a mirror-image) in *mercantesca*. It was common for a person to use different scripts for different purposes; for example, Cellini wrote a clear, book hand for his poetry and autobiography, but used a quick business hand for his account books. It was also not unusual for an individual's handwriting to evolve over the course of a lifetime. But Michelangelo's change of hand may have signaled a conscious effort on his part to write in a more literary style.

Cellini's use of Vasari's life of Michelangelo as a palimpsest is evident in form as well as content. Several features of Cellini's narrative style are similar to stylistic components of Vasari's *Life of Michelangelo*. For example, Cellini follows Vasari in his practice of inserting dialogues between characters as well as long speeches into the prose, although the mingling of indirect discourse with direct discourse is common to historical writing in general and to Villani's *Chronicle*, which Cellini knew, in particular. This element is common to the genre of autobiography, but Cellini normally includes dialogues between himself and a patron, as Vasari does when he relates the dialogues between Michelangelo and Pope Julius II. Cellini also appears to follow the style of Vasari's narrative by including poetry in the prose, although as I have noted, he may have derived this feature from Dante's *Vita nuova*. Cellini includes Latin epigrams, verses by Dante, and sonnets in Tuscan, exactly as Vasari had done in his *Life of Michelangelo*. In his revised biography of Michelangelo for the second edition of the *Lives* (1568) Vasari inserted entire letters into his biography of Michelangelo, precisely as Cellini does in his autobiography. Specifically, Vasari includes eight letters (and two sonnets) that Michelangelo wrote to him personally over the course of his life, and in this way, he aggrandizes himself. Following Vasari, Cellini inserts a letter from Michelangelo himself praising his virtues as a sculptor.

"Benvenuto mio, io v'ho conociuto tanti anni per il maggiore orefice che mai ci sia stato notizia, et ora vi conoscerò per scultore simile. Sappiate che misser Bindo Altoviti mi menò a vedere una testa del suo ritratto, di bronzo, et mi disse che l'era di vostra mano; io n'ebbi molto piacere, ma e' mi seppe molto male che l'era messa a cattivo lume, che se l'avessi il suo ragionevol lume, la si mosterrebbe quella bella opera che l'è." (Bellotto, 678–79)

("My dear Benvenuto, I have known you for many years to be the best goldsmith we know of; but now I shall acknowledge that you are no less a sculptor. I must tell you that Messer Bindo Altoviti took me to see a bust of himself, done in bronze, and told me that it was your work; I took a great deal of pleasure in it, but I thought it very annoying that it should be placed in a poor light, since if it were shown in a reasonable light it would stand out as the beautiful work that it is.")

Both Vasari and Cellini use hyperbole when fashioning literary portraits of the artist(s). Elissa Tognozzi links Cellini's abundant use of superlatives in his *Vita* to his desire to make his life attain an immeasurable standard.[99] Cellini uses many terms that indicate the superlative quality or indefinite nature of something he had created or experienced. Certain of these expressions in Cellini's *Vita* are similar to phrases in Vasari's *Vita* of Michelangelo. For example, Cellini's claim that he saw an "infinite number" of souls in Hell recalls Vasari's insistence that Michelangelo created "an infinite number of fancies" in his genealogies of the Sistine Chapel.

Michelangelo's influence on Cellini the artist is apparent as well. In a letter to Michelangelo dated 3 September 1561, Cellini confessed that it was Michelangelo's virtuous example that inspired him to move beyond goldsmithing to practice "la mirabile scultura."[100] Cellini's masterpiece, the *Perseus*, exhibits three Michelangelesque touches evident in the pose, the banner over the hero's chest, and the presumed inclusion by Cellini of self-portraits. The stance of the *Perseus*, particularly when viewed from behind, is strikingly similar to the pose of the *David* (completed 1504). *David's* body is not straight and stiff, but relaxed and turned ever so slightly, a stance known as *contrapposto*. His left leg is bent, supporting the weight of his body. With his left arm raised holding a sling and the right at his side, he does not directly engage the spectator, but looks to the left. The *Perseus*, too, is turned, almost imperceptibly, with his left knee bent, supporting his weight on one leg. His left arm is raised holding Medusa's head, his right arm at his side, eyes downcast. A three-dimensional computer simulation of the *Perseus* with his body slightly turned, hand raised, and imbalanced weight would display torque. The twistedness and *linea serpentinata* of the *Perseus*, like the elongated feminine body of Cellini's *Nymph of Fontainebleau* (1542), is typical of the Mannerist style. The Latin banner over the *Perseus'* chest proclaiming the date of his "birth," being born of "Benvenutus Cellinis civis Flor. faciebat MDLIII (Made by Benvenuto Cellini, Florentine citizen, 1553 [old style])" recalls the girdle encircling the Madonna of Michelangelo's statue of the *Pietà* in the Basilica of San Pietro in Rome.

David appears to be looking right at *Perseus*. Placed under the Loggia dei Lanzi in the Piazza della Signoria, *Perseus* seems aware of *David's* presence and penetrating gaze. Just as the statue of the *David* had been judged as possessing allegorical meaning in Michelangelo's time, so, too, the *Perseus* was read as political allegory in Cellini's day.[101] Cellini may have derived his use of the four figures of Night, Day, Dawn, and Dusk for his saltcellar from Michelangelo's *Tomb of Lorenzo de' Medici* (ca. 1515). Finally, was Cellini following Michelangelo's new standard of the *non finito*, the unfinished work, when he abruptly ended the story of his life?

The *David* and the *Perseus* signal a shift in views toward sexuality and the body in art. These large, nude male figures of the Renaissance developed out of Donatello's earlier bronzes of *David* and *Judith* of the *Judith and Holofernes*. The *Judith* also stood, with Michelangelo's *David* and Cellini's *Perseus*, in the Piazza della Signoria. The *David*, called a "giant" by Vasari, is over fourteen feet high (ca. 420 cm). The *Perseus*, too, although smaller than *David*, is larger than lifesize, approximately eleven feet high. On its base, it is nearly seventeen feet high (statue ca. 320 cm, base ca. 199 cm). Cellini called him "il mio gigante." Both are shamelessly naked. Donatello's *David*, created after *Judith*, is the first large-scale nude sculpture since antiquity. The pedestals of *Judith* and Michelangelo's *David* are rather plain; in contrast, Cellini's base for the *Perseus* is an art work in itself. Cellini created a grotesque marble base containing four freestanding bronze statues derived from Greek mythology together with large bronze panels depicting mythological scenes from the life of Perseus.

Across Italy ancient coins and statues were being unearthed, while texts by classical authors were being discovered in libraries and monasteries. The humanistic movement gave rise to art works based on classical figures and literature derived from classical texts. But the language of humanism stressed the replication of antique statues in art practice, a replication that was viewed, in a positive light, as a kind of counterfeiting. When Vasari wrote that Michelangelo had made a certain marble "appear an antique," he was paying the sculptor a supreme compliment. Enea Vico paid a similar tribute to Cellini when he praised the artist's ability to fabricate modern copies of ancient coins.[102]

Like many artists of the day, Cellini "completed" an antique statue that had been uncovered in Rome. Another feature of this urge to replicate the ancients was to restore antique fragments that were being unearthed throughout Italy. In Cellini's words,

> Essendo in questi giorni trovato certe anticaglie nel contado d'Arezzo, infra le quale si era la Chimera, che è que lione di bronzo, il quale si vede nelle camere convicino alla gran sala del Palazzo; et insieme con la detta Chimera si era trovato una quantità di piccole statuette, pur di bronzo, le quali erano coperte di terra e di ruggine, et a ciascuna di esse mancava o la testa o le mani o i piedi. (Bellotto, 697–98)

> (At that time certain antiquities were unearthed in the countryside of Arezzo, and among them was the Chimera, that bronze lion which you can see in the rooms near the great hall of the Palace; together with the said Chimera, a number of little statuettes were found, also made of

bronze, which were covered with earth and rust, and each one missing either a head or hands or feet.)

Between 1548 and 1550 Cellini "restored" an antique marble torso of a nude male, creating his *Ganymede* (figures 5 and 6). Cellini also claims to have restored a bronze Chimera that was unearthed in Arezzo in 1554, believed to be the one housed in the Archeological Museum in Florence. The *Ganymede* was brought to the Pitti Palace, the residence of the Medici, in 1570. In a letter dated 11 September 1570 Ammannati judged the "Ganimede di marmo" to be worth eighty *scudi*, noting that it had been placed "sopra una porta nella sala de' Pitti."[103] The torso had been given to Cosimo by Stefano Colonna. As Leonard Barkan has suggested, there is something "unmediated" about Cellini's relationship to antiquity: "Ganymede reflects his own homoerotic desires with no transcendent hermeneutic attached. What is attached to Ganymede for Cellini are rather the prestige and beauty of the ancient world as well as his unmediated identification with its sexual practices, not to mention his own occupation."[104] Barkan has also argued that Cellini felt some emotional attachment to two of the three marble statues he created that were based on Greek mythology, noting that the *Apollo and Hyacinth* (figure 7) as well as the *Narcissus* (figure 8) remained in his workshop during his lifetime. Both are listed in the inventory of his household goods compiled at his death.

Cellini went beyond texts, classical values, and even the real life of Michelangelo in his search for models for his self-portrait in the story of his life. His imaginative life, the *Vita*, parallels the "life" of his own *Perseus*. Like his own *Perseus*, Cellini was "brought back from the dead" ("il resuscitato morto" [Bellotto, 304]). The episode about the fusion of the *Perseus* reveals another component of Cellini's narrative style. The impulse for simile to rupture into metaphor is a common feature of the narrative. Cellini typically uses a simile when comparing himself to an exemplar: for instance, he is like the *Perseus* (and Lazarus) in his resurrection from the dead. Cellini also likens himself to God, claiming during the fusion of the *Perseus* that he raised *Perseus* from the dead just as God resurrected Himself after the crucifixion: "O dDio, che con le tue immense virtù risucitasti da e' morti, et glorioso te ne salisti al cielo!" (Bellotto, 673). However, often the simile slides into metaphor as Cellini himself becomes the exemplar. Cellini was like the devil when he tried to "recreate" nature by attempting to create the *Perseus*; after the *Perseus*' birth and the transgression of Nature's laws, Cellini is the devil himself, at least in the eyes of the majordomo who denounces him in front of Cosimo. Rather than making his life a work of art, as Burckhardt has suggested, instead Cellini made himself a work of art. The physician assures Cellini's friend Giovanni Gaddi after his recovery that Cellini is not a mere mortal made of flesh but rather a statue "not made of marble or bronze, but of pure iron!" (Bellotto, 296). The *Perseus*' lament in a sonnet, "Oh, that unfortunate marble!" in reference to the block destined for Ammannati's *Neptune*, is echoed not once but twice in the *Vita*. Three of Cellini's identities are collapsed in this one utterance. The narrator, the protagonist, and the poet (speaking through Perseus) all join together in unison to express sympathy for that *sventurato marmo* (Bellotto, 740).

It is not wrong to claim Vasari as a model for Cellini, but it would be misleading to view Vasari as Cellini's primary model. Cellini's *Vita* must be studied in relation to plural models rather than just one model, in relation to other literary genres besides autobiography or biography. The *Vita* is based on an exemplar, but the exemplar beyond reach is not a saint or Christ. It is Michelangelo. Yet, Dante was just as important to Cellini's self-expression as Michelangelo. As Cellini believed, he, like Dante, had traveled to France, journeyed to the Otherworld, and envisioned God. Cellini drew inspiration from a variety of sources. Cellini's saintly behavior in prison is reminiscent of tales from the Bible as well as contemporary saints' lives. His mystical visions are similar to the early medieval tradition of vision narratives in which the protagonist journeys to Hell and Heaven. In his *Vita* Cellini mixed the chronicler's concern for historical verisimilitude with the jeweler's predilection for detail. Cellini's interest in necromancy and the demonic status of goldsmithing demonstrates an awareness of Counter-Reformation witchcraft. Like many writers, Cellini participated in the sixteenth-century practice of genre-mixing. The parallels between the *Vita* and the art treatises suggest that the *Vita* is ekphrastic and the manuscript version of the *Two Treatises*, autobiographical. Cellini's *Vita*, ostensibly an art treatise, contains elements of epic, romance, and comedy. In his *Vita* Cellini conflates two chivalric heroes, the romantic knight errant and the epic crusader. The roles he adopts in the story of his life of Dantesque pilgrim, chivalric hero, and *magus* are all forms of claiming status and honor.

CHAPTER 5
HONOR AND MANLINESS

In the story of his life when Cellini is not holding a chisel, he is often clutching a dagger. Cellini is a complex, contradictory figure whose life and work manifest diverse and conflicting impulses. Like Aretino, he composed scandalous works at the same time as he was producing deeply religious ones. The violent persona that Cellini depicts in his *Vita* is not the only posture he adopts. In the *Vita* Cellini employs, for example, the saintly/pilgrim register; one recalls the figure of the Dantesque pilgrim and Otherworld traveler in the prison episodes in Rome. However, viewing the narrative as a whole, these are isolated cases. The sum total of saintly behavior that Cellini exhibits in the story of his life is contained within the prison episodes. In contrast, Cellini's violence does not begin in a particular moment of his life; rather, he acts violently throughout the course of his entire life. As protagonist, Cellini commits assaults and homicides with reckless abandon from adolescence through adulthood to old age. In fact, it is difficult to recall Cellini's imitation of Dante when he boasts so frequently about his violence. In a particularly gruesome episode, for example, Cellini recounts stabbing a man so many times with a large dagger that he renders him paralyzed: "una sera gli detti tanti colpi pur guardando di non lo ammazare, innelle gambe e innelle braccia, che di tutt'a due le gambe io lo privai" (one evening I gave him so many stabs, though being careful not to kill him, in the legs and arms, that I deprived him of the use of both of his legs [Bellotto, 543]). In fact, given Cellini's emphasis on violence, it seems only fitting that he travels to the Otherworld cloaked in a coat of mail and holding a dagger.

A typical, frequently cited violent episode of the *Vita* involves his model and occasional sex partner Caterina, who incurs the wrath of our hero. Cellini's assault on Caterina is just one of many acts of violence he commits as protagonist. Cellini normally confesses acts of murder and assault with a surprising regularity and without expressing the slightest sense of remorse for his actions. Cellini presents many portraits of the artist in the *Vita*. But the principal literary persona is that of a violent, impulsive man who is continually assaulting or murdering other characters whom he encounters in the story of his life.

> Inmentre che io facevo questo mio conto, questa ribalda moltipricava con quelle parole ingiuriose, parlando pure del suo marito; e tanto faceva e diceva, che lei mi cavava de' termini della ragione; e datomi in preda all'ira, la pigliavo pe' capegli e la strascicavo per la stanza, dandogli tanti calci e tante pugna insino che io ero stracco. (Bellotto, 562)
>
> (While I was taking care of things, the slut redoubled her insults, talking even about her husband; what she did and said nearly drove me to the edge of reason; and giving in to my rage, I seized her by the hair and dragged her up and down the room, giving her so many kicks and punches until I was exhausted.)

Critics have attempted to explain the protagonist's violent behavior by taking recourse to the heroic model. Dino Cervigni, for instance, remarks: "The fights, the duels, and the murders constellated throughout the autobiography also evince the same heroic character, for they reveal the protagonist's indomitable courage."[1] This view is shared by many Cellini scholars. James Mirollo elaborates: "It would seem . . . that our two authors [Teresa of Ávila and Cellini] harbor feelings of insecurity about their respective professional roles as measured against a more heroic standard . . . The responses of Teresa and Benvenuto to this crisis in their celebrated autobiographies and other works are thus significant for their own times but also for the influence they subsequently exerted on the genre of autobiography and its images of concepts of heroism."[2] Heroism may explain Cellini's fearless defense of the Church during the Sack of Rome, but it does not explain his assault on Caterina in Paris, his murder of rival jeweler Pompeo in Rome, or his attack on the Roman notary Benedetto. Although urban violence was commonplace in Renaissance Florence, this fact in itself does not explain Cellini's fascination with and ready recourse to violence as protagonist in the story of his *Vita*.[3] Rather, such acts are better explained by contemporary accounts of proper masculine behavior documented in dueling manuals, courtesy books, and legal records. Discourses of honor help explain why Cellini represented his life in this way. In Cellini's day masculinity was fragmentary, multiple, and contradictory. Standards of manliness and honor required Cellini to depict himself as violent and to recount acts of assault and murder. Contemporary ideals of virility and masculinity helped shape Cellini's presentation of himself as dauntless and violent. In his *Vita* Cellini even provides ekphrastic-like accounts of violence.

The episode of the Sack of Rome is clearly marked by a heroic register. Cellini relates how, with the enemy scaling the walls of the city, with soldiers' bodies littering the battlefield, and with the city shrouded in "una nebbia folta quanto inmaginar si possa" (as thick a fog as you could imagine [Bellotto, 129]), he, delegated leader of a band of "cinquanta valorosissimi giovani" (fifty of the most courageous young men), attempts to defend the Christians from the Barbarians:

> Borbone, saputo che a Roma non era soldati, sollecitissimamente spinse l'esercito suo alla volta di Roma... Conparso di già l'esercito di Borbone alle mura di Roma, il detto Alessandro del Bene mi pregò che io andassi seco a farli compagnia... Giugnemmo alle mura di Campo Santo, et quivi vedemmo quel maraviglioso esercito, che di già faceva ogni suo sforzo per entrare. A quel luogo delle mura, dove noi ci accostammo, v'era molti giovani morti da quei di fuora: quivi si combatteva a più potere: era una nebbia folta quanto inmaginar si possa. (Bellotto, 128–29)
>
> (So the Constable of Bourbon, knowing that there were no soldiers in Rome, began marching his army as rapidly as he could toward the city... By this time the Bourbon's army had arrived in front of the walls of Rome. Alessandro del Bene begged me to go along with him... When we arrived at the walls of Campo Santo we caught sight of the Bourbon's impressive army, which was always exerting all its strength to enter the city. At that part of the wall where we stopped, there were many young men already killed by the attackers: the fighting was ferocious: the place was covered by the thickest fog imaginable.)

But this narrative is also punctuated by a rhetoric of masculinity. Alessandro becomes frightened and begins to flee. Outraged at this display of cowardice, Cellini shouts after him to act like a man:

> Il ditto Lessandro spaventato, disse: "Così volessi Idio che venuti noi non ci fussimo!"; et così vòltosi con grandissima furia per andarsene, il quale io ripresi, dicendogli: "Da poi che voi mi avete menato qui, gli è forza fare *qualche atto da uomo.*" (Bellotto, 129–30, emphasis added)
>
> (The said Alessandro frightened, said: "I wish to God we'd never come here!" And then, frightened to death, he started to run away. But I stopped him and told him: "Since you have all brought me here, we must perform *some manly deeds.*")

Cellini's indignation at Alessandro's cowardice exposes a norm of masculine behavior. Cellini justifies the majority of the violent actions to which he confesses throughout his *Vita* by informing the reader that he committed such deeds because he was a man or because he was constrained to act like a man, as in the account of the Sack of Rome. The *Vita* is a litany of proclamations of masculinity: because he was a man, Cellini used Caterina for his own sexual pleasure: "*perché io sono uomo*, me ne son servito ai mia [*sic*] piaceri carnali" (*since I'm a man, I used her for my sexual pleasure* [Bellotto, 545, emphasis added]). Because he was a man, Cellini defended his reputation against the injurious words and insolent gestures of Pompeo through an act of murder: "dissi che le mie brighe *io ero uomo* da per me a saperle finire . . ." (I said that *I was a man* who knew how to settle my own fights [Bellotto, 260, emphasis added]). Because he was a man, he sought vengeance on his brother's murderer. Cellini wrote his *Vita*, he tells us in the opening paragraph, because all virtuous men who have reached the age of forty must do so. These proud declarations remind us that the word virtue derives from a Latin word meaning "manliness" (from *vir*, "man").[4] The *Vita* constructs a virile image of Benvenuto Cellini as a man who boasts of his sexual conquests of women as readily as he does his military feats. Martial prowess and sexual conquests are conventional features of masculinity. But Cellini adds new elements to the Renaissance construction of masculinity, in particular, the contraction of syphilis.[5]

Cellini's *Vita* stands as a corrective to the position of some scholars of sex and gender who claim that all men benefited from a gender system of patriarchy in Renaissance Italy. Recent scholarship on the period has asserted that women were in a unique position to critique gender inequalities in their society and culture. Implicit in much research on women writers, for example, is the assumption that gender affects women more than men. Scholars of gender argue that men and women do not act according to a biological imperative, but in accordance to cultural norms. By exposing the behavioral norms of masculinity, the *Vita* testifies to the notion that gender ideology restricted men as well as women. Sixteenth-century gender ideology required a man use violence in the defense of his honor and manliness.

In his *Vita* Cellini juxtaposes old and new norms of behavior and mixes old and new languages of masculinity: chivalric terms from medieval texts appear alongside the new discourse of genteel courtliness. For men like Cellini, honor is earned at the workshop and confirmed at court. The competition among artists at court has replaced the armed rivalries of men on the battlefield. In Cellini's day, there are new fields of honor: the creation of art objects, too, has become the site for heroic *imprese*. Cellini displaces martial masculinity into artistic enterprise.

Violence

Action and aggression helped define what made a man in the Renaissance. Taking the active role was perceived as masculine, the passive role, feminine. Gender differences were delineated by law and custom and were maintained through a variety of social practices that helped create order and stability, as Ruth Mazo Karras and David Lorenzo Boyd have argued: "[D]ifferences in dress, mannerisms, sexual positions and activities, social pastimes, occupations, familial roles, legal rights, and duties all functioned to distinguish the masculine from the feminine."[6] As we have seen, the active/passive distinction underlies the language of the law in sodomy cases. In Florence where homosexual sodomy was widespread, the sexually dominant role that Cellini played in his relations with boys would have done nothing to detract from his manliness.[7] Cellini's role as the older, active penetrator in sexual intercourse with an adolescent boy did not tarnish his masculine identity; on the contrary, it reaffirmed it. Homoeroticism and masculinity were in harmony in a system where men were deemed superior to women in virtually all respects. In such a world, Dante-pilgrim could express respect and admiration for the sodomites he encounters in *Inferno* 16.[8] Many sodomites of Cellini's time were married, fathered children, and continued to have sexual intercourse with women. Benedetto Varchi, a historian and close friend of Cellini, was widely known at the time for his sexual interest in adolescent boys, and yet, his sexual proclivities did nothing to hinder his successful public career.[9]

Cellini is in the forefront in articulating a new norm of manhood. Several key elements in the passage about the Sack of Rome signal a shift in masculine gender identity, a shift that occurred in the course of the sixteenth century. The "thick fog" of gunpowder that prevents Cellini from seeing the enemy is indicative of a larger historical moment, the fall of the old brand of chivalry. His inability to see the enemy illustrates that there is no longer face-to-face confrontation between adversaries. The knight with a lance on horseback has been replaced by the soldier on foot holding a gun or firing a cannon. This important change in military technology meant that knights were no longer powerful. The man who possessed the new guns and cannons was the one who held the power, and killing could now be done at a distance. Gone were the days when the skill and courage of a knight determined the victor. Now, since Cellini mans the cannon, he holds the power. Contemporaries of Cellini, especially Ariosto, wrote at length about the horror and unchivalrousness of guns.

As John Brackett has shown for Renaissance Florence, there existed "a culture of violence in which just about everyone participated, linked to the defense of honor."[10] The acts of murder and assault that Cellini perpetrates on female models and male rivals throughout the course of his life are linked to his obligations under the male code of honor. In his

Vita Cellini gives numerous accounts of men and women who frustrate and spoil his relations with his patrons, including jealous rivals, major-domos, King Francis's mistress Madame d'Étampes, and the Duchess of Florence Eleonora da Toledo. Men and women alike continually challenge Cellini's honor and manliness. In these moments manliness and honor are inextricably intertwined: Cellini assaults Benedetto because Benedetto had insulted him, and "*io non sono uomo* che sopporti ingiurie" (*I am not the kind of man* who puts up with insults [Bellotto, 242, emphasis added]). Cellini's acts of violence must be analyzed in relation to a code of honor imposed on him. He commits acts of murder and assault in defense of his honor. The *Vita* seeks to dramatize such contests of masculinity in Cellini's day. Cellini's acts of violence against men are primarily against rivals and those who damage his honor or challenge his manliness. The violence he commits against women, epitomized in the episode with Caterina, is linked to misogyny as well as to his own honor.

For centuries in Italy, honor was inextricably intertwined with one's social identity and public reputation.[11] Honor was a concern, at times a preoccupation, for both men and women, irrespective of their class origins. Honor was a public fact and, as such, circulated in the public sphere.[12] Men were responsible for defending the honor of the entire family group, including the women of the lineage—wives, daughters, and sisters—while feminine honor was bound more to women's bodies and predominately to their sexuality.[13] In rape cases in Renaissance Florence, for example, "the most important thing was to publicly repair the damage done to family honor; the feelings of the woman were not the highest priority of concern in a society in which maintaining honor was the primary concern of the family."[14] According to Peter Burke, Italy was a society in which "public reputation defined the individual."[15] In such a society "the public face which one presents defines the individual in terms of honor or dishonor. Honor is maintained, even though a good reputation may or may not be more than a well-known facade, as long as it is not challenged in the public area."[16]

In 1562 Cellini petitioned Cosimo I to carry both offensive and defensive weapons and to wear chainmail (see appendix 3.D).[17] The artist does not specify precisely what these weapons were, but we know that offensive weapons included knives, small swords, and daggers.[18] Wearing chainmail was viewed as a defensive move and "an expectation of some role in violence" and was strictly regulated by the Otto.[19] The inventory of Cellini's household goods at his death reveals a considerable arsenal for an artist: two daggers, a knife "in the Turkish style," two swords, and a *zagaglia*, a special kind of long sword common to the sixteenth century.[20] Clothes made of chainmail were regular items in Cellini's wardrobe. An inventory of his household goods from 1538 in Rome had listed two jackets, a pair of detachable sleeves, a pair of gloves, and a hood, covering the back of the neck, with a coat of arms at its top, all made of chainmail.[21] In his petition to the Duke, Cellini insisted that his request should be granted since he had been allowed to carry weapons in the past. Cosimo did indeed grant the petition on 13 December 1562, declaring that Cellini "possa portare l'arme, come li nostri stipendiati."[22] The granting of this petition, which came after 1557, suggests that Cellini did not lose all status and privilege as a result of the sodomy conviction. A second petition sent to Cosimo's son Francesco in 1566 was also granted. Lelio Torelli indicated that the Duke decreed that Cellini "possa portar l'armi."[23] However, the Eight did order Cellini to turn over two of his weapons, the sword measuring "one and one-half hands" and the exotic *zagaglia*. In the inventory listing of his household goods at his death the functionary wrote, after the *zagaglia* entry, "quale due arme dissono si havevano a mandar alli Octo."[24]

In his petition to the Duke Cellini explains that he must continue to "carry and keep weapons" so that he can "defend his life." In Cellini's day men were constantly challenged to defend their manhood and honor publicly. During this period manly revenge was enacted through violent vendettas or dueling.[25] According to Edward Muir, over the course of the sixteenth century dueling began to replace vendettas as the practice that affirmed honorable masculinity. Muir suggests that during the transition there was a time when both practices overlapped, and it is perhaps for this reason that both duelling and vendettas are evident in Cellini's *Vita*. Although dueling is not prominent in his *Vita*, Cellini does recount in detail being challenged to a duel. Duels were a highly ritualized social practice between men where honor was nego- tiated, exchanged, and reconstituted. Duels were formal, prearranged contests where two men, armed with guns or swords, fought in front of witnesses.[26] Like vendettas, duels were permitted by law but were also restricted by it. Duels and vendettas had to follow specific rules and adhere to precise regulations.[27] Like the witty repartee of Boccaccio's characters and the genteel exchanges of the poetic *tenzone*, exchanges that make up duels were both creative and productive. Duels arise when an offense involving a physical assault or a verbal insult, commit- ted publicly, threatens to diminish the honor of the offended party. Exchanges and communications result from such offenses. After the offense, there must be an exchange of words where the accused party must confess that he committed the said offense. This confession is fundamental to such ritual practices. After the exchange of words that is predicated on a confession, another exchange must take place. One of the two men, usually the injured party, must formally communicate his desire to reconstitute his honor by challenging the other to a duel. This formal challenge must be communicated either in verbal or written form.

An episode about a duel in the *Vita* contains all these elements. As a young man Cellini is challenged to a duel after he strikes another youth in the face for saying "molte parole inoneste della nazione fiorentina" (Bellotto, 89). Cellini and his companions, including the painters Rosso Fiorentino and an apprentice of Raphael, were celebrating the feast of Saint John the Baptist, when an unnamed "giovane isventato, bravaccio" (Bellotto, 88–89), a soldier of captain Rienzo Anguillara da Ceri, passed by, "sbeffando" (Bellotto, 89). Cellini takes his remarks as a personal affront and chases after him. Upon reaching the man, Cellini asks him if he was the man who insulted the Florentines. When the soldier replies without hesitation that he is, in fact, that man, Cellini strikes him in the face. Both men reach for their swords but are separated by passers-by:

> Giunto a llui, lo domandai se egli era quello ardito, che diceva male de' Fiorentini. Subito disse: "Io son quello." Alle quale parole io alzai la mana [*sic*] dandogli in sul viso, et dissi: "Et io son questo." Subito messo mano all'arme l'uno et l'altro arditamente; ma non sì tosto cominciato tal briga, che molti entrorno di mezo . . . (Bellotto, 89)

> (Having reached him, I asked him if he was the fellow who had been so bold, who insulted the Florentines. He immediately retorted: "I'm that very man." When he said that, I lifted my hand, striking him in the face, and said: "Then I'm this very man." Immediately we boldly grabbed for our swords; but no sooner had the fight begun than many bystanders separated us.)

Two elements heighten the tone of the tale: the specific day being celebrated and the duties of the host. The fact that the men were celebrating the festival of the patron saint of Florence when this blasphemy occurred dramatizes the moment and legitimates Cellini's defense of his native land. In addition, Cellini is offended by the young man's words because he is a citizen of Florence as well as the host of the party: "Io . . . guida di quelli tanti virtuosi et uomini da bene" (I [was] host to all those virtuous and honorable men [Bellotto, 89]). The soldier's reply and Cellini's retort mirror in words the blow and parry action of dueling itself. Moreover, Cellini's lexicon contains words and phrases drawn straight from chivalric epics, such as his use of "messo mano all'arme l'uno e l'altro arditamente." Throughout the *Vita* Cellini's characterization of his enemies often derives from chivalric epics; for example, his description of Pierfrancesco Ricci as "nimico mio mortale" identifies him as an enemy whom Cellini must fight to the death. The duel episode demonstrates how manliness and honor are intertwined. Men like Cellini are only too willing to show those like the *bravaccio* what it takes to act honorably. It also illustrates Cellini's attempt to assume the trappings of nobility.

Cellini's blow to the face of his opponent is a formal challenge. The face was the site of honor in Renaissance Italy.[28] Thus, shortly after the incident, Cellini receives a written note challenging him to a duel. He readily accepts: "L'altro giorno a presso mi fu portato un cartello di disfida per conbattere seco, il quale io accettai molto lietamente" (The next day I was brought a *cartello di disfida* [a formal challenge] to fight him, which I accepted very happily [Bellotto, 89]). Although Cellini paints himself as the injured party in the account, the other man's honor was likewise damaged when Cellini struck him in the face in a public space.

Before the duel takes place Cellini talks with a sage old man named Bevilacqua, reputed to be "la prima spada di Italia, perché s'era trovato più di venti volte ristretto in campo franco, e sempre ne era uscito a onore" (the best swordsman in Italy, because he had fought more than twenty duels, and come out of them all with honor [Bellotto, 89–90]). In describing Bevilacqua, Cellini uses terms such as *franco* and *onore*, drawn from, among other places, medieval chivalric texts. The phrase *campo franco*, for example, is also found in Ariosto (OF XLVI, 58), who may have borrowed it from the language of dueling and warfare. Bevilacqua assures Cellini that he will be victorious since he was justly defending the honor of Florence. Moreover, he continues, Cellini will triumph because he is always in the right in matters of honor:

> "Benvenuto mio, se tu avessi da fare con Marte, io son certo che ne usciresti a onore, perché di tanti anni, quant'io ti conosco, non t'ho mai veduto pigliare nessuna briga a torto." (Bellotto, 90)
>
> ("My dear Benvenuto, if you had to fight a duel with Mars, I'm sure you'd come out of it honorably, because for all the many years that I've known you, I've never seen you enter a fight unjustly.")

The duel never takes place because Cellini's adversary withdraws. Nonetheless, Cellini's honor is reconstituted while the other man's is diminished. The soldier loses honor because he displayed cowardice and did not act like a man and defend his honor: "Così prese la mia impresa, et conduttoci in luogo con l'arme in mano, sanza insanguinarsi restando dal mio avversario, con molto onore usci' di tale impresa" (Thus my duel took place, and brought to the place with my sword in hand, without bloodshed, since my adversary desisted from the duel, I came out of the duel with much honor [Bellotto, 90]). The duel allows Cellini, like a good knight of the past, not only to reclaim his own honor, but also that of Florence and the Florentine people. The term *impresa*—repeated twice in the aforementioned passage (a heroic undertaking)—is also common to the language of chivalry.

Contemporary legal judgments, dueling manuals, and courtesy books help elucidate the meanings and limits of honor in Cellini's day as well as Cellini's conception of his obligations under this code. The term *battaglia giudicata* was used in earlier medieval legal codes to designate a public male encounter where disagreements were resolved and injured honor reconstituted in the presence of a sovereign.[29] These medieval judicial duels were legally recognized and had the authority of law. In Renaissance Florence, however, duels were not legally recognized as a space within which to resolve conflicts between men; nonetheless instances of "duel-like" encounters exist in the criminal records. Brackett has discovered cases from the latter part of the century where "men confronted each other, traded insults and challenges, and then proceeded to indulge in armed combat that occasionally resulted in death."[30] For example, a man accused of murder in 1603 was sentenced to only one year of residence in Livorno because the Eight ruled that he had been "provoked" to enter into the exchange that resulted in the death of the other man.[31] In the legal codes of Cellini's day, affronts to honor were considered criminal acts, so "violence could be used in the defense of honor."[32] If the injured party could convince the magistrates that he reacted to an insult to his honor, the authorities often mitigated the penalty. Duels may have been officially prohibited in theory, but they were tolerated in practice. It seems that duels did take place in many Italian cities during the Renaissance. For example, Giovanni Bandini killed Lodovico Martelli in a duel, purportedly over Bandini's affair with Marietta de' Ricci.[33]

Dueling manuals proliferated throughout the sixteenth century in Italy and were intended for an upper-class audience.[34] Anton Francesco Doni's 1550 bibliography of sixteenth-century vernacular books, *La Libraria*, lists dozens of books on dueling and male honor.[35] Many books on dueling and nobility were translations of Spanish texts and reflect the influence of Spanish culture and custom in Italy.[36] Marriages between Spanish royalty and Italian nobility as well as the Spanish papacy of the Borgia solidified the political and cultural ties between Spain and Italy in the Renaissance. Many members of courts read and spoke Spanish in this period: Ariosto and Bembo apparently did, as did courtesans such as Tullia d'Aragona.[37] In his *Memoriale* Bandinelli, in his desire to show the reader his familiarity with Spanish, relates the words spoken to him by the Emperor Charles V when he knighted Bandinelli in 1536.[38] Cosimo's marriage to Eleonora da Toledo in 1539 sealed the union between the Florentine house of Medici and the Spanish family of Don Pedro da Toledo, the Spanish Viceroy at Naples. In Renaissance Italy dueling was viewed as an elite practice. This may help explain why Cellini included such an episode in the story of his life. In the *Vita* Cellini assumes various upper-class postures. The *Vita* narrates Cellini's rise from his lowly professional status, in his words, as a "lavorante libero" (*a free worker*) to the upper-class ranks of sculptor and goldsmith at the courts of Popes, a King, and a Duke. In his real life Cellini's social climb was complete when he was admitted to the Florentine nobility in 1554.[39] This ascension was fueled in no small part by envy over Bandinelli's knighthood in the prestigious order of Santiago by the Emperor Charles V. Cellini's role as social-climbing artist in his imaginative *Vita* is a form of claiming status and honor. The *Vita*, then, constitutes "the struggle of a member of the artisan class to place himself on the same footing as the rulers of Florence."[40]

Courtesy books set down a broad range of prescriptive behaviors for gentlemen in many different social situations. Manner books, like dueling manuals, drew on elements of medieval chivalry, being careful to distinguish between masculine actions that conferred honor and those that conferred dishonor. Books such as Baldassar Castiglione's *Il Libro del Cortigiano* (1528) as well as more practical guides like Giovanni Della Casa's *Il Galateo* (1558) advised gentlemen that the use of violence may be necessary in the defense of honor. Although Castiglione's dialogue is less a practical guide to masculine conduct than an idealized portrait of the perfect courtier, nonetheless an interlocutor asserts that a gentleman who suffers an affront to his honor may be forced into an armed contest with him: "ne sia facile a questi combattimenti, se non quanto per l'onor fosse sforzato."[41] Likewise, even though more practical strategies are glossed over in favor of a discourse about the manly games a courtier should be adept in, including being able to "giocare a canne" and "giostrare," nevertheless the perfect courtier is advised to be knowledgeable about all matters where male honor is potentially damaged.

The interlocutor Galateo of Della Casa's *Il Galateo overo de' costumi* purports to provide counsel to a young man about appropriate public behavior.[42] Galateo's advice is often detailed and quotidian, ranging from correct bodily positions—how to sit at a dinner table, how to cross one's legs—to admonitions against undignified habits such as spitting or making rude noises while eating. Claudia Berra has argued that *Galateo* is a parody of Renaissance etiquette.[43] What is significant is that even these practical texts on male behavior, whether satirical or serious, enumerate the myriad ways in which inappropriate behavior is perceived as an insult. For example, the wise speaker warns his apprentice that not giving suitable honors in public to a man of appropriate age and social status can potentially lead to violence:

> Restami a dire di quelle [cirimonie] che si fanno per debito e di quelle che si fanno per vanità. Le prime non ista bene in alcun modo lasciare che non si facciano, perciochè chi le lascia, non solo spiace, ma egli fa ingiuria e molte volte è occorso che *egli si è venuto a trar fuori le spade solo per questo*: che l'un cittadino non ha così onorato l'altro per via, come si doveva onorare.[44]

> (It's left for me to discuss those ceremonies that are done out of obligation and those done out of vanity. The first should absolutely be done because whoever doesn't do them will not only be sorry but causes insult, and many times it's necessary for *a man to draw his sword just on account of this*: that one citizen did not honor another on the street, who should be honored.)

As a result, Galateo reflects at length on the appropriate "rituals of admiration" that must be performed to prevent such affronts to honor from exploding into violence. Yet, these courtesy books also illustrate that masculinity in Cellini's day is contradictory and fraught with tensions. Dueling manuals admonish men to take up arms to defend their honor, praising action and aggression as masculine. But courtesy books, on the other hand, caution men to show restraint, suggesting a kind of passivity that would be viewed as feminine. The incompatibility of the figure of the courtier with the strictures of masculinity was clearly not lost on contemporary authors of manner books. They continually denounced the courtier who acted "like a woman," and yet in the same breath, however, they encouraged him to temper his behavior.

In the *Vita* Cellini uses violence in the defense of honor. For Cellini, as for Della Casa, the use of violence is permissible in order for a man to behave honorably. Cellini also feels constrained to use violence to avenge the murder of his brother. The *Vita* narrates Cellini's ekphrasis-like account of his revenge for the killing of his brother. Trevor Dean has claimed that vendettas were reserved for "private vengeance" in medieval Florence but over the course of time increasingly received public sanction by the authorities.[45] Cellini's brother Cecchino, a soldier, was shot and killed in Rome by an arquebusier of the chief constable. Cellini is tormented to defend his family's honor and to "seek his vengeance" by murdering his brother's killer. The narrator surfaces and explains to the reader that he is motivated by revenge to kill this other man: "e quella accetta che io feci, fu solo perché non mi scordassi di fare le sue vendette" (And that axe that I made [for my brother's sepulcher] was there only so that I would not forget to avenge him [Bellotto, 191]). After what appears to be a rather brief period of such feverish emotions, however, Cellini decides definitively to kill his brother's murderer in order to rid himself of his torment:

> Cognoscendo io che quella passione di vederlo tanto ispesso mi toglieva il sonno e il cibo et mi conduceva per il mal cammino. . . una sera mi disposi a volere uscire di tanto travaglio. (Bellotto, 192)
>
> (Knowing that that passion of seeing him so often deprived me of sleep and food, and led me down the path of evil. . . one evening I resolved to intend to rid myself of such torment.)

Cellini expresses doubt as to whether the act he is about to perform is honorable: "non mi curando di far così bassa inpresa et non molto lodevole" (not wanting to do such a low and not very honorable deed [Bellotto, 192]). Cellini's brief hesitation and feeling of uneasiness appears linked more to the way in which he plans to avenge his brother's death—sneaking up on a man from behind, stabbing him, and running off—than to the act of vengeance itself.

Cellini's vendetta is intertwined in an infinite web of murders motivated by revenge: Cecchino was murdered defending the honor of his friend and mentor who in turn was murdered by the police while defending the honor of another man. Cellini relates that Cecchino avenged the murder of his friend Bertino Aldobrandi who "era stato allevato e vero discepolo del mio fratello, et il mio fratello voleva a llui tanto smisurato bene" (had been trained and was a true disciple of my brother, and my brother loved him so so much [Bellotto, 183]). One night, unable to contain his feelings for revenge, Cellini waits for the man to exit a brothel. When the man appears, Cellini lunges toward him with a dagger, stabbing him in the neck:

> Io con gran destrezza me gli acostai con un gran pugnal pistolese, e girandogli un marrovescio, pensando levargli il collo di netto, voltosi anche

egli prestissimo, il colpo giunse inella punta della spalla istanca; e fiaccato tutto l'osso, levatosi sù, lasciato la spada, smarrito dal gran dolore, si messe a corsa; dove che seguitandolo, in quattro passi lo giunsi, e alzando il pugnale sopra la sua testa, lui abassando forte il capo, prese il pugnale a punto l'osso del collo e meza la collottola, e inell'una e ne l'altra parte entrò tanto dentro il pugnale, che io, se ben facevo gran forza di riaverlo, non possetti... (Bellotto, 192–93)

(I with great skill ambushed him with my large Pistoian dagger, and aiming a sudden back-strike, with the thought of cutting his head off clean, but he turned in a flash, and the blow landed on the edge of his left shoulder; and shattering the whole bone, he got up, leaving his sword, and dazed by the great pain, he began to run off; where, following him, in a few steps I reached him, and raising the dagger above his head, with his head bent, my blow struck him exactly between his neck bone and the nape of his neck, and the dagger went in so deep that I, even using all my strength to get it out, was not able to pull out the dagger.)

Cellini uses the same narrative style when recounting the murder of his brother's killer as he employs in the art treatises when describing the creation of a work of art. The narrator's description of acts of violence in the *Vita* parallels the ekphrastic descriptions of his art works found both in the *Vita* and in the *Due trattati*. In this ekphrastic-like account of violence Cellini describes the violent act of vengeance with the same precision and minute detail with which he narrates the intricacy and delicate ornamentation of his artistic creations.

When four soldiers arrive on the scene, Cellini flees and takes refuge in Duke Alessandro de' Medici's palace. The soldiers eventually catch up with Cellini, holding the very dagger he had trouble removing from the unfortunate man's neck bone. Cellini's friend Giovanni Bandini happens upon the scene, the same Giovanni Bandini who killed Lodovico Martelli in a duel.[46] Bandini explains to the soldiers that the dagger is his and that "l'avev[a] prestato a Benvenuto, il quale voleva far le vendette del suo fratello" (he had lent it to Benvenuto who wanted to avenge his brother [Bellotto, 194]). When the soldiers hear this, they apologize to Cellini for having interrupted him. Their apologetic stance reveals their implicit acceptance of this element in the male code of honor as well as the place of violence in acts of vengeance: "I ragionamenti di questi soldati furno assai, dolendosi d'avermi impedito..." (The reasonings of these soldiers were such that they were sorry for having stopped me [Bellotto, 194]).

In Florentine law vendettas were prosecuted as a subset of premeditated murder motivated by affronts to "family and personal honor."[47]

Provocation often played an important role in the gravity or levity of the penalty imposed. Verbal or gestural insults were perceived to be harmful enough to tear the texture of the social fabric and thus to promote factions: "Insult could be given to a person directly in word or gesture . . . The law recognized the potential of these acts to cause social disruption."[48] In the *Vita* Cellini recalls Benedetto's *ingiurie* and Caterina's *parole ingiuriose* when attempting to explain his ready recourse to violence. Injurious words found in the autobiography are often linked to the adjective *mordace* or the verb *mordere*, words connoting physical aggression. In Cellini's day civil authorities in Florence and Venice categorized a wide range of verbal acts as speech crimes. These verbal assaults were believed to be divisive enough to contribute to the harboring of vendettas by the injured parties. This, in turn, fostered bitterness and created factions, which could later surface as violent acts directed against the state or its individual members.[49]

Contemporary accounts about the Medici contain similar portraits of violence and masculinity. A common story about Cosimo I is a tale of two murders. An anonymous account in the "Carte Strozziane" collection in the Archivio di Stato, Florence, relates how Cosimo poisoned his daughter Maria after discovering that she had fallen in love with a social inferior:[50]

> essendo in corte un Paggio, figlio del Signor Malatesta da Rimini, s'invaghì di questa figlia, et ella di lui . . . uno spagnuolo . . . [che] assisteva del continuo alla porta della camera, e una mattina la trovò, che ella haveva un braccio al collo a questo giovane, o il giovane a lei, e fattone il rapporto alla Duchessa e la Duchessa al Duca, insomma l'ordinò di avvelenarla, e così fu, e morì.[51]

> (There was at court a page, son of Signor Malatesta da Rimini, who fell in love with this daughter, and she with him . . . a Spaniard . . . who kept watch at the door of the room, one morning found her with her arm around this young man's neck, or his around her, and reported it to the Duchess who in turn told the Duke, who ordered her poisoned, and so it was, and she died.)

The explanation for Cosimo's recourse to violence may be explained by the lowly social status of her purported lover or by Maria's taking her erotic desires into her own hands, thus subverting paternal authority. In this same account Cosimo murders his own son Garzia after learning that Garzia had killed his brother in a duel. Cellini attributed Garzia's death to "quella cattiva aria" that he believed was common in Pisa. Official versions of their deaths claim that Giovanni died of a "malignant fever," while the cause of death of Garzia, who perished a fortnight after Giovanni, was listed as unknown.[52]

Anti-Medici polemics about the violent acts committed by Cosimo's son Francesco, Cosimo's successor and second Grand Duke of Florence, also circulated widely. A contemporary diary by Bastiano Arditi ascribes two murders to Francesco.[53] According to Arditi, Francesco ordered the double murder of Eleonora [Alvarez] de' Toledo, wife of his brother Pietro, and her alleged lover Bernardino Antinori because their act of adultery was perceived as tantamount to a crime of lèse majesté.[54] In addition, Arditi claimed that Francesco killed a Jewish woman, portrayed as a sorceress (*incantatrice*) in the diary, because he believed that she intended to murder his infant son Filippo:

> La causa ch'il Duca fece l'omicidio fu che, interrogando il Duca l'ebrea che gli dovessi dire chi aveva mandato per lei, rispose: "La Bianca [Cappello] m'ha fatto venire." Giustificato del vero (che volevono provare di vita el figliolo del Duca, nominato Filippo) e' subito percosse di morte l'ebrea.[55]

> (The reason the Duke caused this murder was that, when the Duke interrogated the Jewish woman, demanding to know who had sent for her, she replied: "Bianca had me come." Having justified the truth of this (that they wanted to take the life of the Duke's son named Filippo) he immediately punched the woman to death.)

Drawn from diaries and anonymous sources of the day, such accounts, many of which reappear in later periods, deploy an anti-Medicean rhetoric. Francesco Settimanni narrates numerous tales of murders committed by Cosimo's sons. According to Settimanni, it was Pietro who murdered his wife Eleonora by strangling her,[56] while his brother-in-law, the Roman nobleman Paolo Giordano Orsini, Duke of Bracciano, too, strangled his wife Isabella (Cosimo's daughter, 1542–76) in their bed allegedly using a noose that dropped from the ceiling.[57] These narratives functioned primarily to invest "male domination with a powerful mystique."[58] In using violence, Cellini attempts to appropriate princely power.[59] Thus, violence, rather than being a vestige of the artisan class Cellini hopes to leave behind, is a privilege of the aristocratic class he has joined.

Like these tales, Cellini's *Vita* is a kind of fantasy of male power. In the story of his life, Cellini rapes, pillages, and dominates just about everything and everybody in his path. He portrays himself as violent, dominant, and aggressive. Like these accounts of the Medici ruling family, the *Vita* weaves a fantasy of male domination and control.

The tale relating Cosimo's murders of Maria and Garzia exemplifies the complete power that the *pater familias* exerts over his children, especially over his daughters, even to taking life. Still other versions of these tales about the Medici portray Cosimo committing incest by having sexual intercourse with his daughter Isabella or interring his second wife and former mistress Camilla Martelli (1545–90) alive in a convent wall. Cosimo had a son, Giovanni (1567–1621), by another mistress, Eleonora degli Albizzi and two illegitimate daughters. Populated by mistresses, concubines, and illegitimate children, both these "real" and fictitious accounts depict masculine sexual prowess, just as Cellini's *Vita* does. In the *Vita* Cellini relates his numerous sexual encounters with female courtesans, models, and servants as well as his fathering of illegitimate children. For instance, while in Paris Cellini relates how he deflowered a virgin girl who gets pregnant and gives birth to a daughter whom they name Constanza:

> Questa giovanetta era pura e vergine, et io la 'ngravidai, la quale mi partorì una figliuola a' dì sette di giugno a ore tredici di giorno, 1544, quale era il corso dell'età mia appunto de' 44 anni. La detta figliuola, io le posi nome Constanza. (Bellotto, 569)
>
> (This young girl was pure and a virgin, and I got her pregnant. She gave birth to a daughter on the seventh of June, at the thirteenth hour of the day, 1544; and that was precisely the forty-fourth year of my own life. This daughter, I gave her the name Constanza.)

Taken together, these elements create an image of unrestrained male sexuality that is evident in other misogynistic texts of the period, such as Aretino's *Sei Giornate*.

Seduction and even rape are other privileges of the powerful. Cellini's act of deflowering a virgin, like Varchi's alleged seduction of a young girl, was another way for a man to prove his manhood. As Diane Wolfthal has shown, images of what she has called "heroic" rape in high art throughout the early modern period, involving a Greek or Roman god or hero, and displayed in both private and public spaces, "glorify, sanitize, and aestheticize sexual violence."[60] Foundational myths like the "Rape of the Sabines" suggest, ultimately, that social unity is founded on sexual violence. As we have seen, Cellini was familiar with classical mythology. In presenting himself as a rapist in his autobiography, the artist might be attempting to arrogate for himself the power of the gods.

Throughout the story of his life, Cellini's honor, as manifest in his art, writing, and social practice, is on public display. While in Rome, Cellini relates how the Pope decides to present an illuminated manuscript to the Emperor as a gift for the Empress. This Book of Hours was "scritto a mano e miniato per mano de il maggior uomo che mai facessi tal professione" (copied by hand, and illuminated by the greatest craftsman who ever practiced such an art [Bellotto, 328]) but unbound. The Pope wants to complete the artwork by creating a gilt and bejeweled cover for the manuscript ("Al ditto libro voleva fare una coperta d'oro massiccio, riccamente lavorata, e con molte gioie addorna" (For the said book he wanted to commission a solid gold cover, richly ornamented, and thickly studded with jewels [Bellotto, 325])), asking Cellini to create it. In Cellini's day goldsmiths participated actively in this phase of book production.[61] The Pope provides him with the appropriate materials, and Cellini sets to work. Cellini works so vigorously that the Pope marvels at his creation:

> Le gioie valevano incirca seimila scudi; di modo che, datomi le gioie e l'oro, messi mano alla ditta opera, e sollecitandola in brevi giorni io la feci comparire di tanta bellezza, che il Papa si maravigliava. (Bellotto, 325–26)

> (The jewels were worth about six thousand crowns; so having been given the jewels and the gold, I set to work on the said object, and working quickly in a few days I made a work of such beauty that the Pope marveled.)

Here masculine vigor and artistic vigor mirror each other. Artistic honor is at stake here, too.

When it is time to give the manuscript to the Emperor, the book binding, although marvelous, is unfinished due to Cellini's mysterious illness. The Pope orders Cellini to bring the book in its present form and explain that he will complete the work as soon as possible. In a public ceremony filled with formulaic displays of servitude, Cellini presents the gifts of the gilt manuscript and a gold crucifix to the Emperor and Empress. Here Cellini plays the part of the courtier. In his account Cellini and the Emperor discussed a variety of subjects for an entire half-hour, as equals. Cellini himself relates how he came out of the affair with greater honor than even he had anticipated:

> [E] perché a me pareva esserne uscito con molto maggiore *onore* di quello che io m'ero promesso, fatto un poco di cadenza a il ragionamento, feci reverenzia e partimmi. (Bellotto, 329, emphasis added)

> (And because it seemed that I had come out of the affair with greater *honor* than I had anticipated, when the conversation finished, I bowed and left.)

As we noted in chapter 3, Castiglione claims that a courtier must be proficient in both arms and letters. Cellini's *Vita* illustrates how, by the early sixteenth century, art had joined arms and letters as a means of winning honor. Cellini wins honor through his art. But he also acquires honor by virtue of his courtly behavior. This tale of honor and courtiership also testifies to the fact that honor is a kind of disposition.[62] In his account of presenting the gilt manuscript to the Emperor, Cellini insists that he also gave himself as a gift. Before the ceremony with the Emperor, the Pope makes Cellini practice precisely what he will say and do when he actually makes the presentation to the imperial ruler. When Cellini indicates that the binding is unfinished, the Pope seizes the moment to instruct Cellini in the appropriate code of social comportment that he must take toward the Emperor:

A questo il Papa disse che molto gli piaceva, ma che io arrogessi da parte di Sua Santità, faccendogli presente del libro fargli presente di me istesso; e mi disse tutto il modo che io avevo a ttenere, delle parole che io avevo a dire, le qual parole io le dissi al Papa, domandandolo se gli piaceva che io dicessi così. Il quale mi disse: "Troppo bene diresti, se a te bastassi la vista di parlare in questo modo allo Inperadore, che tu parli a me." (Bellotto, 326–27)

(The Pope said that he liked this very much, but he said that I should add something for His Holiness, when presenting the book to him to make a gift of myself; and he told me exactly how I should behave, the words I should say. I repeated these words to the Pope, asking him if he wanted me to speak that way. He said: "If you can speak to the Emperor in the same way as you're speaking to me, you'll do very well.")

Here Cellini's public display of honor is bound to his artistic creations as well as his self-fashioned behavior.

Cellini displays his honor when the *Perseus* (figures 9 and 10) is unveiled in Florence. Cosimo, anxious to gauge public opinion about the statue, exhorts Cellini to unveil the statue partially even though Cellini has not yet finished putting the finishing touches on it. Cellini concedes to his lord and allows the partially unveiled statue to be transported and displayed in the Piazza della Signoria:

Et partitosi, io cominciai a dare ordine di scoprire; et perché e' mancava certo poco di oro, et certe vernice et altre cotai coselline, che si appartengono alla fine dell'opera, sdegnosamente borbottavo et mi dolevo. (Bellotto, 707)

(And when he left, I began to give orders to uncover it; and because there was still some gold missing, and some varnish and a number of other little things, that belong to the last phase of completing an art work, scornfully, I grumbled and complained.)

No sooner is the *Perseus* unveiled than enthusiastic public praise for Cellini resounds:

> Or sì come piacque a dDio, subito che la fu veduta, ei si levò un grido tanto 'smisurato in lode della detta opera, la qual cosa fu causa di consolarmi alquanto. (Bellotto, 707)
>
> (And, then as God would have it, as soon as it was seen, the people let out such an immeasurable cry in praise of the work that I was given some consolation.)

Public acclaim for the statue not only glorifies Cellini as artist but also, by extension, Cosimo. Cosimo's reputation as ruler and patron is intimately intertwined with Cellini's public fame as goldsmith and sculptor at the Medici court. The public display of the *Perseus* is the display of Cellini's honor and artistic virtue. It is also bound to Cosimo's reputation as patron. In addition, the Florentine people validate Cellini's artistic creation socially by praising Cellini's artistic virtues in the Piazza della Signoria, the principal public space in the center of the city of Florence.

But Cellini's artistic talents are also validated socially and publicly by two other social groups: university professors and artists. Both groups wrote sonnets in praise of the *Perseus* and placed them at the base of the statue. The poems placed at the base of the *Perseus* circulated Cellini's honor and displayed the admiration of his peers for all the educated members of the community to see. As noted, the Italian sonnets and Latin epigrams praising the statue were collected and printed as an appendix to his art treatises in 1568. According to Cellini, the erudite professors from the University of Pisa wrote their tributes praising the *Perseus'* beauty and Cellini's virtù in both Latin and Greek, but only the Tuscan and Latin verses were printed in the art treatises:

> [I]l giorno medesimo, che la si tenne parecchi ore scoperta, e' vi fu appiccati più di venti sonetti, tutti in lode smisuratissime della mia opera; dappoi che io la ricopersi ogni dì mi v'era appicati quantità di sonetti, et di versi latini et versi greci; perché gli era vacanza allo Studio di Pisa, tutti quei eccellentissimi dotti e gli scolari facevano a ggara. (Bellotto, 707–08)
>
> (The same day that the statue was uncovered many hours, there were twenty sonnets attached to it, all in immeasurable praise of my statue; so I covered it back up, every day I found a large number of sonnets and

Latin verses and Greek verses attached to it: since there was a vacation at the University of Pisa, all those celebrated professors and students rivaled each other.)

Fellow artists vied with one another in their praise of the statue. Cellini's account underscores how essential the opinion of his peers was to the public display of his honor. For Cellini, both sculptors and painters were important members of the community of artists in Florence who praised his statue.

Ma quello che mi dava maggior contento. . . si era, che quegli dell'arte, cioè scultori et pittori, ancora loro facevano a ggara a chi meglio diceva. Et infra gli altri, quale io stimavo più, si era il valente pittore Iacopo da Puntorno, et più di lui il suo eccellente Bronzino, pittore. (Bellotto, 708)

(But what gave me the most pleasure. . . was the fact that my fellow artists, that is, the sculptors and painters, also rivaled each other to see who could compose the best one. Among them, I especially valued the opinion of the talented painter, Jacopo da Pontormo, and more than his, that of his excellent pupil, the painter Bronzino.)

Bronzino wrote two sonnets praising the *Perseus*; both poems recount the youth's mythical origins, born in an "aurea pioggia" (golden rain), and celebrate the statue's beauty and grace.[63] Bronzino's image of the creation of the *Perseus* by Cellini in a golden rain stands in stark contrast to Cellini's own prose version of the *Perseus'* genesis in a magical and quasi-diabolic ceremony.

This tale of praise and public honor continues when the Perseus is completed and displayed fully. Numerous Florentine social groups are involved in the celebration of Cellini's honor. Foreigners, too, contribute to the circulation of Cellini's honorable reputation and artistic talents. Two Sicilian noblemen pursue Cellini in the Piazza della Signoria, praising him profusely and exhorting to come back with them to Sicily to work at the court of the Spanish Viceroy. Cellini again plays the role of the noble courtier, humbly thanking them but declining their offer. In fact, Cellini uses the occasion to emphasize how pleased he is to work at the court of Cosimo, a great patron and lover of the arts. Cellini's obsequious behavior toward Cosimo is especially marked in this episode:

Infra gli altri e' furno dua gentili uomini, i quali erano mandati dal veceré di Sicilia al nostro Duca per lor faccende. Ora questi dua piacevoli uomini mi affrontorno in piazza, ché io fui mostro loro così passando; di modo che con furia e' mi raggiunsono, et subito, colle lor berrette in mano, e' mi feciono una la più cirimoniosa orazione, la quale saria stata troppa a un papa: io pure, quanto potevo, mi umiliavo... Et infra queste cirimonie eglino furno tanto arditi, che e' mi richiesono all'andare in Sicilia. (Bellotto, 711)

(Among the others were two noblemen, who had been sent by the Viceroy of Sicily to our Duke on a mission. These two agreeable men came up to me in the piazza, since I was pointed out to them as I was passing; and so they ran up furiously, and immediately, with their hats in their hands, they made me one of the most ceremonious orations, which would have been excessive even for a pope: I was as humble as I could be... And in the middle of these ceremonies they were so bold, that they asked me to go to Sicily.)

Male friendships are central to the *Vita*'s construction of masculinity. In the *Vita* relationships among men are of two types: affective and agonistic. The bonds that tie friends was a common theme for Renaissance humanists, no doubt inspired by classical texts such as Cicero's *De Amicitia*, which circulated widely. Closer to Cellini's time, the most articulate formulation of the nature of male friendship and its relation to conjugal and communal life is Leon Battista Alberti's *Della famiglia* (ca. 1430). In *Della famiglia* Alberti takes up the question of friendship, stressing in particular the ties that bind men. For Alberti, friendship bonds, like kinship and patronage ties, are important for maintaining a gentleman's social status and public reputation. In book four Alberti claims that one's friends indicate a man's social position and wealth in society.[64] In this "client system," friendship is an index of a man's status.

Cellini, too, defines friendship as a masculine tie that, although not indissoluble, is a fundamental social bond among men of similar social status.[65] Male friendship is characterized by affection and reciprocity. Throughout the *Vita* Cellini often discloses how much love he feels for a particular young man to whom he is bound in friendship. For example, when recounting his early apprenticeship as a goldsmith in Florence, Cellini relates how he and a certain Francesco di Filippo di Fra Filippo [Lippi] loved each other:

Attesi continuamente in Firenze a imparare sotto la bella maniera di Michelagnolo, et da quella mai mi sono ispiccato. In questo tempo presi pratica et amicizia istretissima con uno gentil giovanetto di mia età, il quale ancora lui stava allo orefice. Aveva nome Francesco, figliuolo di Filippo di Fra Filippo eccellentissimo pittore. Nel praticare insieme generò in noi un tanto amore, che mai, né dì né notte, stavamo l'uno senza l'altro. (Bellotto, 46)

(I waited continuously in Florence to learn Michelangelo's style, and I have never wandered far from it. At this time I formed a close and intimate friendship with a charming young man of my own age, who was also in the goldsmith's trade. His name was Francesco, son of Filippo whose father was the most excellent painter Fra Filippo. In working together there sprung up in us such a great love, that neither night or day we were without each other.)

There are several episodes of same-sex friendships in the *Vita*. For example, Cellini emphasizes how strong his bond is with a young male friend by comparing it to the bonds that bind brothers: "[V]enne a trovarmi insieme con un certo giovane di mia età, il quale si chiamava Piero di Giovanni Landi: ci volevamo bene più che se fratelli fussimo stati" (He came to visit me together with a young man of my own age, whose name was Piero di Giovanni Landi: we loved each other more than if we had been brothers [Bellotto, 63]). Cellini also recounts how a certain Albertaccio del Bene loved him as much as his very self: "a me voleva bene quanto a sé medesimo" (Bellotto, 261). Friendships and homosociability between men were essential components of chivalric epics. It will be useful to recall the friendships between Orlando and Brandimarte as well as between Arthur's knights. The affection between men displayed in the *Vita* may be more than purely platonic, often filled with homoerotic overtones.

This bonding between men calls for a certain style of conduct toward those who are singled out as friends. The mode of existence defined in the *Vita* requires that the men bound by friendship remain loyal to one another. "Fede" (loyalty), another feature of masculinity, involves putting a friend's interests and erotic desires above one's own.[66] This second element in the *Vita*'s construction of masculinity creates a space, indeed, one of the only spaces, where Cellini, not known for his liberality, does not simply take what he desires. On two occasions Cellini acts as a loyal friend, conceding prostitutes to his friends, out of a sense of "fede" to them. The first case involves a Bolognese prostitute Faustina. This narrative is a testimony to masculine fidelity (and vanity):

Accade una sera in fra le altre, un mio confederato compagno menò in casa a ccena una meretrice bolognese, che si domandava Faustina. Questa donna era bellissima, ma era di trenta anni incirca, e seco aveva una servicella di tredici in quattordici. Per essere la detta Faustina cosa del mio amico, per tutto l'oro del mondo io non l'arei toca. Con tutto che la dicesse essere di me forte innamorata, constantemente osservavo la fede allo mio amico. (Bellotto, 100)

(It happened one evening that one of my associates brought home a Bolognese prostitute, whose name was Faustina. The woman was very beautiful, but she was about thirty, and she had with her a little servant girl about thirteen or fourteen. As Faustina belonged to my friend, I would not have touched her for all the gold in the world. Although she told me that she was madly in love with me, faithfully I kept my friend's trust.)

The second passage also takes up how loyalty to friends is an element in a set of duties to the community since lack of fidelity cleaves social relations among men: "Io, che mi pensavo d'esser provisto bene per una giovane molto bella, chiamata Pantassilea, la quali era grandemente innamorata di me, fui forzato a concederla a un mio carissimo amico, chiamato il Bachiacca" (I, who thought I was well provided for with a very beautiful young woman, whose name was Pantisilea, madly in love with me, had to concede her to a dear friend of mine, Bachiacca [Bellotto, 106]). The masculine fidelity articulated by Cellini requires a self-sacrifice typical of a courtier. But such friendships do not preclude a man's use of violence against his friends: when Firenzuola, laughing, refuses to pay Cellini money owed to him, Cellini retorts that he can brandish a sword as well as a chisel. The dispute between them was finally settled when Firenzuola paid up and the two men return to being friends: "[F]ui pagato; et con ispazio di tempo il ditto Firenzuola et io fummo amici, et gli battezzai un figliulo, richiesto da llui" (I was paid; and later on the said Firenzuola and I were friends, and I stood as godfather at his son's baptism, at his request [Bellotto, 53]).

The matrix of friendship posited by Cellini also registers agonistic forces: the inversion of male bonding is male competition. Cellini's *Vita* dramatizes contests of masculinity in numerous spheres. Men challenge each other in the public sphere to reconstitute damaged honor on the one hand; on the other, artists compete with each another to win commissions from patrons. While in Rome Cellini relates how he and a Sicilian priest, a noted necromancer, conjured demons in the Coliseum. Before he agrees to participate in this magical ritual, Cellini tells the cleric that he must finish a medal he has been working on. He postpones their encounter with demons because he cannot concentrate on anything else:

Essendomi io disposto in tutto e per tutto di voler prima finir la mia medaglia, di già eramo vicini al fine del mese; al quale, per essere invaghito tanto inella medaglia, io non mi ricordavo più né di Angelica né di null'altra cotal cosa, ma tutto ero intento a quella mia opera. (Bellotto, 240)

(Being disposed to first want to finish my medal once and for all, since we were already at the end of the month; being so in love with the medal, I forgot about both Angelica and any other thing, and was completely engrossed by my art work.)

Cellini desperately wants to finish this medal because another artist who recently arrived in Rome is reputed to be a master in creating medals:

> Io, che ne cominciavo avere più voglia di lui, gli dissi che per essere venuto in Roma un certo maestro Giovanni da Castel Bolognese, molto valentuomo per far medaglie di quella sorte che io facevo, in acciaio. (Bellotto, 240)

> (I, who was beginning to have more interest than him, told him that a certain Master Giovanni da Castel Bolognese had come to Rome, a very distinguished man who made the kind of medals that I did, in steel.)

Cellini views their artistic competition as a duel. He uses the language of dueling and chivalry to describe their heroic undertaking (again referred to as *una tale impresa*). Cellini relates how he hopes to "kill" his opponents with works of art not swords:

> [N]on desideravo altro al mondo che di fare a gara con questo valentuomo, e uscire al mondo a dosso con una tale impresa, per la quale io speravo con tal virtù, e non con la spada, amazzare quelli parechi mia nimici. (Bellotto, 240)

> (I wanted nothing else in the world than to compete with this distinguished man, and come out on top with such a feat, so I hoped to kill all those many enemies of mine with my virtue and not with my sword.)

Cellini's use of the verb "ammazzare" to describe how he will "win" the competition through the metaphorical "murder" of Giovanni by creating a more beautiful medal illustrates the potential violence underlying these artistic rivalries between men. For Cellini, contests of masculinity are charged with potential violence. Like his account of his revenge for the killing of his brother, Cellini's assault on Caterina is ekphrastic. Here, too, Cellini's honor is on public display. In the episode recounting Cellini's violence against Caterina, the themes of sex and art are tied to honor.

Misogyny

The notion of honor, however, does not fully explain the motives for Cellini's violent behavior. For Cellini, violence against women is also permissible behavior for a man. Violence against women was a generalized feature of the society of Renaissance Florence. Although acts of sexual violence were prohibited by law and condemned with a harsh rhetoric, it appears that rape was commonplace. In Venice, for example, the distant and antiseptic language of rape was tied to "the mild penalties rape garnered," and reflected "a continuing low evaluation of the crime and in turn an enduring tradition of limited concern for protecting a woman's sexuality and personality."[67] In Florence, punishments varied according to the social status of the victim. Often, without a confession, defendants were acquitted or freed.[68] Brackett has argued that "rape was viewed as an extremely serious offense, meriting the death penalty when bodily injury occurred, but the penalties imposed by the Otto do not seem to accord with the stated degree of seriousness."[69] Furthermore, within the code of masculinity, the seduction or rape of girls could enhance, rather than damage, a man's reputation. Varchi's prosecution and conviction for seducing a young girl did nothing, it seems, to damage his reputation.[70] Lorenzo Venier composed a venomous, misogynistic, and widely circulated poem titled *Il Trentuno della Zaffetta* (1531) celebrating the gang-rape of the Venetian courtesan Angela del Moro, known as *La Zaffetta*.[71]

The dynamics of power and dominance may help explain Cellini's act of violence against Caterina. Violent acts are part of a pattern of correlative practices in which aggression involves art as well as sex. Cellini uses women as sexual objects, models, and servants.[72] As Tylus has noted, for Cellini, artistic creation is dependent upon violence.[73] In the episode involving Caterina violence is enacted upon the bodies of women.

> Ancora vedevo lei esser tutta lacerata, livida e enfiata, pensando che, se pure lei tornassi, essere di necessità di farla medicare per quindici giorni, innanzi che me ne potessi servire . . . Aprendo la porta, questa bestia ridendo mi si gittò al collo, abbracciommi e baciommi, e mi dimandò se io era più crucciato con essa. Io dissi che no . . . Dipoi mi messi a ritrarla, et in quel mezo vi occorse le piacevolezze carnali, e dipoi a quell'ora medesima del passato giorno, tanto lei mi stuzicò, che io l'ebbi a dare le medesime busse; e così durammo parechi giorni, faccendo ognidì tutte queste medesime cose, come che a stampa: poco variava dal più al manco. (Bellotto, 563–64)

> (Besides this, I saw that she was all torn up, bruised and swollen, thinking that even if she did come back, it would be necessary to have her treated for fifteen days, before I could use her again . . . Opening the door, the creature, laughing, threw her arms around my neck, hugging and kissing me, and asked me if I was still angry at her. I said, no . . . Then I began to draw her, and in the middle of this time we had

sex, and then, at the same time as she did the day before, she teased me so much, that I had to give her the same beating; and this went on for several days, like a printing press, doing the same thing every day, with little variation.)

For Cellini, sexual conquests of boys may have been perceived as less masculine than conquests of women. In his *Vita* Cellini does not recount assaulting his male models, only his male (and female) servants. Violence is permitted against servants in a specific and charged moment, during the fusion of the *Perseus*. Cellini attacks his group of male and female servants with impunity because domestic workers were his social inferiors and prosecutions for such acts were rare.

In the violent episode with the model Caterina, the narrator comments on the "strangeness" he feels when relating this episode. This strangeness is evidenced in the narrative style itself: surprisingly, the author enumerates the precise levels of revenge he enacts upon Paolo and Caterina, going so far as to number them in his account:

> [O]gnidì le davo trenta soldi; e faccendola stare ignuda, voleva la prima cosa che io li dessi li sua dinari innanzi; la siconda voleva molto bene da far colezione; la terza io *per vendetta* usavo seco. . . la quarta si era che io la facevo stare con gran disagio parechi e parechi ore. (Bellotto, 561, emphasis added)
>
> (Every day I gave her thirty soldi; and making her pose in the nude, first, she wanted me to give her the money in advance; second, she wanted me to give her a good meal; third, *I had my revenge* by having sex with her . . . the fourth thing I did was to make her pose for hours and hours in great discomfort.)

Is the "strangeness" linked to a sadomasochistic impulse? After the initial assault, a ritualized pattern of sex, artistic creation, and violence is established between Caterina and Cellini. For Cellini, violence is, as Ivan Arnaldi has argued, both a natural outlet and a pleasure.[74]

The violent episode of Cellini's assault on Caterina is also bound to the notion of male honor. Cellini continues his detailed account of the violent episode, emphasizing how honor is bound to artistic creation:

> [E] stando in questo disagio a llei veniva molto a ffastidio, tanto quanto a me dilettava, perché lei era di bellissima forma e *mi faceva grandissimo onore*. (Bellotto, 561, emphasis added)
>
> (And, staying in this position gave her great discomfort, she was as annoyed as I was pleased, since she was very beautiful and *won me the greatest honor*.)

Cellini believes that Paolo has damaged his honor and made him a cuckold by having sexual relations with Caterina, whom everyone recognizes as Cellini's sexual partner. To be cuckolded was a typically male injury, involving women as pawns "in a battle between male sexual rivals."[75] Cellini feels compelled to take vengeance on Paolo by having sexual relations with Caterina after she and Paolo have married. In fact, he refers to this act as a "dual act" of vengeance. By having sexual relations with Caterina, Cellini makes Paolo a cuckold and simultaneously inflicts pain on Caterina. Cellini commits a sadistic act by forcing her to pose for hours on end in uncomfortable positions:

> [D]a me dicevo: "Io fo qui *dua diverse vendette*: l'una per esser moglie: queste non son corna vane, come eran le sua quando lei era a me puttana: però se io fo questa vendetta sì rilevata inverso di lui; et inverso di lei ancora tanta istranezza, faccendola stare qui con tanto disagio."(Bellotto, 562, emphasis added)

> (I said to myself: "I get *two kinds of revenge* out of this: first, she's married: these horns are not in vain, unlike hers when she was playing the whore with me: so I'm taking an excellent revenge against him; and an extravagant one against her, by making her pose here in such discomfort.")

Art is directly linked to honor: in addition to the pleasure Cellini gets from Caterina's pain, he relates how he will acquire honor by creating works of art using Caterina as his model. With a rhetorical flourish, the narrator addresses the reader directly in an imaginary monologue: "[I]l quale, oltra al piacere, mi resulta tanto onore e tanto utile, che poss'io più desiderare?" (Which gave me, besides pleasure, so much honor and profit, what more could I possibly want? [Bellotto, 562]). Here pain, pleasure, art, honor, and sex are all bound together.

Cellini's *Vita* dramatizes power conflicts between men and women. In addition to courtesy books and dueling manuals, many texts in diverse genres dealing with the concept of virtù articulated forms of masculinity in sixteenth-century Italy. In these texts metaphors of power are expressed in terms of male domination. For instance, Machiavelli's famous formulation that since "la fortuna è donna, è necessario, volendola tenere sotto, batterla e urtarla" (*The Prince*, 1532) (because Fortune is a woman, it is necessary, in order to keep her down, to beat her and to struggle with her) expresses the conflict between virtù and fortune as a sexual one and the exercise of power as an assault.[76] Here Machiavelli articulates virtù specifically in terms of the physical domination of women.

Cellini's *Vita* repeats negative representations of women circulating in the culture of Renaissance Florence. In general, his portrayals of both upper- and lower-class women, like those of other male writers of his time, are imbued with misogyny and stereotypes. Three commonplaces about women in the *Vita* are exemplary. The first narrates how women are vain and materialistic: "Angelica mi pregò che io li comperassi una vesta di velluto nero" (Angelica begged me to buy her a black velvet dress [Bellotto, 251]). Women are portrayed as prattling: at a party in Rome Cellini met two women who, during a poetry reading "non mai restate di cicalare" (never stopped chattering [Bellotto, 110]). And finally, women are depicted as downright evil: "[M]adama de Tanpes [desiderava] maggiormente invelenire a far contro a di me, dove io portai gran pericolo della vita mia" (Madame d'Étampes increased her venomous desire to do me harm to such an extent that I felt that my life was in great danger [Bellotto, 534]).

In the story of his life Cellini's encounters with women of any social rank precipitate diatribes on the nature of Woman and her destructive forces. Throughout the *Vita* women are continually the cause of his various misfortunes. Madame d'Étampes is to blame for Cellini's loss of a commission: "Potettono tanto quelle argute ragione [*sic*], con il grande aiuto di madama di Tampes e con il continuo martellare giorno e notte, or Madama, ora il Bologna, . . . [che] conpiacque tutto quello che dimandato egli avevano" (They used such cunning arguments, with the great help of Madame d'Étampes, they hammered away continuously day and night, now Madame, now Bologna . . . so that he agreed to everything that they had asked [Bellotto, 539–40]). The Duchess of Florence is responsible for his loss of favor with the Duke: "[Sua] Eccellenzia . . . a mme aveva ordinato che io me n'andassi per la sua guardaroba . . . dove che inn-ispazio di pochi giorni la Duchessa me ne privò" (His Excellency . . . had told me that I was to make my way there through his wardrobe . . . then, inside the space of a few days, the Duchess took this privilege away [Bellotto, 699]). These "injustices" are a result of "quelle vie che possono le donne innegli uomini" (those things that women do to men [Bellotto, 575]).

But the literary tradition of misogyny is not a static repertory of commonplaces. Rather, it is a litany that changes over time as new elements emerge and common elements are deployed in new ways. The *Vita* testifies to the emergence of new elements as social conditions changed and sexual roles were redefined. One particular element in Cellini's *Vita* illustrates how a new element was added to the litany of misogyny: soon after its appearance, women were soon blamed for the spread of syphilis. Cellini himself blames a servant girl for giving him the French disease: "La infirmità gli era il vero che io l'avevo, ma credo che l'avessi guadagnata mediante quella bella giovane serva che io tenevo nel tempo in cui fui rubato" (It was true that I had caught the disease, but I think I must have acquired it from that pretty young servant girl I was keeping at the time I was robbed [Bellotto, 214–15]).

Cellini's contraction of syphilis may be a new element in the construction of masculinity. In this new version, contracting syphilis is not something that a man should be ashamed of, but rather, demonstrates sexual promiscuity and prowess. His use of the verb "guadagnare" (to earn or gain) to describe the act of contracting the disease evokes precisely this image of virile manhood: "l'avessi guadagnata" from "that young servant girl." Indeed, he earned it. In this new norm of manhood, syphilis signified a badge of honor and allowed entrance into an illicit cult where sexual promiscuity and domination over one's sexual partners reigned.[77]

Over the course of the sixteenth century in Italy prostitutes were commonly blamed for the spread of syphilis.[78] A negative view of prostitutes as carriers of disease was one factor among many that led to the increasing criminalization of prostitution over time.[79] The cultural association of prostitutes with disease, and specifically with syphilis, can be traced to a much earlier period. But negative images of prostitutes proliferated, almost immediately following the discovery of the disease by the philosopher and physician Girolamo Fracastoro. Fracastoro's poem titled "Syphilis sive morbus gallicus" (Rome, 1531) is a treatise on the origins and nature of syphilis. By the 1540s "syphilis appears to have been considered an eminently suitable (and highly topical) subject for artistic productions emanating from, and intended for, an elite courtly audience."[80]

Berni's poem "Sonetto delle Puttane" (ca. 1518), discussed in chapter 3, in addition to being a parody of Petrarchism, illustrates nicely the identification of prostitutes with disease in general and with syphilis in particular.[81] The sonnet opens with the male poet lamenting the impossible demands made on him by a female prostitute. The prostitute, who is never given a name, and whom he barely knows ("E per averla conosciuta a pena"), asks him to give her clothes and jewels: "Or la veste, or l'anello, or la catena." Ultimately, she is never satisfied with whatever object(s) he presumably gives her for she really desires to take all of his possessions, wanting, as the male speaker claims, to "tutta tòr la robba [sua]." The second quatrain follows the pattern of the first, with the male interlocutor voicing the demands being made on him by the prostitute, this time for companionship and food ("un voler che'io gli facci compagnia, / . . . / Un dargli desinar, albergo, e cena"), which evokes feelings of anger in him (". . . nell'inferno non è maggior pena, / . . . / Come se l'uom facesse l'osteria"). The male poet surmises that she has syphilis ("Un sospetto crudel del mal franzese"), and then begins his diatribe against her. Besides associating her with syphilis, the poet uses metaphors of filth and disease, calling her "un morbo, un puzzo, un cesso." The male speaker concludes by implying that he will no longer bother with female prostitutes anymore and will instead masturbate: "un toglier a pigion ogni palazzo / son le cagioni ch'io mi meni il cazzo."

As we have seen, the male poet's "lady" is characterized as a prostitute only in the final tercet. A member of the "whorish sex" (*puttanesco sesso*), she is identified as a prostitute through recurring images of filth. The repetition of the verbs "tôr"/"toglier" emphasizes the violent rupture and perhaps potential castration that the prostitute's demands make on the male poet's material, psychological, and sexual self. The melancholy lament created by the vowel sounds in the words "tôr"/"onor"/"torno" echoes the male interlocutor's state of mind and seems to produce his breathy lament. "Pigion" could also connote sodomy, suggesting that the male poet will seek male sexual partners or male prostitutes from now on. The term is used, for instance, in a sonnet by the poet Burchiello (Domenico di Giovanni, 1404–49) to signify sodomitical sexual intercourse.[82]

The discourse of syphilis in the sixteenth century reveals instances of both cultural associations and national stereotyping. From its first appearance onwards, Italians referred to the disease as "il mal francese," an association that Cellini continually makes in the autobiography. In the *Vita* Cellini refers to the disease as either the "morbo gallico" or "mal franzese," claiming that the disease is particularly fond of priests: "[Q]uesti mali [franzesi] in Roma sono molto amici de' preti, massime di quei più ricchi . . ." (This particular disease in Rome is very fond of priests— especially very rich priests [Bellotto, 97]). Ironically, the French called it the "Neapolitan" disease. This anticlerical theme is common throughout the medieval and Renaissance periods in Italy, as in, for example, Boccaccio's tales. In Cellini's day syphilis became a prevalent motif in images as well as texts, and so, it is not surprising to find it in Cellini's writings. Margaret Healy has claimed that Bronzino's painting, *An Allegory of Venus and Cupid*, directly takes up the theme of the consequences of the venereal act by depicting a syphilitic man behind the two lovers.[83]

Being a Renaissance Man

Contemporary ideals of virility and masculine honor shaped Cellini's presentation of himself in the *Vita* as dauntless and violent. In his day violence, honor, sexuality, and male friendships all helped construct masculine gender identity. This culturally induced process of self-fashioning influenced the persona Cellini sought to portray in his *Vita*. Both honor and manliness inform his literary persona.

Cellini articulated a new norm of manhood by displacing martial masculinity into artistic enterprise. His artistic honor was constantly at stake. The *Vita* also reveals that gender ideology restricted male behavior. In Cellini's world, honor is a kind of ideological imposition. It inspires male violence. To expand on the insight of Joan Kelly who first argued that the position of women worsened during the Renaissance, perhaps there was no Renaissance for men of certain groups either. Cellini's *Vita* reveals that gender restrictions affected male behavior, too.

Cellini reformulated the traditional quest of the hero of epic or romance by undertaking a metaphorical quest to prove his own and his art's problematic relationship to the world of an aristocratic elite. In the *Vita* Cellini tries throughout to assume the trappings and codes of nobility even though he is from an artisan background. Cellini's application for admission to the Florentine nobility demonstrates his quest for social advancement; likewise, the artist's lengthy retelling of this intellectual elite's praise for his *Perseus* illustrates his desire for social legitimation by this group.

Cellini wrote his *Vita* during a transitional period in European history, between the medieval world and the late Renaissance one. His *Vita* expresses the tensions inherent in this period of transition by juxtaposing the old and the new. Medieval chivalric terms appear alongside the new language of genteel courtliness; the medieval journey to the Otherworld in prison takes its place alongside the Counter-Reformation journey involving necromancers and demons in the Coliseum; the medieval chivalric code of honor won on the battlefield has been replaced with the new code of honor displayed in art and social practice. Moreover, in the *Vita* Cellini mixes high (elite) and low (popular) elements. Learned necromancy appears alongside popular magical practices, ignoble assaults find a place alongside upper-class duels.

The *Vita* also expresses nostalgia for a lost world and its values. Tylus has argued that Cellini longs for a return to the medieval economic system of patronage that has been replaced by a new pre-capitalistic mode of production. Following Tylus, Amelang has suggested that the

Vita stands strangely apart from the autobiographies of its time in its insistence on work and physical labor.[84] Artists, too, sought to downplay labor or even to avoid it altogether. Waldman has noted that Bandinelli in particular "seems to have regarded the dirty and time-consuming work of carving his own sculptures with a certain measure of disinterest."[85] The *Vita* also expresses a Don-Quixotesque nostalgia for a lost world of heroic deeds, a world where men were judged by their deeds not their words, a world where men were asked to perform manly deeds rather than exhibit courtly manners. Cellini may have insisted that deeds were more important than words, but it is predominately words that he has left us. Unable to follow the old chivalric code, Cellini adheres to a new one; rather than defending women, he assaults them. The *Vita* also reveals that masculinity is fragile and must be reaffirmed constantly. It also suggests that the misogyny evident in this and other contemporary texts such as those of Aretino may be a result of the tension created by the requirements on men like Cellini to be both a feminine courtier and a masculine defender of honor.

Contemporary understanding of the artistic temperament may also help explain Cellini's violent self-portrait. The goldsmith and sculptor Leone Leoni (ca. 1509–90) was convicted of assault; the painter Caravaggio (1573–1610) murdered a man.[86] The miniaturist Cesari di Francesco from Perugia was condemned to death for homicide but was pardoned.[87] Artists were believed to live and work under the influence of Saturn and as such were viewed as melancholic.[88] In his *Vita* Cellini tells the reader that he had a natural melancholic disposition: "Essendo io per natura malinconico" (Bellotto, 95). The topos of melancholy helps explain some facets of Cellini's self-representation, including his use of violence. Here, too, in the concept of melancholy, we find, as Juliana Schiesari first proposed, a tension between masculine artistic genius and feminine melancholia.[89] Fifteenth-century theories of "noble rage" and sixteenth-century discourses of wrath and anger may also help explain Cellini's ready recourse to violence. The *Vita* recounts the story of a man who commits acts of murder and assault in the defense of his honor and manliness. Contemporary standards of honor and masculinity require Cellini to depict himself as violent. In presenting himself as a murderer and rapist in the story of his life, Cellini attempted to appropriate both princely and divine power. For Cellini, being a man, concretized in his proud affirmation "sono uomo" (I am a man), and performing "qualche atto da uomo" (manly deeds), attests to a cultural poetics of manhood that constructed masculinity in terms of how dominant men were both on the battlefield and in the bedroom.

CONCLUSION

In a letter to the Duke of Ferrara in 1545, Giulio Alvarotti, the Ferrarese Ambassador to France, relates a story about an encounter between Cellini and Madame d'Étampes at Francis's court at Fontainebleau.[1] The tale contains a clever pun by Cellini on *fornire*, a verb denoting "to supply" or "furnish," but here filled with sexually charged connotations. Alvarotti narrates a contentious clash between Cellini and Madame d'Étampes in which she berates him in front of the king and his attendants. The king had asked Cellini to bring his life-size silver statue of *Jupiter* to Fontainebleau so that he might see its beauty and grace. But while Francis was praising Cellini's craftsmanship and the statue's beauty, Madame d'Étampes began to mock Cellini for completing only one statue rather than the twelve that the king had commissioned. In fact, she insinuates that Francis has paid Cellini for a full four years of labor during which time he has produced just this one work of art. Alvarotti relates: "Disse Madama di Tampes, disse forte che a Sua Maestà e tutti la odirano: sono queste quelle opere che costano 10 m franchi e che si sono fornite in quattro anni?; e questo disse per pugnere Benvenuto perchè favorisce un certo chiamato il Bologna, che fa professione di pittore e di scultore" (Madame d'Étampes said, and said loudly so that His Majesty and everyone else could hear: are these those works that cost ten thousand francs and that were finished in four years?; and this she said to punish Benvenuto because she favored a certain young man called Il Bologna, who was a painter and sculptor by profession). To this Cellini replies, "questa è una delle opere che in quattro anni si sono fornite" (this is one of the works that was finished in four years). She continues badgering him, insisting on knowing if the small cloth below the statue's waist was put there to hide some flaw: "che vol dir quella camisa, che le ha posto in dosso? Rispose Madama di Tampes: l'averà fatto per coprirle qualche falta" (what does this cloth mean, that was placed down here? Madame d'Étampes asked: you must have put it here to cover up some defect). To this Cellini replies that he put the cloth there for modesty's sake, but since she clearly does not like it, he claims, he will remove it. In a flash he tears it off in one motion, exposing the male genitalia, turns toward her and asks, "parvi che e' sia ben fornito?" (do you think it's finished/do you think he's well endowed?)

Cellini's shocking exposure of the well-endowed *Jupiter*'s genitalia, with his lively double entendre on *fornito* as both "endowed" and "finished," elegantly parallels the strategy Cellini himself employed in the story of his own life. In fact, this tale stands as a kind of allegory. In his *Vita*, Cellini exposed himself as sodomite, misogynist, rogue, and rebel for his contemporaries and for posterity. Cellini's shocking exposé of male gender stereotypes, of a life filled with sex and violence, stands as a monument in the history of first-person testimonies.

This book has sketched the many modes of self-expression available to Renaissance artists and has charted the shift in self-expression for Cellini from self-expression in art to self-expression through writing and violence. I began by speculating on the reasons Cellini put down the chisel and took up the pen, focusing on the pivotal and determining event in his life, his conviction of sodomy in Florence in 1557. After his trial and conviction Cellini began a prolonged assault on his enemies and, to some extent, on the literary tradition. In Cellini's case, writing was closely allied with subjectivity. In fact, Cellini seems to act out and live out his experiences in writing. I have sought to view his writings as a poetics, analyzing his works in prose (*Vita*) and in verse (*Rime*) together. Cellini worked in a variety of media, including marble, gold, and bronze, and in a range of literary genres, including ekphrastic writing, autobiography, and lyric poetry. I have examined texts and images together in an attempt to fuse the two sides of Cellini's worlds, the visual and the verbal.

Paradoxically, Cellini's *Vita* fits and does not fit in its sixteenth-century context. Its association of masculinity with violence and domination as well as its gender fluidity were common in his day. But the autobiography is unusual in its time for its lack of a definitive religious conversion and for its insistence on physical labor. The *Vita* is also unique for addressing the reader directly as "gentle readers," a rhetorical technique commonly associated with the rise of the modern novel in the eighteenth century. In this way, the artist as author linked early modernity and modernity.

Cellini wrote in a period of transition, and his writings manifest diverse and conflicting impulses. He seems to look forward and backward simultaneously, to express desire for both old and new values. For instance, as Tylus has argued, in his *Vita* Cellini expresses nostalgia for an economy based on patronage rather than capitalism. But the autobiography also celebrates new technologies such as guns as well as new norms of manhood. Cellini's writings illustrate the mingling of high and low culture, of both popular and elite forms. These ambiguities suggest that the self is not unified but rather fragmented.

In his *Vita* Cellini drew on many literary traditions, including chivalric epics, theatrical drama, Otherworld journeys, and late medieval visions. In borrowing from sources as diverse as Dante's *Comedy* and Florentine comedies, his *Vita* reveals a breadth of culture hitherto unacknowledged by scholars. Cellini's poetry, too, displays a sophistication that, to date, critics have not fully unrecognized. In his lyric Cellini parodies Petrarch and personifies Dante. He took the traditional *poetic tenzone* and used it innovatively by deploying it in an artistic forum. Cellini's lyrics illustrate the popularity of the sonnet in his day. In Florence poetry functioned as a kind of broadsheet—what would become the popular pamphlets that circulated gossip, scandal, and rumor in the seventeenth century—and as a kind of chronicle. Cellini's literary accomplishments demonstrate that the interactions between artists and men of letters at the court of Cosimo I were close and frequent. Cellini's *Vita* and *Rime* together reveal that the *Tre Corone* of Dante, Petrarch, and Boccaccio had a profound influence on professional authors such as Ariosto but also on artists like Cellini as well.

I have argued that Cellini's frequent use of violence is best understood through the lens provided by gender studies. His self-presentation as dauntless and violent is linked to contemporary standards of proper masculine behavior rather than, as critics argue, to notions of heroism. Cellini's *Medal for Francis I* (1537) nicely illustrates iconographically the manly themes of chapter 5. On its reverse the medal, which carries the artist's signature, depicts an armed man on horseback with lance raised trampling a nude reclining woman. The inscription reads "Fortunam virtue devicit" (He has conquered Fortune with virtù). Masculine virtù triumphs over feminine *fortuna*.

Cellini was a great artist, a brilliant and versatile craftsman who displayed consummate skill in a wide variety of materials and media. A successful sculptor, metalsmith, jeweler, and minter, Cellini created artworks of rare and inimitable beauty. He was a very polysemous individual. The *Vita's* excessive detail and obsession with minutiae parallels both the intricacy of the jeweler and the meticulousness of the bookkeeper.

The artist may not be among the great authors of the sixteenth century, but he was a prolific writer and poet who was able to compose Petrarchan verses as well as burlesque ones. His poetry is both imitative and fashionably innovative. Cellini may not have the consciousness of genre that we expect from professional writers or men of letters who obtained a formal education, nonetheless in his extensive written corpus Cellini showed his versatility and adaptability by playing with a broad range of genres. In the *Vita* Cellini conflates two types of chivalric heroes—the knight errant and the epic crusader—and presents himself as a character from chivalric romance, as a Dantesque pilgrim, and as a necromancer.

Cellini's appeal has endured through the centuries. He has enthralled scholars through the ages, from Goethe and Stendhal to Wilde and D'Annunzio. It was Burckhardt who cemented Cellini's fame as a thoroughly modern man when, in 1860, he selected the artist as "a significant type of the modern spirit."[2] When the winds of psychoanalysis blew across Europe, Cellini seemed a perfect case study for evidence, historically, of various types of psychopathology, including paraphrenia (late-onset schizophrenia) and paranoia.[3] Interest in Cellini spans a wide range of cultures and media and has furnished subject matter for a 1924 Broadway play, *The Firebrand*, starring veteran stage actor Joseph Schildkraut as Cellini (figure 16), a Broadway operetta, *The Firebrand of Florence*, with lyrics by Ira Gershwin and music by Kurt Weill (1945), and a *Classics Illustrated* comic book titled *Adventures of Cellini* (1947, reprint 1961).[4] In modern America comic rather than serious treatments of Cellini's life and writings have proved to be the most popular.

The allure of Cellini, as myth and icon, continues its hold on the American imagination. Cultural fascination with the great artist continues to the present day, as evidenced by the recent Off-Broadway play *Cellini*, written and directed by John Patrick Shanley (ran 21 January to 4 March 2001). His self-presentation as a violent braggart and swaggering adventurer pre-figures *The Three Musketeers* and Casanova. The artist sought to shock and expose his own and his society's transgressions and limitations. The Truman Capote of his day, Cellini allows us all entry into the fascinating and disturbing (under)world we call the Renaissance.

Appendix 1:
Unpublished Archival Document

Letter of Supplication Written by Cellini to
Duke Cosimo I de' Medici, Dated 3 March 1557

ASF, Magistrato degli Otto di Guardia e Balìa (granducal period),
vol. 2232 (*Suppliche*), fol. 552r.

Illustrissimo et Eccellentissimo Signor Duca Patron Mio Osservandissimo,
Essendo stato dal Magistrato delli Signori Otto giudicato et condannato in
scudi cinquanta et di più per anni quattro alle Stinche: ora ricordatomi
siccome io ho servito 12 anni Vostra Eccellentia Illustrissima con quello
amore et fede et suffitienza d'arte che Lei stessa ha visto et siccome Mio
Signiore et Patrone sempre conosciutolo clementissimo et piatosissimo et
più volte ho sentito et visto che Vostra Eccellentia Illustrissima a molti altri
ha fatte delle gratie: genuflesso mi getto dinanzi a quella pregandoLa che
tal confino converta dentro alle mura della Sua città o si veramente nella
casa mia per quel tempo che a Vostra Eccellentia Illustrissima piacessi che
così io potrei finire il Cristo di marmo il quale si è in procinto di fine quale
sarà Sua stessa gloria o qual che exilio fuori del Suo dominio. Solo
pregandoLa per l'amor di Dio che non voglia che in questa età di 57
anni non avendo mai in nella mia giovinezza avutomi a vergoniare di
nissuno accidende d'essa che ora con maggior mio danno et vergogna
io non abbia a pagare la gabella d'essa giovinezza. Così faccendomi gratia
io Le donerò il resto delli mia anni, sempre pregando Dio per la Sua
felicità.

Di carcere. Il dì 3 di Marzo 1557.
Il fidelissimo servo di Vostra Eccellentia Illustrissima,
Benvenuto Cellini

(Most Illustrious Lord, Most Excellent and Most Worthy of Reverence,
My Duke and Master, Having been by the Magistrates of the Eight judged
and condemned to pay fifty scudi and moreover to spend four years in the

Stinche: I recall now that since I served Your Most Illustrious Excellency for twelve years with that love and faith and worthiness of art that You yourself have witnessed, and since I have always known My Lord and Master to be most merciful and compassionate and I have seen and heard that Your Most Illustrious Excellency has granted pardons to many others: genuflecting, I throw myself before you, begging you to convert the incarceration to confinement within the walls of Your city or even to my own house, or into exile beyond the boundaries of Your dominion, for that amount of time that pleases Your Most Illustrious Excellency so that I will be able to finish a marble Christ which is near completion that will be Your true glory. I only ask for the love of God— given that never in my youth did I have to be ashamed of any misfortune on this account—that you don't wish that now at fifty-seven with greater damage and shame that I should have to pay the tax of such youthful folly. So, if you grant this pardon, I will donate the rest of my life to You, always praying to God for Your happiness.

From prison. 3 March 1557.
The most faithful servant of Your Most Illustrious Excellency,
Benvenuto Cellini)

APPENDIX 2: UNEDITED SONNETS ATTRIBUTED TO CELLINI

Two Newly Discovered Sonnets in the BNCF

BNCF, Conv. Soppr. B 8 1657, fols. 252v, 253r (mod. num.)

"A Don Gabriello Fiamma Benvenuto Cellini."
   Nuova fiamma dal ciel discesa in terra
Per dimostrare l'immortal fattore
Qual ch'il cognosce vive, e mai non muore
Quel ci apre il ciel e l'inferno ci serra.
   Tromba se' gloriosa a tanta guerra
Al pover gregge se' guida e pastore
Di spirto santo in fiammi l'alma e core
Mostrando il ver sentier qual mai non erra.
   Fiamma tu se' di quei più cari a Cristo
Vestita dell'immenso spirto santo
felice è chi t'ascolta e chi t'ha visto.
   Che fia quel gran splendor se quest'è tanto
Angiol col gran saper di Dio commisto
Quel sente stesso chi t'ascolta alquanto.

"Del Medesimo"
   Ghiaccio terrestre ch'alle fiamm'ardente
Lontan ti sta e più piacer ne prendi
Gelato l'herbe abbrusci e tanti incendi
Corpi diversi alle divine mente.
   Calor ci mostra il sol tu' più possente
Ne' caldi petti tua virtù risplendi
Rischiari l'Alme et all'hor vita attendi
Gloria d'ogn'alta ed ogni bassa gente.
   Tu nodrisci ogni frutto ch'a noi piace
Non ti possa lodar con la mia voce
Pur cantar voglio i tua divin precetti.
   Natura gli dà a te veri e perfetti
Rimedia Amor tu se' puro e verace
Come colui che per noi morì in croce.

Description of the Manuscript

The provenance of this manuscript, Conventi Soppressi B 8 1657, is given as SS. Annunziata (where Cellini is buried); the title, *Poesie sacre varie*, from BNCF Sala MSS Cat. 1 (F. Bencini, *Indice dei MSS: Indice alfabetico del Fondo Conventi Soppressi*, page 123) and Cat. 2 (*Inventario dei MSS dei Conv. Soppr.*, page 8). This manuscript is also listed in *Monumenta Ordinis Servorum Sanctae Mariae*, 6, no. 2 (1903–04): 175. It passed from the monastery of the Annunziata to the Biblioteca Magliabechiana (now the BNCF) during the Napoleonic era.

The ms. is *cartaceo* (paper), bound in *cartapecora*, and *in quarto*. It contains various sheets of paper bound together in a random manner.

The two sheets of the alleged poems by Cellini are contained within a group of three *fascicoli*—one *fascicolo* of eight sheets (fols. 245–60), one *binione* (fols. 261–64), and one *senione* (fols. 273–84)—that at one time formed one *fascicolo* of sixteen sheets. When it was bound, the original *fascicolo* was separated into the three aforementioned *fascicoli* and did not retain the old and, most likely, original numbering.

The hands present are seventeenth century. The binding in *cartapecora* appears to date from the second half of the Seicento, and appears to be the work not of the original owner but of a later, unknown successor.

The original numbering of the two sonnets attributed to Cellini is fols. 16v–17r.

On the original fol. 1, an annotator added a title, "Principio della raccolta di varie composizioni . . . tiche di diversi celebri autori." In the *fascicolo* containing the two poems by Cellini there is another title added by an annotator, "Raccolta di varie composizioni di diversi celebri autori."

These sheets contain primarily encomiastic verse, to rulers and clerics, as well as prayers to specific saints. Poems are claimed to be by poets such as Bembo, Varchi, Bronzino, and Laura Battiferra. The anonymous copyist identified many of the poems as by an unknown poet ("D'Incerto").

I tried to verify if the copyist was correct in some of the poems where a poet is identified. Four sonnets identified as by Battiferra are indeed by her ("Deh se quel vivo, chiaro sol," "Razzi gentil, che qual candida," "Con duo vari pensier sovente," and "Al gran merto dell'alma eletta," fols. 250v, 254v, 256r, and 257r). In addition, two *risposte* to Battiferra by Varchi and Bronzino are also correct, "come 'l puro di voi cortese" by Varchi (fol. 255v) and "S'al nostro alto valor famosa" by Bronzino (fol. 257r). But four sonnets labeled as unknown by the copyist are, in fact, by Battiferra ("Quando nell'ocean l'altera fronte," "Lascia, o Diana il tuo cerchio," "O di casta bellezza esempio," and "Dolce verde fiorito e sacro monte", fols. 250r, 252r, 251r, 251v). I collated the incipits of these sonnets by and to Battiferra with Victoria Kirkam's appendix II of her article

"Laura Battiferra degli Ammannati's First Book of Poetry: A Renaissance Holograph comes out of Hiding," *Rinascimento* 36 (1996): 386–91.

Cellini's sonnets are not labeled as "D'Incerto." But because more information needs to be uncovered in order to verify Cellini's authorship of one or both of these sonnets, I have called them attributions.

Neither of these sonnets appears in the CD-ROM *Archivio della tradizione lirica da Petrarca a Marino (Testi di poesia lirica italiana, sec. xiv-xvi)*, ed. Amedeo Quondam, nor in the IUPI (*Incipitario Unificato della Poesia Italiana*, ed. Marco Santagata). The second new sonnet attributed to Cellini contains a few copyist errors (verse 5 "tu' " [tuo] and verse 7 "hor" [a lor]), making it difficult to discern the poem's meaning. Verse 14 of the first sonnet also contains a copyist's error (quel sente stesso).

Gabriello Fiamma, a Venetian patrician (1531–86), was abbot of the Carità in Venice and, from 1584, Bishop of Chioggia. His *Rime spirituali* with his own commentary were published in 1570 and 1575. Many poets of the day exchanged sonnets with Fiamma, and Cellini belonged to this circle of poets. Battiferra included two exchanges with Fiamma in her *Primo libro*; Varchi addressed a sonnet to him in his *Sonetti spirituali*. Since encomiastic sonnets represent one of the largest groups of sonnets penned by Cellini and since the artist wrote his compositions on separate sheets of paper and circulated them among friends, it is plausible that one or both of these new sonnets are by Cellini.

The second new sonnet contains a striking parallel to two of the sonnets that constitute one of the poetic exchanges between Laura Battiferra and Gabriello Fiamma and published in Battiferra's *Primo libro*. Battiferra's sonnet addressed "A Don Gabriello Fiamma" beginning "Fiamma del Ciel, che dal divino ardente" has exactly the same fourteen word-endings as Fiamma's *risposta* beginning, "Donna onor delle donne, che d'ardente" (Guidi, ed., 96–97). The endings of each verse in both sonnets are: ardente, prendi, 'ncendi, mente, possente, splendi, attendi, gente, piace, voce, precetti, perfetti, verace, croce. These endings are, with one exception (*risplendi* rather than *splendi*), the same as the endings of the new Sonnet 2 attributed here to Cellini: ardente, prendi, incendi, mente, possente, risplendi, attendi, gente, piace, voce, precetti, perfetti, verace, croce. This may signal that this poetic exchange involved more than the traditional two poets.

I would like to thank Franca Petrucci Nardelli for helping me with the transcriptions of these sonnets as well as with the description of the manuscript. I would also like to thank Victoria Kirkham for sharing information about Battiferra and Fiamma with me, which is drawn from her edition with commentary of the complete poems of Laura Battiferra (in progress).

Appendix 3: Published Documents

3.A   Sentence of the Otto di Guardia Convicting
        Cellini of Sodomy, Dated 27 February 1557

Published in Luigi Greci, "Benvenuto Cellini nei delitti e nei processi fiorentini ricostruiti attraverso le leggi del tempo," *Archivio di Antropologia Criminale* 2nd ser., 50, no. 4 (1930): 530, but slightly modified.

Adì XXVII di febbraio 1556 in Sabato. *Item* simile modo et vista una querela posta contro Benvenuto di Maestro Giovanni Cellini scultore, cittadino fiorentino, come ne appare al libro di querele n. 287 a carte 32, perchè circa di cinque anni or sono passati esso ha tenuto per suo ragazzo Fernando di Giovanni da Montepulciano, giovanetto con il quale ha usato carnalmente moltissime volte col nefando vitio di soddomia, tenendolo in letto come sua moglie, etiam et perchè consta al magistrato per la confessione di detto Benvenuto fatta in scritto come si vede in filza di querele n. 154 dove confessa di essere vero di avere soddomitato detto Fernando, però in obedienza delle leggi condannano detto Benvenuto in scudi 50 d'oro da pagarsi al fisco di Sua Excellenzia Illustrissima secondo gli ordini et più lo confinano a stare quattro anni in le Stinche dal dì vi sarà presentato et lo privano in perpetuo delli offitii, secondo il tenore di dette leggi. Vinto per fave 7 nere per lo sì. Notificata a lui adì 2 di marzo per me cancelliere infrascritto. Si mandò al fisco adì 26 di marzo come dissi. Vedi la permuta di confine in questo a carte 106. Rapportò il segretario si assegnasse un tale confine in casa perchè di lì porrà andare detto condannato come li disse Sua Eccellenzia.

(Saturday 27 February 1557. *Item* in the same manner because this magistracy has examined a denunciation against Benvenuto, son of Master Giovanni Cellini, sculptor and Florentine citizen, as it appears in the book of denunciations numbered 287 on page 32 [which states that] for about the last five years this Cellini had kept as his boy Fernando di Giovanni da Montepulciano, a youth who he used most frequently sexually engaging in the despicable vice of sodomy, keeping him in bed as if he was his wife, and also because there is in the possession of the court the written confession of the said Benvenuto, as can be read in the files of the complaint numbered 154, where he confesses that it is true that he sodomized the said Fernando; thus in accordance with the law this court condemns the said Benvenuto to pay a fine of 50 golden scudi to the Treasury of His Most Illustrious Excellency as is the protocol and to serve four years in the prison known as the Stinche from the day he will have presented himself there and strips him for life of holding public office, following the tenor of the said laws. Convicted with a vote of seven black beans. Notified on 2 March by me the undermentioned chancellor. Sent to the Treasury on 26 March as requested. See the change in the confinement in this volume on page 106. The Secretary [Francesco Borghini] noted that his confinement is assigned to his house because he can serve there the said sentence as His Excellency ruled.)

3.B   Poetic Exchange Between Cellini and Laura Battiferra degli Ammannati

Published in *Laura Battiferri degli Ammannati, Il Primo libro delle opere toscane*, ed. Enrico Maria Guidi (Urbino, 2000), 116–17.

Di Messer Benvenuto Scultore
    Con quel soave canto e dolce legno
ne corse ardito Orfeo per la consorte,
Cerber chetossi e le tartaree porte
s'aperser, che Pluton ne lo fe' degno;
    poi gli rendette il prezioso pegno,
ma d'accordo non fu seco la morte.
Voi, gentil Laura, quanto miglior sorte
aveste al scendere al superno regno.
    Lassù v'alzò il Petrarca, e dietro poi
ne venne a rivedervi in Paradiso,
sete scesi in un corpo ora ambidoi.
    Felice Orfeo, s'avea tale avviso
cangiar la spoglia, aria fatto qual voi,
ch'amor, vita e virtù non v'è diviso.

RISPOSTA
    Volesse pure il ciel ch'all'alto segno,
ove giungeste voi per piane e corte
vie, che sono ad altrui sì lunghe e torte,
giugnesser l'ali del mio basso ingegno,

che, come paurosa e debil vegno
a dir di voi, sicura allora e forte
verrei, né punto temeria di morte
l'ultimo assalto, ch'or temer convegno.
E direi come in un sceser fra noi
Pirgotele e Lisippo, onde conquiso
fu 'l vento, prisca età, degli onor tuoi,
e perché 'l sacro Apollo mai diviso
da' più cari non v'ebbe amici suoi,
tal ch'io co' più perfetti in voi m'affiso.

3.C Sonnet by Cellini on the Death of Benedetto Varchi

Published by Bruno Maier, ed., *Opere* (Milan, 1968), 936–37.

Benedetto quel dì che l'alma varchi,
lasciando omai la spoglia di lei sazia;
e reverente a Dio renda ogn'or grazia
d'essere scarsa di sì grevi incarchi.
Se ben con doglia par di lei si scarchi,
quanto maggior, s'a Dio fusse in disgrazia,
saria la pena! ch'or, del ben non sazia,
è pur cagion che manco uom si rammarchi.
Vostre alte prose, vostre dolci rime,
che voi fra tutti gli altri han fatto solo,
al ciel per dritta via sen vanno prime;
e voi ven gite a Dio col maggior volo
che fesse uom mai, e con più ricche stime,
chiaro dall'uno infino all'altro polo.

3.D Petition of Cellini to Carry Weapons, Dated 20 August 1562

Published by Guido Biagi, *Due lettere di Benvenuto Cellini sul portar l'armi* (Florence, 1911), unnumbered page.

Illustrissimo et Eccellentissimo Signor Duca patron mio sempre osservandissimo,

Io lauldo et ringratio Iddio e V[ostra] E[ccellenza] I[llustrissima] che e' sono diciasette anni quasi passati che io servo V.E.I. dalla quale io fui molto ben veduto, nè mai mi si ricorda di averle dato causa di vedermi altrimenti. V.E.I. si ricordi che insieme colla mia servitù, sì come agli altri suoi buon servitori, Quella mi conciesse che io portassi le armi; et perchè in ispatio di circa a uno anno il cardinale Capodiferro di Roma mi fecie intendere che mi farebbe dispiacere in tutti i luoghi dove io fussi, per alcuna diferenza che io ebbi seco, e per questa cagione io missi la mia spada accanto et di più feci venire una mia camicia di maglia, la quale io avevo lasciata in Lione. La quale venuta che la fu, al magistrato et segretario degli Otto, quello con buona gratia di V.E.I. me la mandorno a casa mia; et così l'ho sempre tenuta. Et di più io feci fare dua guanti et una mezza testa perchè io mi volevo potere difendere. Hora egli è in circa a uno anno passato che io mandai la ditta camicia a Roma al mio messer Libradoro. Ora che il detto se n'è servito, e' me l'ha rimandata; la quale è si come si usa venuta alle mani di ser Lorenzo Corboli, il quale come persona diligentissima m'ha fatto intendere che non me la vole rendere per tenere come per il passato, sanza la parola di V.E.I. la quale io priego che le piaccia che io la possi tenere come io ho fatto insino a ora; et quando a Quella non piacessi, io sono contento di stare a ubbidienza, sempre mantendendomi in sua buona gratia, la quale Iddio felicissima conservi.

(Lord Most Illustrious, Most Excellent and always Most Worthy of Reverence, My Duke and Master, I praise and thank God and Your Most Illustrious Excellency that for about the last seventeen years I have served Your Most Illustrious Excellency who held me in great esteem, nor do I recall ever giving you a reason to feel any other way about me. Your Most Illustrious Excellency will remember that together with my servitude, just as you had done for all your good servants, You granted me the right to carry weapons, and because in the span of about a year the Cardinal Capodiferro from Rome let me know that he would harm me wherever I might be because of certain conflicts that I had with him, so for this reason I wore my sword by my side and moreover sent for a shirt made of mail that I had left in Lyon. This chainmail shirt having arrived at the magistracy and secretary of the Eight, he with the good grace of Your Most Illustrious Excellency sent it to my house, and thus I have always kept it. In addition, I had two gloves and a hood of chain-mail made for me because I want to be able to defend myself. About a year has passed since I sent this shirt to my friend Messer Libradoro, but now that he has made use of it, he has sent it back, as a result as is customary here it has come into the hands of ser Lorenzo Corboli [the present secretary of the Otto who was in charge of controlling the entry of weapons in Florence], who being a most officious person has informed me that he is not willing to give it to me to keep as in the past without the permission of Your Most Illustrious Excellency. So I pray that it pleases you that I can carry weapons as I have done up until now and if it does not please You, I am happy to obey your command, as I always follow your will, so I pray to God to preserve you long in happiness.)

NOTES

Introduction

1. The ceremony is described in an anonymous account by one of the brothers who attended the burial service. See *Vita* (Milan, 1873), 399.
2. Oscar Wilde, *The Portable Oscar Wilde*, eds. Richard Arlington and Stanley Weintraub, rev. ed. (New York, 1981), 52.
3. Cited in George E. Price, "A Sixteenth-Century Paranoic: His Story and His Autobiography," *New York Medical Journal* 99 (1914): 728.
4. See, for example, the anthology by Gregory Woods, A *History of Gay Literature: The Male Tradition* (New Haven, 1998).
5. In this book, Italian text of the *Vita* is taken from *Benvenuto Cellini, La Vita*, ed. Lorenzo Bellotto (Parma, 1996) but replaces Bellotto's raised dot with a space—to indicate phonosyntactic doubling (for instance, "a·llui" in Bellotto became "a llui" in this book)—for the sake of legibility; text of the art treatises and minor writings on art are from *Benvenuto Cellini, La Vita, I Trattati, I Discorsi*, ed. Pietro Scarpellini (1967; Milan, 1987). Occasionally, I have inserted "[*sic*]" into passages taken from Bellotto's edition in order to identify Cellini's unique spellings of words rather than errors in transcription or typographical errors. See the foreword for other conventions used in this book.
6. The body of literature on New Historicism and Gender Studies is vast and continually growing. On New Historicism as a methodology, see in particular Jean E. Howard, "The New Historicism in Renaissance Studies," *English Literary Renaissance* 16, no. 1 (1986): 13–43; Louis Adrian Montrose, "Renaissance Literary Studies and the Subject of History," *English Literary Renaissance* 16 (1986): 5–12; and Margaret A. Gallucci, "Intervista a Stephen Greenblatt: Il Nuovo Storicismo e Il Futuro della Letteratura," *Allegoria* 8, no. 24, n.s. (1996): 130–43. On gender as an analytical tool, see especially Merry E. Wiesner, "Beyond Women and the Family: Towards a Gender Analysis of the Reformation," *Sixteenth Century Journal* 18, no. 3 (1987): 311–21 and Joan Wallach Scott, "Gender: A Useful Category of Historical Analysis," in *Gender and the Politics of History* (New York, 1988), 28–50. For critical works that I believe are close to mine in their theoretical underpinnings and uses of historicist and/or gender models, see Stephen J. Greenblatt, *Renaissance Self-Fashioning: From More to Shakespeare* (Chicago, 1980), Caroline Walker Bynum, *Holy Feast and Holy Fast: The Religious Significance of Food to Medieval Women* (Berkeley, The New Historicism: Studies in

Cultural Poetics, 1988), and especially Margaret F. Rosenthal, *The Honest Courtesan: Veronica Franco, Citizen and Writer in Sixteenth-Century Venice* (Chicago, 1992).
7. Judith Butler, *Bodies that Matter: On the Discursive Limits of "Sex"* (New York, 1993), 232.
8. Apart from Dino Cervigni's *The Vita of Benvenuto Cellini* (Ravenna, 1979), there is no other book in English on Cellini's writings, and his is limited to Cellini's autobiography only.

1   Benvenuto Cellini, Life and Works

1. Nino Borsellino, "Benvenuto Cellini," *Dizionario Biografico degli Italiani* (Rome, 1979) 23: 440.
2. Gene Brucker, *Florence: The Golden Age, 1138–1737* (1984; Berkeley, 1998), 70–71. Cellini's three other designs for Alessandro de' Medici that were minted as coins are the silver *giulio* (or *barile*), the silver *mezzo giulio* (or *grossone*), and the gold *scudo*. For more on Cellini's coins, see Philip Attwood's forthcoming article, "Cellini's Medals and Coins," in *Benvenuto Cellini 1500–71: Sculptor, Goldsmith, Writer*, eds. Margaret A. Gallucci and Paolo L. Rossi (Cambridge, 2004).
3. Nancy K. Vickers, "The Mistress in the Masterpiece," in *The Poetics of Gender*, ed. Nancy K. Miller (New York, 1986), 28.
4. R. Burr Litchfield, *Emergence of a Bureaucracy: The Florentine Patricians 1530–1790* (Princeton, 1986), 27.
5. "A Virgin made of wood with Saint Anthony." Eugène Plon, *Benvenuto Cellini, orfèvre, médailleur, sculpteur: Recherches sur sa vie, sur son oeuvre, et sur les pièces qui lui sont attribuées* (Paris, 1883), 382.
6. On both the clandestine and legitimate marriages, see Piero Calamandrei, *Scritti e inediti celliniani, ed. Carlo Cordié* (Florence, 1971), 364–66.
7. Paul F. Grendler, *Schooling in Renaissance Italy: Literacy and Learning 1300–1600* (Baltimore, 1989), 78.
8. Timothy J. McGee, "In the Service of the Commune: The Changing Role of Florentine Civic Musicians, 1450–1532," *Sixteenth Century Journal* 30 (1999): 736.
9. Timothy J. McGee, "Giovanni Cellini, piffero di Firenze," *Rivista italiana di musicologia* 32, no. 2 (1997): 220–21.
10. Gene Brucker, *Renaissance Florence* (Berkeley, 1969), 133.
11. Cellini's description of the family coat of arms in his *Vita* is slightly different from the heraldic image accepted by scholars such as the one reproduced in Orazio Bacci's *La Vita di Benvenuto Cellini* (Florence, 1920), unnumbered page.
12. "E a dì 28 d'aprile 1554 si schoperse una figura posta nella loggia di piaza in verso el palazo la quale fece Benvenuto orefice diligente omo, *el ducha lo fece cittadino fiorentino* e chostò 5000 scudi d'oro o più sanza la provisione che eral data anzi che penò a fare 10 scudi altrove, chiamasi Perseo che amazò Medusa inchantatrice." *Francesco di Andrea Buonsignori, Memorie*

(1530–1565), eds. Sandro Bertelli and Gustavo Bertoli (Florence, 2000), 93, emphasis added. Buonsignori probably means that Cellini was admitted to the Florentine nobility. For a discussion of this, see chapter 5.

13. Christian Bec, *Les livres des Florentins (1413–1608)* (Florence, 1984), 61–62.

14. Eugène Plon, *Benvenuto Cellini* (Paris, 1883), 384.

15. "[U]n libro scritto in penna, copiato da uno del gran Lionardo da Vinci . . . Questo libro era di tanta virtù e di tanto bel modo di fare, secondo il mirabile ingegno del detto Lionardo (il quale io non credo mai che maggior uomo nascessi al mondo di lui), sopra le tre grandi arti, scultura, pittura, ed architettura."

16. "Il caso del Cellini risulta, dunque, assolutamente anomalo non solo per l'entità della documentazione, ma anche perché egli è autore di una autobiografia." Dario Trento, *Benvenuto Cellini. Opere non esposte e documenti notarili* (Florence, 1984), 44.

17. The account books are in the BRF and include manuscripts Ricc. 2788, 2789, 2790, 2791, and 3617.

18. Julius Magnino Schlosser, *La letteratura artistica: Manuale delle fonti della storia dell'arte moderna*, trans. Filippo Rossi, 3rd ed. (1924; Florence, 1964), 104–20, 375–76. Louis Alexander Waldman has recently argued that Bandinelli's *Memoriale* was not written by him at all: "the apocryphal *Memoriale* [is] attributed to the sculptor himself but in all probability largely the work of his grandson Baccio the Younger" (Waldman, "Bandinelli and the Opera di Santa Maria del Fiore," 235).

19. Tylus, "The Merchant of Florence," 52. Petrarch, humanist and poet, is certainly another example of an "obsessive writer" and is considered by some the first great self-fashioner.

20. BMLF, Med-Pal. 234², unnumbered leaf. This manuscript is only part-autograph since the entire manuscript is not in Cellini's hand. The artist often signed documents written for him by an amanuensis. This practice was common in his day; in fact, many authors created a clean copy of their manuscripts for the printer, but others hired copyists and only supervised the project. The so-called autograph of the artist's art treatises at the BNMV (MSS It. Cl. IV. cod. 44) serves as an example. It is wholly written in another's hand, with the exception of one small insertion in the manuscript that is in Cellini's hand (fol. 143v). Nonetheless, scholars refer to this manuscript as an autograph, following the designation by Carlo Milanesi in 1857 that it was based on what he called "the original dictation." Technically speaking, however, it is not an autograph.

21. Paolo L. Rossi, "*Sprezzatura*, Patronage, and Fate: Benvenuto Cellini and the World of Words," in *Vasari's Florence*, 58–59.

22. Plon, *Benvenuto Cellini*, 380–84.

23. BNCF, Pal. 988 (Scipione Ammirato il Giovane, *Zibaldone di spogli*).

24. On the autograph, see Orazio Bacci, "Il codice mediceo-palatino 234² della R. Biblioteca Medico-Laurenziana," *Rivista delle Biblioteche e degli Archivi* 7, no. 1 (1896): 1–11.

25. ASF, *Carteggio d'Artisti* vol. 21, insert 18, letter 2.

26. *Vocabolario degli Accademici della Crusca. Compendiato. Secondo la quarta ed ultima impression di Firenze corretta ed accresciuta, cominciata l'anno 1729 e terminata nel 1738* (Venice, 1741), 1: xvii.
27. Eric Cochrane, *Florence in the Forgotten Centuries 1527–1800* (Chicago, 1973), 324.
28. *Vocabolario degli Accademici della Crusca*, 1: xvii.
29. *Vita di Benvenuto Cellini*, Colonia [Naples], n.d. [1728], unnumbered page.
30. ASF, *Notarile Moderno* vol. 15383 (1655), fols. 38r–42v.
31. ACBF, *Testamenti* vol. 6, fols. 409r–413v.
32. BNCF, *Banco Rari* 353.
33. ACBF, *Inventorio* titled, *Estratto dei documenti e carte dell'archivio della Congregazione dei Buonuomini di San Martino*, section *Aggiunti*, entry 1358. This inventory confirms the donation of "Cellini, Benvenuto. Documenti originali di esso" to the Biblioteca Palatina and lists all the items donated.
34. ACBF, *Libro dei Capitoli e Indulgenze*, unnumbered page.
35. *Vita*, ed. Orazio Bacci (Florence, 1901), 426–27. This list corresponds to an entry in the *Appendix* of the ACBF inventory, *Estratto dei documenti e carte*, unnumbered page. However, the reference in the Buonuomini document to Leopold II, Grand Duke of Tuscany (1765–90) and later Holy Roman Emperor (1790–92), is unclear since he died in 1792.
36. Trans. mine of the passage reproduced in *Opere*, ed. Bruno Maier (Milan, 1968), 942–43, note 12.
37. *Opere*, ed. Bruno Maier (Milan, 1968), 942–43, note 12.
38. Giulio Negri, *Istoria degli Scrittori Fiorentini* (Ferrara, 1722), 99 (postumous edition).
39. Cited in Mabellini, *Delle Rime di Benvenuto Cellini* (Florence: Paravia, 1885), 294. Alfieri made a marginal note in his copy of Cellini's *Vita* next to the sonnet that opens the story of the artist's life beginning "Questa mia vita travagliata io scrivo." Alfieri was praising verse eight of this sonnet ("che molti io passo, e chi mi passa arrivo").
40. Adolfo Mabellini's *Delle Rime* was followed by his *Benvenuto Cellini, Le Rime, pubblicate ed annotate per cura di Adolfo Mabellini* (Turin, 1891).
41. Special issue of *Il Marzocco* 5, no. 44 (Nov. 4, 1900): unnumbered page.
42. Bruno Maier, "Le *Rime* di Benvenuto Cellini," *Annali Triestini* 22 (1952): 307–58.
43. John Pope-Hennessy, "A Bronze Satyr by Cellini," *The Burlington Magazine* 124 (1982), 409.
44. Michael W. Cole, "Cellini's Blood," *Art Bulletin* 81, no. 2 (1999): 223. Cole's new book, *Cellini and the Principles of Sculpture* (2002), is a welcome addition to Cellini scholarship and promises to provide new insights into his art. Unfortunately, his book had not yet been published when mine went to press.
45. Paolo L. Rossi, "The Writer and the Man. Real Crimes and Mitigating Circumstances: Il caso Cellini," in *Crime, Society, and the Law in Renaissance Italy*, eds. Trevor Dean and K.J.P. Lowe (Cambridge, 1994), 157–83.

46. Patricia L. Rubin, *Giorgio Vasari: Art and History* (New Haven, 1995), 53.
47. Ingrid Rowland, "The Real Caravaggio," *NYRB* 46, no. 15 (1999), 14.
48. Pope-Hennessy, *Cellini* (London, 1985), 254.
49. Michel Foucault, *The History of Sexuality*, trans. Robert Hurley (New York, 1980), 68–69.
50. Eds. Renzo Paris and Antonio Veneziani (Milan, 1982).
51. "Since there is an important and large literature about loving boys in Greek culture, some historians say, 'Well, that's the proof that they loved boys.' But I say that proves that loving boys was a problem. Because if there was no problem, they would speak of this kind of love in the same terms as love between men and women." *The Foucault Reader*, ed. Paul Rabinow (New York, 1984), 344–45.
52. Michael Rocke, *Forbidden Friendships*, 12.
53. *The Divine Comedy of Dante Alighieri, I: Inferno*, ed. and trans. Robert M. Durling (New York, 1996), 235 (Inf. 15, 101–02, 106–08).
54. James M. Saslow, "'A Veil of Ice Between my Heart and the Fire': Michelangelo's Sexual Identity and Early Modern Constructs of Homosexuality," *Genders* 2 (1988): 77–90.
55. On Michelangelo, see Saslow, Wallace, and Barolsky; on Bronzino, see Parker and Healy; on Bandinelli, see Barkan and Waldman.
56. John Sturrock, "Fame and Fortune: Cellini, Cardano," in *The Language of Autobiography: Studies in the First Person Singular* (Cambridge, 1993), 64–74; and Jane Tylus, "The Merchant of Florence: Benvenuto Cellini, Cosimo de' Medici, and the *Vita*," in *Writing and Vulnerability in the Late Renaissance* (Stanford, 1993), 31–53.
57. Jonathan Goldberg, "Cellini's *Vita* and the Conventions of Early Autobiography," *MLN* 89 (1974): 71–83, and Dino S. Cervigni, "Cellini's *Vita* and Cervantes' *Don Quixote*: An Inquiry into Prose Narrative and Genre," in *Il Rinascimento*, ed. Vittore Branca (Florence, 1979), 275–98.
58. Another contribution to the study of the *Vita*'s spiritual aspects is the article by Yemin Chao, "Two Renaissance Lives: Benvenuto Cellini and Teresa of Jesus," *Renaissance and Reformation* new ser. 23, no. 2 (1999): 29–44.
59. Cervigni, Dupré, Guglielminetti, and Rossi have all written on various aspects of the *Vita*'s rhetorical style.
60. Benedetto Croce, "Sul Cellini scrittore," in *Poeti e scrittori del pieno e tardo rinascimento* (Bari, 1952), 3: 169: "è notissimo che la prosa semplice e ingenua suol essere la più a lungo travagliata."
61. Compare the Italian, "'Ella vuol dire che tu hai usato seco fuora del vaso dove si fa figliuoli'" (Bellotto, 551) with the Bull translation: "'She means that you did it by another way than the way for begetting children'" (Bull, 282). The revised edition of 1998 provides the same translation (Bull, rev. ed., 283). Two other English translations of the twentieth century come no closer to Cellini's explicit language. Symonds translated this sentence as "He demurred: 'She means that you improperly abused her'" (*The Life of Benvenuto Cellini*, 313), while MacDonell translated it as "Whereupon the judge replied that the accusation was quite other" (*The Life of Benvenuto Cellini*, 241). I do not mean to criticize the efforts of translators who have

struggled with Cellini's difficult language, but I believe that more literal translations capture the rawness of the language.

62. I refer to Vasari's tondo of Cosimo and his artists in the Salone dei Cinquecento in the Palazzo Vecchio in Florence (ca. 1559). Following Charles Davis and Pope-Hennessy, I believe that Cellini is one of the two figures in the background to the viewer's left (Charles Davis, "Benvenuto Cellini and the Scuola Fiorentina," *North Carolina Museum of Art Bulletin* 13, no. 4 (1976), 21, and Pope-Hennessy, *Cellini*, plate 1). These two figures are face-to-face. Cellini is the white-bearded figure on the right-hand side. I believe Ammannati is the dark-haired, bearded man to the viewer's right. Davis explains how Vasari's early descriptions of the tondo in his writings, which differ from the finished artwork, led to the misidentification (65, note 32). In addition, the figures are inscribed with names— which I am aware that the Wittkowers refute—and the face-to-face figures indicate that they are "Bandinelli" on the viewer's left and "Benvenuto" on the viewer's right.

63. For the characteristics of Cellini's hand that are different from the hand of the copyist of the Laurenziana manuscript, see Orazio Bacci, "Il Codice Mediceo-Palatino 234² della R. Biblioteca Mediceo-Laurenziana," *Rivista delle biblioteche e degli archivi* 7, no. 1 (1896): 10, note 6.

64. The Pierpont Morgan Library, New York, MA 973, f. 2. The illustration shows the first page of a two-page autograph memorandum and letter, dated [Florence], to Cosimo I de' Medici, through his majordomo Pier Francesco Ricci, 16 December 1549. For a transcription of this document, see I *Trattati dell'Oreficeria e della Scultura di Benvenuto Cellini*, ed. Carlo Milanesi (Florence, 1857), 280–81.

65. The Newberry Library, Newberry Case MS 5A 56, dated 27 November 1565.

66. *Study for the Seal of the Accademia del Disegno*, Florence (Pope-Hennessy, pl. 144). It survives as one of several drawings made by Cellini. Another drawing with the secret code is in the British Museum, London.

67. "La cura meticolosa quasi maniaca" of Cellini's writings was first noted by Piero Calamandrei (cited in Trento, *Benvenuto Cellini*, 43).

2 Criminal Acts and Literary Practice

1. My translation of Luigi Greci, "Benvenuto Cellini nei delitti e nei processi fiorentini ricostruiti attraverso le leggi del tempo," *Archivio di Antropologia Criminale* 2nd ser., 50, no. 4 (1930): 530, but I have modified it where I believe it contains errors of transcription or typographical errors after studying the original document (ASF, Magistrato degli Otto di Guardia e Balìa (granducal period), vol. 75 ("Partiti e Deliberazioni"), fols. 74r/v). Greci gives the page number in the book of denunciations as 82, but Piero Calamandrei gives it as 32 (Piero Calamandrei, *Scritti e inediti celliniani*, ed. Carlo Cordié (Florence, 1971), 342). I believe it is 32. Following Pope-Hennessy, I have translated the phrase "circa di cinque anni or sono passati" as "for about the last five years" rather than "about five years ago" because

documents show that Fernando was with Cellini in 1555 and 1556 (Pope-Hennessy, *Cellini*, 253). For more on Cellini's sex crimes, see Greci, "Benvenuto Cellini nei delitti," 50, no. 3 (1930): 355–63 and no. 4 (1930): 528–39; Calamandrei, *Scritti e inediti celliniani*, 179, 189, 342–44, 351–52; and Paolo L. Rossi, "The Writer and the Man. Real Crimes and Mitigating Circumstances: *Il caso Cellini*," 174–80, in *Crime, Society and the Law in Renaissance Italy*, eds. T. Dean and K.J.P. Lowe (Cambridge, 1994). The title "Maestro" indicates an artist who was master of his own establishment.

2. Tzvetan Todorov, *Genres in Discourse*, trans. Catherine Porter (Cambridge, 1990).

3. Guido Ruggiero, *The Boundaries of Eros: Sex Crime and Sexuality in Renaissance Venice* (New York, 1985), 109.

4. Rocke, *Forbidden Friendships* (New York, 1996), 14.

5. Guido Ruggiero, *The Boundaries of Eros*, 114.

6. Rocke, *Forbidden Friendships*, 46.

7. Rocke, *Forbidden Friendships*, 10.

8. Rocke, *Forbidden Friendships*, 4.

9. Rocke, *Forbidden Friendships*, 234. For a copy of this law, see *Legislazione Toscana raccolta et illustrata dal 1532 al 1705*, ed. Lorenzo Cantini (Florence, 1800), 1: 211–13.

10. John K. Brackett, *Criminal Justice and Crime in Late Renaissance Florence, 1537–1609* (Cambridge, 1992), 67.

11. For similar such constructions, see Ruth Mazo Karras and David Lorenzo Boyd, "'Ut cum muliere:' A Male transvestite prostitute in fourteenth-century London," in *Premodern Sexualities*, eds. Louise Fradenburg and Carla Freccero (New York, 1996), 103.

12. ASF, Magistrato degli Otto di Guardia e Balìa (granducal period), vol. 2232 ("Filze di Suppliche"), fol. 552r.

13. ASF, Magistrato degli Otto di Guardia e Balìa (granducal period), vol. 418 ("Giornale delle Faccende Quotidiane"), fol. 53r.

14. Rocke, *Forbidden Friendships*, 107–09.

15. Marvin E. Wolfgang, "A Florentine Prison: Le Carceri delle Stinche," *Studies in the Renaissance* 7 (1960), 150.

16. G. Baccini, "Scarperia. L'arresto di Benvenuto Cellini," *Bollettino storico-letterario del Mugello* 1 (1892): 27–29.

17. "The voting procedure of the Otto involved the use of black or white beans, which were secretly deposited in a cup by each judge. The secretary did not vote. A vote of seven black beans was needed to convict, seven white to acquit" (Brackett, *Criminal Justice*, 64).

18. For the earlier sodomy conviction, see Greci, "Benvenuto Cellini nei delitti," 355–63; Calamandrei, *Scritti inediti*, 179, 351–52; and Rossi, "The Writer and the Man," 177–78. Extant documentation on this earlier case is very slight; to my knowledge, only the very brief sentence survives. The title "Ser" (shortened from "Messer") most likely indicates a notary or lawyer, although it was sometimes used rather generically as a sign of respect to mean simply "Mister." A note on terminology: following Ruggiero, Rocke, and Brackett, I will use "homosexual sodomy" and "heterosexual

sodomy" to refer, respectively, to anal intercourse between males and anal intercourse between males and females. I am avoiding referring to Cellini as a "homosexual" because I believe the term carries too many modern connotations.

19. Rocke, *Forbidden Friendships*, 234.

20. The phrase "for quite some time" is taken from a summary of the charge on the back of his letter of supplication (see below). ASF, Magistrato degli Otto di Guardia e Balìa (granducal period), vol. 2232 ("Filze di Suppliche"), fol. 552v.

21. ASF, Magistrato degli Otto di Guardia e Balìa (granducal period), vol. 2232 ("Filze di Suppliche"), fol. 552r. To my knowledge, this letter is unpublished. It does not appear in Greci's article, nor is it mentioned by either Pope-Hennessy or Rossi. Calamandrei mentioned it but did not publish it. On page 189 of *Scritti inediti* Calamandrei incorrectly gives the date of Cellini's letter as 13 March, but on page 342 he gives the correct date of 3 March. 3 March is correct because there are marginal annotations by Lelio Torelli dated 5 March and 13 March. Torelli was Cosimo's chief legal adviser.

22. Brackett, *Criminal Justice*, 74.

23. Trento, *Benvenuto Cellini* (Florence, 1984), 48.

24. Ruth Wedgwood Kennedy, "Cellini and Vincenzo de' Rossi," *Renaissance News* 4, no. 3 (1951), 36. Borghini's animus toward Cellini was also displayed when he excluded Cellini from any involvement in the planning of the 1565 festivities for the wedding of Giovanni d'Austria and Francesco I.

25. Annibal Caro, *Lettere familiari*, ed. Aulo Greco (Florence, 1957), 1: 162. The Pope is Paul III.

26. Giorgio Vasari, *Lives of the Painters, Sculptors, and Architects*, trans. Gaston du C. de Vere (New York, 1996), 2: 886. The original is: "[Benvenuto Cellini] è stato in tutte le sue cose animoso, fiero, vivace, prontissimo, e terribilissimo, e persona che ha saputo pur troppo dire il fatto con i principi, non meno che le mani e l'ingegno adoperare nelle cose dell'arti." From Giorgio Vasari, *Le vite de' più eccellenti pittori, scultori e architettori nelle redazioni del 1550 e 1568*, eds. Rosanna Bettarini and Paola Barocchi (Florence, 1966), 6: 246.

27. The sonnet begins "Già tutti i Santi, ancor Saturno e Giove" [Maier, 900]. For more on this sonnet, see below.

28. Michel Plaisance, "Culture et politique à Florence de 1542 à 1551: Lasca et les *Humidi* aux prises avec l'Académie Florentine," in *Les Écrivains et le Pouvoir en Italie à l'époque de la Renaissance*, eds. André Rochon et al., 2nd ser. (Paris, 1974), 155, note 23.

29. ASF, *Manoscritti* vol. 126, fol. 303r. I would like to thank John Brackett for sharing this reference and for discussing the supplication process in Cellini's day with me.

30. Bernardo Segni, *Istorie fiorentine dall'anno MDXXVII al MDLV* (Florence, 1857), 409.

31. John K. Brackett, "The Florentine Onestà and the Control of Prostitution, 1403–1680," *Sixteenth Century Journal* 24, no. 2 (1993), 291.

32. Rubin, *Giorgio Vasari*, 48.
33. Referring to Cosimo, Cellini claims, "Le legge [*sic*] non si posson dare a chi è padron di esse," *Vita* (1996), 323.
34. Giovanni Antonelli, "La magistratura degli Otto di Guardia a Firenze," *Archivio Storico Italiano* 112 (1954), 35.
35. Brackett, "The Florentine Onestà," 291–95.
36. Plaisance, "Culture et politique à Florence," 228.
37. Judith Bryce, "The oral world of the early Accademia Fiorentina," *Renaissance Studies* 9, no. 1 (1995), 102.
38. Francesco Guicciardini, *Consolatoria, Accusatoria, Defensoria: Autodifesa di un politico*, ed. Ugo Dotti (Bari, 1993). The *Defensoria* is incomplete. For more on Guicciardini, see Randolph Starn, "Francesco Guicciardini and His Brothers," in *Renaissance Studies in Honor of Hans Baron*, eds. Anthony Molho and John Tedeschi (Florence, 1971), 409–44.
39. Todorov, *Genres in Discourse*, 19.
40. Margaret W. Ferguson, *Trials of Desire: Renaissance Defenses of Poetry* (New Haven, 1983), 4.
41. Paolo Prodi, *Una storia della Giustizia: Dal Pluralismo dei Fori al Moderno Dualismo tra Coscienza e Diritto* (Bologna, 2000), 53.
42. Ferguson, *Trials of Desire*, 24–25, and Thomas M. Greene, *The Light in Troy: Imitation and Discovery in Renaissance Poetry* (New Haven, 1982), 8–11.
43. Alan Bray," Homosexuality and the Signs of Male Friendship in Elizabethan England," *Queering the Renaissance*, ed. Jonathan Goldberg (Duke, 1994), 55.
44. Leonard Barkan, *Transuming Passion*, 105.
45. Saslow, "Homosexuality in the Renaissance," 101.
46. The technical term "intaglio" makes possible another rendering of the second sentence into English: "the engraving of his head was more beautiful than the ancient one of Antinous, and many times I have portrayed him/it." Antinous was the beautiful Bithynian boy loved by the Emperor Hadrian.
47. Cellini did not capitalize the word "ganimede" in the autograph, Ricc. 2353, fol. 26v.
48. Rocke, *Forbidden Friendships*, 33.
49. *The Penguin Book of International Gay Writing*, ed. Mark Mitchell (Harmondworth, England, 1995) and Woods, *A History of Gay Literature* (New Haven, 1998).
50. *The Penguin Book of International Gay Writing*, xiii.
51. Woods, *A History of Gay Literature*, 4, 198.
52. http://calvin.usc.edu/~trimmer/famous_names.html. Compiled by the American Library Association.
53. Annamarie Jagose, *Queer Theory: An Introduction* (Washington Square, NY, 1996), 98.
54. Saslow, *Ganymede in the Renaissance*, 48.
55. Saslow, *Ganymede in the Renaissance*, 48.
56. *The Gay and Lesbian Literary Heritage: A Reader's Companion to the Writers and Their Works, from Antiquity to the Present*, ed. Claude J. Summers (New York, 1995), x.

57. Joseph Cady, " 'Masculine Love,' " 9.
58. Woods, *A History of Gay Literature*, 8–9.
59. Information about this film was provided to me in a phone interview with Kristine Krueger of the National Film Information Service at the Margaret Herrick Library in Los Angeles on 14 September 2001.
60. Halperin, "Questions of Evidence," 40–41.
61. Ruggiero, *The Boundaries of Eros*, 121–25, and Rocke, *Forbidden Friendships*, 101–09. See also Brackett, *Criminal Justice and Crime*, 131–32.
62. Cady, " 'Masculine Love,' " 30–33.
63. BNMV, MSS Ital., Cl. IV, cod. 44.
64. Avery and Barbaglia, *L'opera completa del Cellini*, 92.
65. Pope-Hennessy, *Cellini*, 217.
66. Aristotle, *Generation of Animals*, trans. A.L. Peck (1943; Cambridge, MA, 1953), 738b.
67. Tylus, "The Merchant of Florence," 40–41.
68. *La Vita*, ed. Lorenzo Bellotto (Parma, 1996), 610, notes 19–20, concern this folio of Laur. Med-Pal. 234².
69. Bacci, "Il codice Mediceo Palatino 234²," 9.
70. *Vita di Benvenuto Cellini orefice e scultore fiorentino* . . . (Colonia [Naples]: Pietro Martello [Paulo Kuhzio], n.d. [1728]), 247.
71. Benvenuto Cellini, *La Vita*, ed. Carlo Cordié (Milan, 1996), 368.
72. Bellotto, 625; *Vita* (1728), 254.
73. Bellotto, 628; *Vita* (1728), 256.
74. *Vita di Benvenuto Cellini orefice e scultore fiorentino, da lui medesimo scritta, nella quale molte curiose particolarità si toccano appartenenti alle arti ed all'istoria del suo tempo, tratta da un'ottimo manoscritto, e dedicata all'Eccellenza di Mylord Riccardo Boyle* (Colonia [Naples]: Pietro Martello [Paulo Kuhzio], n.d. [1728]). On the printer, see Mario Emilio Cosenza, *Biographical and Bibliographical Dictionary of Italian Printers, and of Foreign Printers in Italy from the Introduction of the Art of Printing in Italy to 1800* (1967; Boston, 1968), 461.
75. Cited in George E. Dorris, *Paolo Rolli and the Italian Circle in London 1715–1744* (The Hague, 1967), 265. I would like to thank Tom Willette for this reference.
76. *Vita di Benvenuto Cellini* (Colonia: Pietro Martello, n.d.), 289. In the manuscript (BMLF Med-Pal. 234², fol. 492r), the four verses are vigorously crossed out.
77. Plon, *Benvenuto Cellini* (Paris, 1883), 380–84.
78. Eric Cochrane, *Florence in the Forgotten Years, 1527–1800* (Chicago, 1973), 324. Cochrane implies that Cellini's *Vita* was suppressed because it was embarrassing to Cosimo. I suspect also that it was perceived as a controversial manuscript, and thus, hidden away, coming to light in the eighteenth century only when the people involved had been long dead.
79. For other voices from the Renaissance competing with the silence perceived by many scholars in gay studies, see Cady, " 'Masculine Love,' " 9–40.
80. "Benvenuto erupts and spits poison and throws fire from his eyes, and dares the duke with his tongue." From *Il Carteggio di Michelangelo*, eds. Paola Barocchi and Renzo Ristori (Florence, 1983), 5: 232.

3 Cellini's Poetics I: The *Rime*

1. *Opere*, ed. Maier, 900–01. In the original (BRF, Ricc. 2353, fol. 8r), the word "Ganymede" is not capitalized. Cellini's sonnets normally follow this rhyme scheme: *abba abba* for the octave, *cdc dcd* for the sestet.
2. Cited in Richard Fisher, "'Ein Repräsentant Seines Jahrhunderts,'" 95.
3. Fisher, "'Ein Repräsentant Seines Jahrhunderts,'" 89.
4. Adolfo Mabellini, *Delle Rime di Benvenuto Cellini* (Rome, 1885), 20–21. On grace (*gratia*) as the product of ornateness and variety, see Michael Baxandall, *Painting and Experience in Fifteenth-Century Italy*, 2nd ed. (New York, 1988), 127 ff.
5. Special issue of *Il Marzocco* 5, no. 44 (1900): unnumbered page.
6. Bruno Maier, "Le *Rime* di Benvenuto Cellini," *Annali Triestini* 22 (1952), 307–58.
7. Giulia dell'Aquila, "Benvenuto Cellini lirico," *Rivista di letteratura italiana* 18 (2000): 47–69; Paolo Paolini, "Le Rime di Benvenuto Cellini," *Rivista di letteratura italiana* 18 (2000): 71–89; and Margaret A. Gallucci, "A New Look at Benvenuto Cellini's Poetry," *Forum Italicum* 34 (2000): 343–71. For a useful discussion of Cellini's poetry, see also Michael W. Cole, "Grazzini, Allori and Judgment in the Montauti Chapel," *Mitteilungen des Kunsthistorischen Institutes in Florenz* 45 (2001): 302–12, as well as his "Cellini's Blood," 222–27.
8. *Le Rime di Benvenuto Cellini*, ed. Adolfo Mabellini (Turin, 1891); *Benvenuto Cellini, Opere*, ed. Bruno Maier (Milan, 1968); and *Benvenuto Cellini, Rime*, ed. Vittorio Gatto (Rome, 2001). Other Cellini scholars, such as Francesco Tassi, have published collections of Cellini's complete writings, but did not write extensively on his poetry.
9. BRF, Ricc. 2728, fol. 12r.
10. Glauco Cambon, *The Poetry of Michelangelo: Fury of Form* (Princeton, 1985), 56–57.
11. According to Gregory L. Lucente, Michelangelo's sonnets were modified to appear as religious sonnets: *signor* (referring to Tommaso Cavalieri) became *Signor* (Lord). See his "Lyric Tradition and the Desires of Absence: Rudel, Dante, and Michelangelo ('Vorrei uoler')," *Comparative Review of Canadian Literature* 10, no. 3 (1983): 305–32, especially 324, note 22.
12. On the manuscript circulation of verse, see Walter LL. Bullock, "Some notes on the manuscript circulation of verse in sixteenth-century Italy," in *Essays in Honor of Carleton Brown* (New York, 1940), 220–41.
13. Sonnets by Cellini appeared in Battiferra's *Il primo libro dell'opere toscane* (1560) and in Varchi's *Sonetti spirituali* (1573).
14. BNCF, *Conventi Soppressi* B 8 1657, fols. 252v, 253r. I am indebted to Kelly Harness for sharing these newly discovered sonnets with me; she came upon them in the course of her research at the BNCF on an unrelated topic. For modernized transcriptions of these unedited sonnets, see appendix 2. For an illustration of one of the sonnets, see figure 15.
15. BRF, MS Ricc. 2728, fol. 22r, for example, contains accounting entries; BRF, Ricc. 2353 fols. 85v–86r contains six drawings of a tomb, which Michael Cole argues were intended for Cellini's own tomb, "Benvenuto

Cellini's Designs for His Tomb," *The Burlington Magazine* 140, no. 1149 (1998): 798–803.

16. Gatto, likewise, retains these artificial divisions.

17. Charles Davis, "Benvenuto Cellini and the Scuola Fiorentina," *North Carolina Museum of Art Bulletin* 13, no. 4 (1976), 19.

18. Deitlef Heikamp, "Poesie in vituperio del Bandinelli," *Paragone* 15, no. 175 (1964): 59–68.

19. On the *tenzone*, see Giovan Mario Crescimbeni, *L'istoria della volgar poesia* (Venice, 1730–31), 1: 178–82, and Ruggero Stefanini, "Tenzone sì e tenzone no," *Lectura Dantis* 18–19 (1996): 111–28.

20. For an overview of this debate, see John White, "Paragone: Aspects of the Relationship between Sculpture and Painting," in *Art, Science, and History in the Renaissance*, ed. Charles S. Singleton (Baltimore, 1967), 43–109.

21. Zygmunt Wazbinski, "Artisti e pubblico nella Firenze del Cinquecento. A proposito del topos 'cane abbaiante,'" *Paragone* 28 (1977): 15. For more on Borghini, see later, especially note 31.

22. Cellini did not capitalize "iddio" in verse 1. This sonnet contains three alternate endings, written in Cellini's hand, and each one crossed out. They are: "Come fannoggi e frati e quel priore," "Come fan giorgio e gli altri e quel priore," as well as "Come fa giorgio e gli altri oggi el priore." Apparently, Cellini favored a more general claim about sculptors over an attack on specific individuals, in this case Vasari and Borghini. Neither Maier's edition nor Gatto's contains a note about these alternate endings. The autograph folio is BRF, Ricc. 2353, fol. 43r.

23. *Scritti d'Arte del Cinquecento*, ed. Paola Barocchi (Turin, 1978), 3: 594, note 1.

24. Barocchi, *Scritti d'Arte*, 3: 506.

25. Barocchi, *Scritti d'Arte*, 3: 522. Note, too, the reference to the platonic doctrine of increasingly remote copies of an essential original.

26. Franco Sacchetti, *Il Trecentonovelle*, ed. Valerio Marucci (Rome, 1996): 649–54.

27. Baldassarre Castiglione, *Il Libro del Cortigiano*, ed. Ettore Bonora (Milan, 1976), 95.

28. ASF, Carte Bardi, 3rd ser., vol. 58, insert 12, n. 23, section 109.

29. Giorgio Vasari, "Baccio Bandinelli," in *Lives of the Painters, Sculptors, and Architects*, trans. Gaston de Vere (New York, 1996), 2: 299.

30. See especially Piero Calamandrei, "Sulle relazioni fra Giorgio Vasari e Benvenuto Cellini," in *Studi Vasariani/Convegno Internazionale Vasariano* (Florence, 1952), 195–214.

31. On Borghini, see Philip Gavitt, "Charity and State Building in Cinquecento Florence: Vincenzio Borghini as Administrator of the Ospedale degli Innocenti," *Journal of Modern History* 69, no. 2 (1997), 230–70.

32. Karen-edis Barzman, *The Florentine Academy and the Early Modern State* (Cambridge, 2000), 35.

33. Pope-Hennessy, *Cellini* (London, 1985), 277.

34. The date change caused a printing error to occur: most exemplars of the book on the obsequies for Michelangelo display the actual date of the

ceremony (14 July 1564), but some rare ones show the wrong date of 28 June. See Enzo Orvieto, "Un raro esemplare delle *Esequie* di Michelangelo nella Biblioteca dell'Università di Pennsylvania," *Library Chronicle* 39, no. 2 (1973): 76–80.

35. Barocchi, *Scritti d'Arte*, 3: 599, note 2.
36. Barocchi, *Scritti d'Arte*, 3: 611–73, especially 642–44.
37. See the "Medaglia di Pietro Bembo," in *L'opera completa del Cellini*, eds. Charles Avery and Susanna Barbaglia (Milan, 1981), 88–89.
38. William J. Kennedy, *Authorizing Petrarch* (Ithaca, NY, 1994), 84.
39. Heikamp, "Rapporti fra accademici ed artisti nella Firenze del '500," *Il Vasari* 15, no. 4 (1957), 140. Like the majority of other artists who were members of the Florentine Academy, Cellini did not apply for readmission to the Academy after reformers expelled most of the artists from it in 1547.
40. Francesco Berni, "Sonetto delle puttane (1518?)," *Rime*, ed. Danilo Romei (Milan, 1985), 30. A member of the "whorish sex" is not necessarily a prostitute, but the final tercet establishes her as such by associating her with disease (syphilis). On the changing vision of the prostitute, see John K. Brackett, "The Florentine Onestà and the Control of Prostitution, 1403–1680," *Sixteenth Century Journal* 24 (1993): 273–300, as well as chapter 5. A caudate sonnet was a traditional fourteen-line sonnet followed by a *coda* of tercets.
41. The meaning of this sonnet, particularly the last *terzina*, is ambiguous. Maier felt that the last *terzina* referred to Cellini abandoning Fortune when he left France, so she won vindication against the artist when he lived in Florence (901, notes 13–14). I believe, however, that since the sonnet is captioned "in prison" and was written in Florence, Cellini is referring to his first conviction for sodomy in Florence in 1523 ("that first injury in my youth"). At that time, the magistrates imposed a fine alone on him, not incarceration, so he avoided prison. This time, Fortune no longer favored the artist, so she abandoned him, letting the magistrates impose a harsh prison sentence.
42. *Grande Dizionario della Lingua Italiana* (hereafter, GDLI), ed. Salvatore Battaglia, 13 (Turin, 1986), 893; 14 (Turin, 1988), 1070.
43. GDLI, 2 (Turin, 1962), 620.
44. Jean Toscan, *Le Carnaval du Langue: Le lexique érotique des poètes de l'équivoque de Burchiello à Marino (XVᵉ–XVIIᵉ siècles)* (Lille, 1981), 1: 161.
45. On the theme of arms and letters, see Castiglione, *Il libro del cortigiano*, ed. Ettore Bonora (Milan, 1976), 87–90, as well as Stefano Prandi, *Il cortigiano ferrarese: I Discorsi di Annibale Romei e la cultura nobiliare nel Cinquecento* (Florence, 1990), 185–210.
46. Sonnet 11 in *Petrarch's Lyric Poems: The Rime sparse and other lyrics*, trans. and ed. Robert M. Durling (Cambridge, MA, 1976), 46–47.
47. Deborah Parker, *Bronzino: Renaissance Painter as Poet* (New York, 2000), 21.
48. Toscan, *Le Carnaval*, 1: 409.
49. Lynne Lawner, *I modi, The Sixteen Pleasures: An Erotic Album of the Italian Renaissance* (Evanston, IL, 1988).

50. Pietro Aretino, *Ragionamenti. Sei giornate*, ed. Romualdo Marrone (Rome, 1993).

51. Aretino, *Lettere, Tomo I, Libro I*, ed. Paolo Procaccioli (Rome, 1997), 303–04.

    Cellini and Tribolo had visited Venice together in 1535.

52. Giulia dell'Aquila, "Benvenuto Cellini lirico," 66: "I tradizionali lemmi che circoscrivono normalmente il campo semantico affettivo-amoroso sono qui, invece, utilizzati in riferimento al sentimento religioso: 'amore' (6 volte), 'amori' (1 volta), 'amor' (8 volte), come pure 'cuore' (10 volte), 'cuor' (5 volte), 'cor' (5 volte), e 'cor' (1 volta) [*sic*], sono quasi sempre usati a proposito della fede in Dio."

53. Victoria Kirkham, "Laura Battiferra degli Ammannati's *First Book* of Poetry: A Renaissance Holograph Comes Out of Hiding," *Rinascimento*, 2nd ser., 36 (1996), 351–91.

54. *Laura Battiferri degli Ammannati, Il primo libro delle opere toscane*, ed. Enrico Maria Guidi (Urbino, 2000), 116. Cellini's sonnet to Laura begins, "Con quel soave canto e dolce legno."

55. *Il primo libro dell'opere toscane* (Florence, 1560), 75. See appendix 3.B.

56. *Sonetti spirituali di M. Benedetto Varchi. Con alcune risposte, et proposte di diversi eccellentissimi ingegni. Nuovamente stampati* (Florence, 1573), 91. See appendix 3.C.

57. Kirkham, "Laura Battiferra degli Ammannati's *First Book* of Poetry," 356, n. 12.

58. Accademia della Crusca, *Concordanze del* Canzoniere *di Francesco Petrarca*, ed. Ufficio Lessicografico (Florence, 1971), 2: 1791. Sonnet 329 begins "O giorno, o ora, o ultimo momento," in Durling, *Petrarch's Lyric Poems* (Cambridge, MA, 1976), 517.

59. For Bronzino's sonnet, see *L'opera completa del Cellini* (Milan, 1981), 10.

60. *La Vita* (Milan, 1873), 383. For a discussion of these figures in Vasari's tondo, see chapter 1, note 62.

61. Waldman, "Bandinelli and the Opera di Santa Maria del Fiore," 232.

62. Bette Talvacchia, *Taking Positions: On the Erotic in Renaissance Culture* (Princeton, 1999), 91.

63. "i quai sonetti fra gli altri mia si conservano," in "Il Memoriale di Baccio Bandinelli," ed. Arduino Colasanti, *Repertorium für Kunstwissenschaft* 28 (1905), 424.

64. "Pecoron" (literally, "big sheep") most likely connotes "country bumpkin." Waldman has argued that the term "ox" in a vituperative sonnet about Bandinelli's *Hercules and Cacus* signifies "blockhead" (" 'Miracol Novo et Raro,' " 422).

65. *Opere di Anton Francesco Grazzini*, ed. Guido Davico Bonino (Turin, 1974), 441, 443, 444.

66. Jonathan Goldberg, "Cellini's *Vita* and the Convention of Early Autobigraphy," *MLN* 89 (1974): 71–83.

67. Cervigni likewise notes that Cellini's narrative lacks elements of "archetypal spiritual autobiographies in which conversion and divine revelation require confession of sinfulness" (*The* Vita *of Benvenuto Cellini*, 37), and criticizes Goldberg for overemphasizing the genre of spiritual autobiography in his analysis of the *Vita* (*The* Vita *of Benvenuto Cellini*, 33, n. 21; 39).

68. Trento, *Benvenuto Cellini* (Florence, 1984), 50.
69. Trento, *Benvenuto Cellini*, 51.
70. Maier, *Opere*, 953–61; Trento, *Benvenuto Cellini*, 51; Calamandrei, "Inediti celliniani: nascita e vendita del 'Mio Bel Cristo,'" *Il Ponte* 6 (1950): 378–93, 487–99.
71. Paolo Paolini, "Le Rime," 86.
72. Inf. 7, 1–3 from *La Divina Commedia*, ed. C.H. Grandgent, rev. by Charles S. Singleton (Cambridge, MA, 1972), 64–66.
73. *The Divine Comedy of Dante Alighieri, I: Inferno*, trans. Allen Mandelbaum (Toronto, 1980), 1: 334.
74. Jacopo della Lana, *Commento all'Inferno*, BRF, Ricc. 1009, fol. 3v. The phrase "diavolo lo sa" could also figuratively mean "who the Hell knows."
75. Plon, *Benvenuto Cellini* (Paris, 1883), 381.
76. Some Dante scholars now hold that Dante never actually traveled to France, but Cellini, like many of his contemporaries, believed that Dante did. Boccaccio also held this belief.
77. Bernard Weinberg, "The Quarrel over Dante," in *A History of Literary Criticism in the Italian Renaissance* (Chicago, 1961), 2: 819–911.
78. Weinberg, 2: 820.
79. *Veronica Franco, Poems and Selected Letters*, eds. and trans. Ann Rosalind Jones and Margaret F. Rosenthal (Chicago, 1998), 7.
80. "Dante est considéré tout à la fois comme théologien, philosophe et poète. On peut tirer de son oeuvre un enseignement encyclopédique et opérer à partir d'elle une large diffusion culturelle répondant aux aspirations d'un humanisme *volgare*." Michel Plaisance, "Une première affirmation de la politique culturelle de Côme Ier: La transformation de l'Académie des 'Humidi' en Académie Florentine (1540–42)," in *Les Écrivains et le Pouvoir en Italie a l'Époque de la Renaissance*, eds. André Rochon et al., (Paris, 1973), 425.
81. GDLI 4: 1023 (Turin, 1966).
82. "Ingannacontadini: opera d'arte di scarso valore ma di grande effetto." Cited in Battaglia, GDLI 7: 1009 (Turin, 1972).
83. The dozen words in the GDLI are: baiate (1: 948), babbuasso (1: 920), fummo (6: 451), omaccioni (11: 903), pappolate (12: 525), pedantuzo (12: 918), pigliare (13: 450), scannapagnotte (17: 808), scannapane (17: 808), spagnolescamente (19: 674), sparpagliò (19: 716), and statuare (20: 106). The three individual entries are for bordellerie (2: 310), broccardo (2: 387), and sodomitaccio (19: 252).
84. *Leonardo omo sanza lettere*, ed. Giuseppina Fumagalli, 2nd ed. (Florence, 1970).

4 Cellini's Poetics II: The *Vita*

1. Victoria C. Gardner, "*Homines non nascuntur, sed figuntur*: Benvenuto Cellini's *Vita* and the Self-Presentation of the Renaissance Artist," *Sixteenth Century Journal* 28, no. 2 (1997): 447–65.
2. Allodoli, "Appunti di storia e letteratura," 166–78.
3. Plon, *Benvenuto Cellini*, 384: "18 pezzi di libri di stampa di varie sorte."

4. Maier, "L'elemento comico-realistico: il boccaccismo e il cosidetto 'realismo' celliniano," *Umanità e stile*, 95–110.
5. Ginzburg, "Titian," 77–95, 197–200.
6. Paul F. Grendler, "Chivalric Romances in the Italian Renaissance," 59.
7. Anton Francesco Doni, *La Libraria*, ed. Vanni Bramanti (Milan, 1972), 229–30.
8. Barbara Mori, "Le vite ariostesche del Fornari, Pigna e Garofalo," *Schifanoia* 17–18 (1997): 135–39.
9. I refer to Schlosser's *La letteratura artistica*. See also Peter Burke, "Representations of the Self," 17–28.
10. Guglielminetti, *Memoria e scrittura: L'autobiografia da Dante a Cellini* (Turin, 1977), 295, 300.
11. Guglielminetti, *Memoria*, 296–97.
12. Cited in Guglielminetti, *Memoria*, 299.
13. Howard Saalman, "Introduction," in *The Life of Brunelleschi by Antonio di Tuccio Manetti* (University Park, PA, 1970), 26.
14. Saalman, *Life of Brunelleschi*, 26.
15. Bruno Maier, "Il frammento autobiografico di Raffaello da Montelupo e la *Vita* di Benvenuto Cellini," in *Problemi di esperienze di critica letteraria* (Siena, 1950), 48.
16. Fisher, " 'Ein Repräsentant Seines Jahrhunderts,' " 89.
17. See especially Gene Brucker, *Two Memoirs of Renaissance Florence: The Diaries of Buonaccorso Pitti and Giorgio Dati*, 2nd ed. (Prospect Heights, IL, 1991), 9–18, and Christian Bec, *Les marchands écrivains: affaires et humanisme à Florence 1375–1434* (Paris, 1967), 49–179.
18. T.C. Price Zimmerman, "Confession and Autobiography in the Early Renaissance," *Renaissance Studies in Honor of Hans Baron*, eds. A. Molho and J. Tedeschi (Dekalb, IL, 1971), 1: 119.
19. "Il *Memoriale* di Baccio Bandinelli," ed. Arduino Colasanti, *Repertorium für Kunstwissenschaft* 28 (1905): 406–43.
20. Natalie Zemon Davis, "Fame and Secrecy: Leon Modena's *Life* as an early modern Autobiography," in *Essays in Jewish Historiography*, ed. Ada Rapoport-Albert (Atlanta, 1991), 108. I am comparing these two genres to demonstrate the fluidity among genres in Cellini's day.
21. Philippe Lejeune, *On Autobiography*, trans. Katherine Leary (Minneapolis, 1989), 4, emphasis added.
22. On genre theory in Cellini's day, see Rosalie Colie, *The Resources of Kind: Genre-Theory in the Renaissance* (Berkeley, 1973); Bernard Weinberg, *A History of Literary Criticism in the Italian Renaissance* (Chicago, 1961); and Baxter Hathaway, *Marvels and Commonplaces: Renaissance Literary Criticism* (New York, 1968).
23. Ferguson, *Trials of Desire* (New Haven, 1983), 54.
24. On the evolution of autobiography in early modern Europe, see especially Weintraub, *The Value of the Individual*; May, *L'Autobiografie*; Olney, ed. *Autobiography*; and Amelang, *The Flight of Icarus*.
25. On Spini and the printers' involvement, see Trento, *Benvenuto Cellini*, 54–56.

26. Tylus, "The Merchant of Florence," 34.
27. Tylus, "The Merchant of Florence," 42, 39.
28. Cited in Tylus, "The Merchant of Florence," 225, note 40.
29. William Eamon, *Science and the Secrets of Nature: Books of Secrets in Medieval and Renaissance Culture* (Princeton, 1994), 10.
30. Bec, *Les livres des Florentins* (Florence, 1984), 67–68.
31. Eamon, *Science and the Secrets of Nature*, 8.
32. Grillot de Givry, *Witchcraft, Magic, and Alchemy*, trans. J. Courtenay Locke (1931; New York, 1971), 347.
33. *Leonardo, I codici*, eds. Carlo Pedretti and Marco Cianchi (Florence, 1995), 6.
34. Tylus, "The Merchant of Florence," 53.
35. Paul F. Grendler, "Chivalric Romances in the Italian Renaissance," *Studies in Medieval and Renaissance History*, eds. J.A.S. Evans and R.W. Unger, 10, n.s. (New York, 1988), 59–102.
36. Ruth House Webber, "Towards the Morphology of the Romance Epic," in *Romance Epic: Essays on a Medieval Literary Genre*, ed. Hans-Erich Keller (Kalamazoo, MI, 1987), 1–10. On epic and romance in the Italian Renaissance in general, see also Patricia Parker, *Inescapable Romance Studies in the Poetics of a Mode* (Princeton, 1979), and Sergio Zatti, *Il Furioso fra epos e romanzo* (Lucca, 1990) and his *L'ombra del Tasso: Epica e romanzo nel Cinquecento* (Milan, 1996).
37. On the blending of romance and epic in the *Furioso*, see especially Albert Russell Ascoli, *Ariosto's Bitter Harmony: Crisis and Evasion in the Italian Renaissance* (Princeton, 1987), as well as P. Parker, *Inescapable Romance*, and Zatti, *Il Furioso fra epos e romanzo* (Lucca, 1990).
38. Dennis Looney, *Compromising the Classics*, 15.
39. For a concise account of this debate see Bernard Weinberg, "Quarrel over Ariosto and Tasso," in *A History of Literary Criticism in the Italian Renaissance* (Chicago, 1961), 2: 954–1073. On the popularity of the *Furioso*, see Daniel Javitch, *Proclaiming a Classic: The Canonization of Orlando Furioso* (Princeton, 1991), 11–14.
40. Grendler, "Chivalric Romances," 80.
41. Allaire, *Andrea da Barberino*, 21.
42. Gabrielle M. Spiegel, "Genealogy: Form and Function in Medieval Historical Narrative," *History and Theory* 22, no. 1 (1983), 48.
43. Giovanni Villani, *Nuova Cronica*, in *Cronisti del Trecento*, ed. R. Palmarocchi (Milan, 1935), 159–61.
44. On the legendary origins of Florence, see Nicolai Rubinstein, "The Beginnings of Political Thought in Florence," *JWCI* 5 (1942): 198–227, and Donald Weinstein, "The Myth of Florence," in *Florentine Studies*, ed. Nicolai Rubinstein (Evanston, IL, 1968): 15–44.
45. See Randolph Starn and Loren Partridge, *Arts of Power: Three Halls of State in Italy 1300–1600* (Berkeley, 1992), 238 for a black and white reproduction, as well as 174–78 (with notes 347–48) for a discussion of this image.
46. On the miraculous origins of heroes, see Mario Martelli, "Schede sulla cultura di Machiavelli," *Interpres* 6 (1985–86): 283–330.

47. The scorpion was also associated in the zodiac with sexuality, in the melothesia. Melothesia is the correspondence of parts of the body to the constellations of the zodiac. Cellini seems to have had a lifelong interest in astrology, as attested by the astrology chart kept among his papers in the Biblioteca Riccardiana, Florence, as well as by his refrain about the "malevolent stars." On the cultural interest among artists and the Medici in these new sciences, see especially, Paolo L. Rossi, "*Sprezzatura*, Patronage, and Fate," 62–69.

48. Michael Murrin, *History and Warfare in Renaissance Epic* (Chicago, 1994), 123.

49. Grendler, "Chivalric Romances," 71.

50. Heinrich Cornelius Agrippa Von Nettesheim (1486?–1535), *Three Books of Occult Philosophy of Magic. Book One: Natural Magic*, ed. Willis F. Whitehead (New York, 1971), 187.

51. Richard C. McCoy, *The Rites of Knighthood: The Literature and Politics of Elizabethan Chivalry* (Berkeley, 1989), 16–17.

52. William L. Howarth, "Some Principles of Autobiography," in *Autobiography: Essays Theoretical and Critical*, ed. James Olney (Princeton, 1980), 97–104.

53. Maria Galetta, "Tradizione ed innovazione nella *Vita* di Benvenuto Cellini," *Romance Review* 5, no. 1 (Spring 1995), 68.

54. Richard Andrews, *Scripts and Scenarios: The Performance of Comedy in Renaissance Italy* (Cambridge, 1993), 271–79.

55. Judith Bryce, "The Oral World of the Early *Accademia Fiorentina*," *Renaissance Studies* 9, no. 1 (1995), 86.

56. See especially Winfried Schleiner, "Male Cross-Dressing and Transvestism in Renaissance Romances," *Sixteenth Century Journal* 19, no. 4 (1988): 605–19, and John C. McLucas, "'Faccio o nol faccio?' Cross-Dressing Initiatives in the *Orlando furioso*," *Italian Culture* 14 (1996): 35–46.

57. *Pietro Aretino, Tutte le Commedie*, ed. G.B. De Sanctis, 3rd ed. (Milan, 1973), 29–112.

58. Maier, *Umanità e stile*, 100–05.

59. Deborah Parker, *Commentary and Ideology: Dante in the Renaissance* (Durham, NC, 1993), 132.

60. Maier, *Umanità e stile*, 22, note 15.

61. Howard Rollin Patch, *The Other World, According to Descriptions in Medieval Literature* (Cambridge, MA, 1950), 1–5.

62. *The Aeneid*, ed. J.W. MacKail (Oxford, 1930), 222.

63. Gardiner, *Visions of Heaven and Hell*, xiii.

64. Jacques Le Goff, *The Birth of Purgatory*, trans. Arthur Goldhammer (Chicago, 1984), 198.

65. On the relationship between Dante's Otherworld journey and medieval visions, see also Caroline W. Bynum, "Faith Imagining the Self: Somatomorphic Soul and Resurrection Body in Dante's *Divine Comedy*," in *Faithful Imagining: Essays in Honor of Richard R. Niebuhr*, eds. Sang Hyun Lee et al. (Atlanta, 1995), 81–104.

66. Gardiner, *Visions of Heaven and Hell*, xix. There are some late medieval visions of travel to Purgatory, for example, the widespread folk tale of Saint

Patrick's journey to Purgatory. Concern with travels to Purgatory in Sicily dates from the seventh through the thirteenth century (Le Goff, *The Birth of Purgatory*, 201). Whether these stories were known in an Italian context is unclear. The *Tractatus de Purgatorio Sancti Patricii*, composed between 1190 and 1210, was translated into English and French (Le Goff, *The Birth of Purgatory*, 198–99). Cellini's visions are also very close in content and tone to the dramatic genre known as the *sacre rappresentazioni* that flourished in Tuscany in the fifteenth and sixteenth centuries. These sacred dramas, usually written in *ottava rima*, were staged outdoors in public spaces. Often commissioned by confraternities, they were performed on municipal occasions. There were no fixed stages or sets, but they contained elaborate machinery and effects. On this genre, see the *Encyclopaedia of the Italian Renaissance*, ed. J.R. Hale. repr. (London, 1989), 285.

67. James V. Mirollo, "The Lives of Saints Teresa of Ávila and Benvenuto of Florence," *Texas Studies in Language and Literature* 29 (1987), 57.

68. The singing of portions of psalms is reminiscent, for example, of certain passages in Boccaccio's *Decameron*, for example, the tale of Rinaldo d'Asti (II, 2). "I conversed with God for a while" is, in the Italian, "ragionai con Idio un pezo" [Bellotto, 433].

69. Leandro Perini, "Libri e Lettori nella Toscana del Cinquecento," in *Firenze e la Toscana dei Medici nell'Europa del '500, I: Strumenti e veicoli della cultura, Relazioni politiche ed economiche* (Florence, 1983), 113.

70. Michel Plaisance, "Culture et politique à Florence de 1542 à 1551: Lasca et les *Humidi* aux prises avec l'Académie Florentine," in *Les Écrivains et le pouvoir en Italie a l'Époque de la Renaissance*, ed. André Rochon, 2nd ser. (Paris, 1973), 209.

71. Ruth Martin, *Witchcraft and the Inquisition in Venice 1550–1650* (New York, 1989), 87.

72. Martin, *Witchcraft and the Inquisition*, 44.

73. Martin, *Witchcraft and the Inquisition*, 86–101.

74. Martin, *Witchcraft and the Inquisition*, 97.

75. John A. Tedeschi, "Toward a Statistical Profile of the Italian Inquisitions, Sixteenth to Eighteenth Centuries (with William Monter)," in *The Prosecution of Heresy: Collected Studies on the Inquisition in Early Modern Italy* (Binghamton, NY, 1991), 89–126.

76. C.P. Brand, *Ludovico Ariosto: A Preface to the "Orlando Furioso"* (Edinburgh, 1974), 46–57.

77. Weinberg, *A History of Literary Criticism* (Chicago, 1961), 2: 958.

78. David Quint, "The Figure of Atlante: Ariosto's and Boiardo's Poem," *MLN* 94 (1979): 81, and Ascoli, *Ariosto's Bitter Harmony*, 371–75.

79. Julia M. Kisacky, "Chaos and Order: Magical and Anti-Magical Books in Boiardo and Ariosto," *Romance Languages Annual* 8 (1997), 208.

80. "Certain words pronounced with a quite strong emotion have great force to aim the effect of images precisely where the emotional words are directed." Cited in Kennedy, *Authorizing Petrarch* (Ithaca, 1994), 96–97.

81. Claude Lévi-Strauss, "A Writing Lesson," in *Tristes Tropiques*, trans. John Russell (New York, 1971), 286–97, and Jacques Derrida, "The Violence of

the Letter: From Lévi-Strauss to Rousseau," in *Of Grammatology*, trans. Gayatri C. Spivak (Baltimore, 1976), 101–40.

82. J.L. Austin, *How to Do Things with Words* (Cambridge, MA, 1962).

83. Martin, *Witchcraft and the Inquisition*, 144.

84. Martin, *Witchcraft and the Inquisition*, 107.

85. Martin, *Witchcraft and the Inquisition*, 65.

86. Anton Francesco Grazzini, "A Trick Played by the Scheggia on Gian Simone Berrettaio," in *Renaissance Comic Tales of Love, Treachery, and Revenge*, eds. and trans. Valerie Martone and Robert L. Martone (New York, 1994): 174–99.

87. Valerie and Martone, *Renaissance Comic Tales*, 177.

88. Valerie and Martone, *Renaissance Comic Tales*, 181.

89. E.H. Gombrich, "Leonardo and the Magicians: Polemics and Rivalry," in *New Light on Old Masters, Studies in the Art of the Renaissance IV* (Chicago, 1986), 66. On Leonardo's diatribes against necromancy and alchemy, see 67–68.

90. *The Malleus Maleficarum of Heinrich Kramer and Jacob Sprenger*, trans. Montague Summers (1928; New York, 1971), 80.

91. *Il Carteggio di Michelangelo*, eds. Paola Barocchi and Renzo Ristori (Florence, 1965), 1: 346.

92. Margherita Orsino, "Il fuoco nella *Vita* di Benvenuto Cellini: Aspetti di un mito dell'artista-fabbro," *Italian Studies* 52 (1997): 104.

93. For a reproduction and brief discussion of this painting, see Mario Scalini, *Benvenuto Cellini* (Florence, 1995), 35, 41.

94. Giorgio Vasari, *Lives of the Painters, Sculptors, and Architects*, trans. Gaston de Vere, 2 vols. (New York, 1996), 2: 654–55.

95. Gardner, "*Homines non nascuntur*," 455.

96. Lisa Pon, "Michelangelo's *Lives*: Sixteenth-Century Books by Vasari, Condivi, and Others," *The Sixteenth Century Journal* 27, no. 4 (1996): 1033.

97. Gardner, "*Homines non nascuntur*," 454–55.

98. Armando Petrucci, "Lettere di artisti italiani del Rinascimento: Osservazioni paleografiche ed ecdotiche," public lecture delivered at the University of California, Berkeley, on 8 September 1993. Petrucci analyzed the autograph contained in Carlo Pini's three volume set *La scrittura di artisti italiani (sec. xiv–xvii) riprodotta con la fotografia* (Florence: Presso l'editore, 1869–73), 3: 181.

99. Elissa A. Tognozzi, "The Heterodoxy of Benvenuto Cellini: Emblematic Symbol of the Renaissance or Isolated Case of Excessive Indulgence" (Ph.D. diss., UCLA, 1993), 144–71.

100. *Il Carteggio di Michelangelo*, eds. Paola Barocchi and Renzo Ristori (Florence, 1983), 5: 266.

101. Corinne Mandel, "Perseus and the Medici," *Storia dell'arte* 87 (1996): 168–87.

102. Enea Vico, *Discorso sopra le medaglie de gli antichi* (Venice, 1555), 1: 67.

103. *La Vita di Benvenuto Cellini* (Milan, 1873), 376.

104. Barkan, *Transuming Passion*, 105.

5 Honor and Manliness

1. Dino S. Cervigni, "Cellini's *Vita* and Cervantes' *Don Quixote*: An Inquiry into Prose Narrative and Genre," in *Il Rinascimento*, ed. Vittore Branca (Florence, 1979), 288.
2. Mirollo, "The Lives of Saints Teresa of Avila and Benvenuto of Florence," 57.
3. David Herlihy, "Some Psychological and Social Roots of Violence in Tuscan Cities," in *Violence and Civil Disorder in Italian Cities 1200–1500*, ed. Lauro Martines (Berkeley, 1972), 145–52.
4. *OED* 19 (Oxford, 1989), 675.
5. Guido Ruggiero first suggested that "certain males began to see syphilis as a mark of belonging to an illicit world" of sex. See his "Marriage, Love, Sex, and Renaissance Civic Morality," in *Sexuality and Gender in Early Modern Europe*, ed. James Grantham Turner (Cambridge, 1993), 20.
6. Ruth Mazo Karras and David Lorenzo Boyd, " 'Ut cum muliere,' "109.
7. Rocke, *Forbidden Friendships*, 101–11.
8. Robert Hollander, "Dante's Harmonious Homosexuals," www.princeton.edu/~dante/rh.html.
9. Pope-Hennessy, *Cellini*, 254–55.
10. Brackett, *Criminal Justice and Crime*, 107–08.
11. Ruggiero, *The Boundaries of Eros*, 17–22, 43–49, 70–75.
12. Pierre Bourdieu, *Outline of a Theory of Practice*, trans. Richard Nice (Cambridge, 1977), 10 ff.
13. Guido Ruggiero, " 'More Dear to Me than Life Itself': Marriage, Honor, and a Woman's Reputation in the Renaissance," in *Binding Passions: Tales of Magic, Marriage, and Power at the End of the Renaissance* (New York, 1993), 57–87, and Lucia Ferrante, "L'onore ritrovato: Donne nella casa del Soccorso di San Paolo a Bologna," *Quaderni Storici* 53 (1983): 499–527.
14. Brackett, *Criminal Justice and Crime*, 113.
15. Cited in Brackett, "The Florentine Onestà," 275.
16. Brackett, "The Florentine Onestà," 275, note 7.
17. Guido Biagi, *Due lettere di Benvenuto Cellini sul portar l'armi* (Florence, 1911).
18. Brackett, *Criminal Justice and Crime*, 103.
19. Brackett, *Criminal Justice and Crime*, 103.
20. Plon, *Benvenuto Cellini*, 381: "Dua pistolesi, una coltella alla turchescha, una spada, uno pugniale con fornimenti argentati, una spada a una mano e mezzo, una zagaglia."
21. *L'opera completa del Cellini*, 85. I would like to thank Ann Rosalind Jones for help in translating these items of clothing made of chainmail. For more on chainmail clothing, see Cesare Vecellio, *Degli Habiti Antichi et Moderni di Diverse Parti del Mondo* (Venice, 1590), 59 (for the picture) and 20, 60–61 (for the commentary).
22. Biagi, *Due lettere*, unnumbered page.
23. *La Vita* (Milan, 1873), 373.
24. Plon, *Benvenuto Cellini*, 381.

25. Edward Muir, "The Double Binds of Manly Revenge in Renaissance Italy," in *Gender Rhetorics: Postures of Dominance and Submission in History*, ed. Richard C. Trexler (Binghamton, NY, 1994), 65–82.

26. On duels and honor in the Renaissance, see especially Francesco Erspamer, *La Biblioteca di Don Ferrante: Duello e Onore nella cultura del Cinquecento* (Rome, 1982), and Frederick R. Bryson, *The Point of Honor in Sixteenth-Century Italy: An Aspect in the Life of a Gentleman* (Chicago, 1935).

27. For instances of vendetta in late medieval court cases, see "The Vendetta" in *The Society of Renaissance Florence: A Documentary Study*, ed. Gene Brucker (New York, 1971), 106–20.

28. Thomas V. Cohen and Elizabeth S. Cohen, *Words and Deeds in Renaissance Rome: Trials Before the Papal Magistrates* (Toronto, 1993), 25.

29. GDLI, 2: 105–06.

30. Brackett, *Criminal Justice and Crime*, 106.

31. Brackett, *Criminal Justice and Crime*, 106.

32. Brackett, *Criminal Justice and Crime*, 107 ff.

33. Caroline Elam, "Art in the Service of Liberty: Battista della Palla, Art Agent for Francis I," in *I Tatti. Essays in the Renaissance* 5 (1993): 65.

34. On duels in general, see Jacopo Gelli, *Bibliografia generale della scherma con note critiche biografiche e storiche* (Milan, 1895) and Giorgio Enrico Levi, *Bibliografia del duello* (Milan, 1903).

35. Doni, *La Libraria*, 197–230.

36. On the Spanish influence in Italy in Cellini's day, see especially Benedetto Croce, *La Spagna nella vita italiana durante il Rinascimento* (Bari, 1917), Gian Luigi Beccaria, *Spagnolo e spagnoli in Italia. Riflessi ispanici sulla lingua italiana del Cinque e del Seicento* (Turin, 1985), as well as Thomas James Dandelet, *Spanish Rome, 1500–1700* (New Haven, 2001).

37. Gloria Allaire, "Tullia d'Aragona's *Il Meschino altramente detto il Guerrino* as Key to a Reappraisal of Her Work," *Quaderni d'Italianistica* 16, no. 1 (1995), 41.

38. Colasanti, "Il Memoriale di Baccio Bandinelli," 424.

39. *Le Opere di Benvenuto Cellini* (Florence, 1843), 355, refers to a Cellini diary entry for 12 December 1554.

40. Gwendolyn Trottein, "Battling Fortune in Sixteenth-Century Italy: Cellini and the Changing Faces of Fortuna," in *Artful Armies, Beautiful Battles: Art and Warfare in Early Modern Europe*, ed. Pia Cuneo (Leiden, 2002), 227.

41. Castiglione, *Il Libro del Cortigiano*, 56.

42. Giovanni Della Casa, *Galateo overo de' costumi*, ed. Giancarlo Rati (Rome, 1993).

43. Claudia Berra, "Il Galateo fatto per scherzo," in *Per Giovanni della Casa. Ricerche e contributi*, eds. Gennaro Barbarisi and Claudia Berra (Bologna, 1997), 271–335.

44. Della Casa, *Galateo*, 43, emphasis added.

45. Trevor Dean, "Marriage and Mutilation: Vendetta in Late Medieval Italy," *Past and Present* 157 (1997): 10–11.

46. Elam, "Art in the Service of Liberty," 65–66.

47. Brackett, *Criminal Justice and Crime*, 104.

48. Brackett, *Criminal Justice and Crime*, 113–14.
49. Guido Ruggiero, *Violence in Early Renaissance Venice* (New Brunswick, NJ, 1980), 137.
50. ASF, *Carte Strozziane*, Serie I, vol. 28. There are numerous versions of the same events with variations on the general themes in other collections of the ASF, such as the *Miscellanea Medicea* and *Manoscritti* collections.
51. ASF, *Carte Strozziane*, Serie I, vol. 28, fol. 4.
52. Christopher Hibbert, *The Rise and Fall of the House of Medici* (New York, 1979), 269.
53. Bastiano Arditi, *Diario di Firenze e di altre parti della Cristianità (1574–1579)*, ed. Roberto Cantagalli (Florence, 1970).
54. Arditi, *Diario di Firenze* (Florence, 1970), 105–06.
55. Arditi, *Diario di Firenze* (Florence, 1970), 219.
56. ASF, *Manoscritti*, vol. 129, fol. 80r. Settimanni's diaries are not contemporary with the events narrated.
57. ASF, *Manoscritti*, vol. 129, fol. 86v. Following Settimanni, modern historians from Saltini (1898) to Hibbert (1975) continue to repeat this tale. Orsini allegedly killed his wife to defend his honor after he found out she was having an affair with his cousin Troilo.
58. Judith R. Walkowitz, *City of Dreadful Delight: Narratives of Sexual Danger in Late-Victorian London* (Chicago, 1992), 199.
59. It has come to my attention that another scholar, Horst Bredekamp, delivered a lecture in Frankfurt in November of 2000 where he, independently, came to similar conclusions concerning Cellini's use of violence. I originally developed this idea in my 1995 dissertation.
60. Diane Wolfthal, *Images of Rape: The "Heroic" Tradition and its Alternatives* (Cambridge, 1999), 7 (citation); also 5, 26.
61. Franca Petrucci Nardelli, personal communication.
62. Bourdieu, *Outline of a Theory of Practice*, 15.
63. Bronzino's two sonnets beginning, "Giovin'altier, che Giove in aurea pioggia" and "Ardea Venere bella, e lui ch'in pioggia," were both printed in the 1568 edition of Cellini's two art treatises. Note here the reference to Danae, mother of Perseus, seduced by Jove descending as a shower of gold.
64. Alberti, *I Libri della famiglia*, eds. Ruggiero Romano and Alberto Tenenti, 2nd ed. (Turin, 1972), 319–425.
65. On friendship, see James M. Najemy, *Between Friends: Discourses of Power and Desire in the Machiavelli-Vettori Letters of 1513–15* (Princeton, 1993); Barry Weller, "The Rhetoric of Friendship in Montaigne's Essais," *New Literary History* 9 (1978): 503–23; and Michel Rey, "Communauté et individu: L'Amitié comme Lien Social à la Renaissance," *Revue du Histoire Moderne et Contemporaine* 38 (1991): 617–25.
66. *Fede* was an important theme in the writings of many of Cellini's contemporaries. See, for instance, Ascoli's discussion of faith for Ariosto in his *Ariosto's Bitter Harmony*, 284–86.
67. Ruggiero, *The Boundaries of Eros*, 90, 108.
68. Brackett, *Criminal Justice and Crime*, 111.
69. Brackett, *Criminal Justice and Crime*, 112.

70. Pope-Hennessy, *Cellini*, 254–55.
71. On Lorenzo Venier, see Giovanni Aquilecchia, "Pietro Aretino e altri poligrafi a Venezia," in *Storia della cultura veneta*, eds. Girolamo Arnaldi and Manilo Pastore Stocchi (Vicenza, 1982), 2: 85–86. On *La Zaffetta*, see Rosenthal, *The Honest Courtesan*, 37–39.
72. Vickers, "The Mistress in the Masterpiece," 36.
73. Tylus, "The Merchant of Florence," 50.
74. Ivan Arnaldi, *La vita violenta di Benvenuto Cellini* (Bari, 1986), 121: "La violenza per Cellini, è bisogno naturale . . . costituiva anche un piacere quasi fine a se stesso."
75. Vickers, "The Mistress in the Masterpiece," 23.
76. Niccolò Machiavelli, *Tutte le opere storiche e letterarie di Niccolò Machiavelli*, eds. G. Massoni and M. Casella (Florence, 1929), chapter 25, paragraph 8. English translation from *The Portable Machiavelli*, eds. and trans. Peter Bondanella and Mark Musa (New York, 1979), 162.
77. Ruggiero, *Binding Passions*, 5–7, 10–13, 179–85.
78. On syphilis in Cellini's day, see Bruce Thomas Boehrer, "Early Modern Syphilis," *Journal of the History of Sexuality* 1, no. 2 (1990): 197–214, and Anna Foa, "Il nuovo e il vecchio: l'insorgere della sifilide," *Quaderni Storici* 55 (1984): 11–34.
79. Brackett, "The Florentine Onestà," 288.
80. Margaret Healy, "Bronzino's London Allegory and the Art of Syphilis," *Oxford Art Journal* 20, no. 1 (1997): 6.
81. Berni, *Rime*, ed. Danilo Romei (Milan, 1985), 30.
82. Toscan, *Le Carnaval du langage*, 3: 1571–72.
83. Margaret Healy, "Bronzino's London *Allegory* and the Art of Syphilis," *Oxford Art Journal* 20, no.1 (1997): 3–11.
84. Amelang, *The Flight of Icarus*, 120.
85. Waldman, "Bandinelli and the Opera di Santa Maria del Fiore," 233.
86. Rudolph and Margot Wittkower, *Born under Saturn: The Character and Conduct of Artists, A Documented History from Antiquity to the French Revolution* (New York, 1969), 190.
87. John W. Bradley, *A Dictionary of Miniaturists, Illuminators, Calligraphers, and Copyists* (New York, 1958), 1: 213.
88. Rudolph and Margot Wittkower, *Born under Saturn*, 187–90.
89. Juliana Schiesari, *The Gendering of Melancholia: Feminism, Psychoanalysis, and the Symbolics of Loss in Renaissance Literature* (Ithaca, 1992).

Conclusion

1. Orazio Bacci, "Per un documento inedito su Benvenuto Cellini in Francia," *Miscellanea d'Arte* 1, no. 2 (1903): 24.
2. Jacob Burckhardt, *The Civilization of the Renaissance in Italy*, trans. S.G.C. Middlemore (New York, 1935), 330.
3. General psychological diagnoses of Cellini include Paul Courbon's *Étude Psychiatrique sur Benvenuto Cellini* (Paris, 1906) and Francesco Querenghi's *La psyche di Benvenuto Cellini* (Bergamo, 1913). More specific case studies

were conducted by Luigi Roncoroni, "Benvenuto Cellini (Contributo allo studio delle parafrenie)," *Minerva Medicolegale* 26 (1905): 271–97 and George E. Price, "A Sixteenth Century Paranoic: His Story and His Autobiography," *New York Medical Journal* 99 (1914): 727–31.

4. For more on Cellini's popularity in twenieth-century America, see my forthcoming article, "Benvenuto Cellini as Pop Icon," in *Benvenuto Cellini 1500–71: Sculptor, Goldsmith, Writer*, eds. Margaret A. Gallucci and Paolo L. Rossi (Cambridge UP, 2004). For details about Cellini as a comic book hero, see William B. Jones Jr., *Classics Illustrated: A Cultural History, with Illustrations* (Jefferson, NC, 2002), 75–76, 164, 218.

BIBLIOGRAPHY

Archival and Manuscript Sources

Archivio della Confraternità dei Buonuomini di San Martino, Florence

Inventario
Libro dei Capitoli e Indulgenze
Testamenti

Archivio di Stato, Florence

Carteggi d'Artisti
Carte Bardi
Carte Strozziane
Manoscritti
Mediceo del Principato
Miscellanea Medicea
Notarile Moderno
Magistrato degli Otto di Guardia e Balìa (granducal period)
   Filze di Suppliche
   Giornale delle Faccende Quotidiane
   Partiti e Deliberazioni

Biblioteca Medicea Laurenziana, Florence

Mediceo-Palatino 234[2]

Biblioteca Nazionale Centrale, Florence

Autografi Palatini Cellini
Banco Rari
Codici Magliabechiani
Conv. Soppr. B 8 1657
Gonnelli
Pal. 988
Poligrafo Gargani

Biblioteca Nazionale Marciana, Venice

MSS It. Cl. IV. cod. 44

Biblioteca Riccardiana, Florence

Ricc. 2353
Ricc. 2728
Ricc. 1009

The Newberry Library, Chicago

Newberry Case MS 5A 56

The Pierpont Morgan Library, New York

MA 973

Published Sources

Accademia dei Lincei. *Benvenuto Cellini artista e scrittore*. Rome, 1972.
Accademia della Crusca. Opera del Vocabolario. *Concordanze del* Canzoniere *di Francesco Petrarca*. Ed. Ufficio Lessicografico. 2 vols. Florence, 1971.
———. *Vocabolario degli Accademici della Crusca. Compendiato. Secondo la quarta ed ultima impression di Firenze corretta ed accresciuta, cominciata l'anno 1729 e terminata nel 1738*. 4th ed. 2 vols. Venice, 1741.
Adventures of Cellini. Classics Illustrated No. 38. New York: The Gilberton Company, June 1947.
Adventures of Cellini. Classics Illustrated No. 38. Rev. ed. New York: The Gilberton Company, October 1961; reprint, December 1963.
The Affairs of Cellini. 1934. Dir. Gregory La Cava.
Agrippa, Heinrich Cornelius Von Nettesheim. *Three Books of Occult Philosophy and Magic. Book One: Natural Magic*. Ed. Willis F. Whitehead. New York, 1971.
Alberti, Leon Battista. *I Libri della Famiglia*. Eds. Ruggiero Romano and Alberto Tenenti. 2nd ed. Turin, 1972.
Alighieri, Dante. *La Divina Commedia*. Ed. C.H. Grandgent. Rev. by Charles S. Singleton. Cambridge, MA, 1972.
———. *Rime*. Ed. Gianfranco Contini. Turin, 1965.
———. *Vita nova*. Ed. Guglielmo Gorni. Turin, 1996.
———. *The Divine Comedy of Dante Alighieri*. 3 vols. Trans. Allen Mandelbaum. Toronto, 1980. Vol. 1: *Inferno*.
———. *The Divine Comedy of Dante Alighieri*. 3 vols. Ed. and trans. Robert M. Durling. New York, 1996. Vol. 1: *Inferno*.
Allaire, Gloria. "Tullia d'Aragona's *Il Meschino altramente detto il Guerino* as Key to a Reappraisal of her work." *Quaderni d'Italianistica* 16 (1995): 33–50.

——. *Andrea da Barberino and the Language of Chivalry.* Gainesville, FL, 1997.
Allodoli, Ettore. "Appunti di storia e letteratura (I. Una lettera dell'Aretino e una pagina del Cellini—II. La morte di Ramus secondo Marlowe—III. Il duca di Guisa e Giulio Cesare)." *La Rinascita* 6, no. 2 (1943): 166–78.
Amelang, James S. *The Flight of Icarus: Artisan Autobiography in Early Modern Europe.* Stanford, 1998.
Ames-Lewis, Francis and Mary Rogers, eds. *Concepts of Beauty in Renaissance Art.* Brookfield, VT, 1998.
Andrews, Richard. *Scripts and Scenarios: The Performance of Comedy in Renaissance Italy.* Cambridge, 1993.
Antonelli, Giovanni. "La Magistratura degli Otto di Guardia a Firenze." *Archivio Storico Italiano* 112 (1954): 3–39.
Aquilecchia, Giovanni. "Pietro Aretino e altri poligrafi a Venezia." In *Storia della cultura veneta.* Eds. Girolamo Arnaldi and Manlio Pastore Stocchi. Vol. 3. Vicenza, 1982. 61–98.
Archivio della tradizione lirica da Petrarca a Marino. See Quondam, Amedeo, ed.
Arditi, Bastiano. *Diario di Firenze e di altre parti della Cristianità (1574–1579).* Ed. Roberto Cantagalli. Florence, 1970.
Aretino, Pietro. *Tutte le commedie.* Ed. G.B. De Sanctis. 3rd ed. Milan, 1973.
——. *Ragionamenti. Sei giornate.* Ed. Romualdo Marrone. Rome, 1993.
——. *Lettere. Tomo I. Libro I.* Ed. Paolo Procaccioli. Rome, 1997.
Ariosto, Ludovico. *Orlando furioso.* Ed. Lanfranco Caretti. 2nd ed. 2 vols. Turin, 1992.
Aristotle. *Generation of Animals.* Trans. A.L. Peck. 1943; Cambridge, MA, 1953.
Armstrong, Nancy and Leonard Tennenhouse, eds. *The Violence of Representation: Literature and the History of Violence.* London, 1989.
Arnaldi, Ivan. *La vita violenta di Benvenuto Cellini.* Bari, 1986.
Arrizabalaga, Jon, John Henderson, and Roger French. *The Great Pox: The French Disease in Renaissance Europe.* New Haven, 1997.
Ascoli, Albert R. *Ariosto's Bitter Harmony: Crisis and Evasion in the Italian Renaissance.* Princeton, 1987.
Attwood, Philip. "Cellini's Medals and Coins." Forthcoming in *Benvenuto Cellini 1500–71: Sculptor, Goldsmith, Writer.* Eds. Margaret A. Gallucci and Paolo L. Rossi. Cambridge, 2004.
Augustine. *Confessions.* Trans. Henry Chadwick. Oxford, 1991.
Austin, J.L. *How to Do Things with Words.* Cambridge, MA, 1962.
Bacci, Orazio. "Il Codice Mediceo-Palatino 234² della R. Biblioteca Mediceo-Laurenziana." *Rivista delle biblioteche e degli archivi* 7, no. 1 (1896): 1–11.
——. "Per un documento inedito su Benvenuto Cellini in Francia." *Miscellanea d'Arte* 1, no. 2 (1903): 22–24.
Baccini, G. "Scarperia. L'arresto di Benvenuto Cellini." *Bollettino storico-letterario del Mugello* 1 (1892): 27–29.
Baldacci, Luigi. *Il Petrarchismo Italiano nel Cinquecento.* 2nd ed. 1957; Padua, 1974.
Baldini, Gianni. "Un ricordo del Cellini a Reggio Emilia." *Mitteilungen des Kunsthistorischen Institutes in Florenz* 32, no. 3 (1988): 554–56.

Bandinelli, Baccio. "Il Memoriale di Baccio Bandinelli." Ed. Arduino Colasanti. *Repertorium für Kunstwissenschaft* 28 (1905): 406–43.

Barbaro, Francesco. "On Wifely Duties." In *The Earthly Republic: Italian Humanists on Government and Society*. Eds. Benjamin G. Kohl and Ronald G. Witt. Trans. Benjamin G. Kohl. Philadelphia, 1986. 189–228.

Barbina, Alfredo, ed. *Concordanza del* Decameron. 2 vols. Florence, 1969.

Barkan, Leonard. *Transuming Passion: Ganymede and the Erotics of Humanism*. Stanford, 1991.

———. *Unearthing the Past: Archaeology and Aesthetics in the Making of Renaissance Culture*. New Haven, 1999.

Barker, Emma, Nick Webb and Kim Woods, eds. *The Changing Status of the Artist*. New Haven, 1999.

Barocchi, Paola, ed. *Scritti d'Arte del Cinquecento*. Vol. 3. 1971; Turin, 1978.

——— and Renzo Ristori, eds. *Il Carteggio di Michelangelo*. Edizione postuma di Giovanni Poggi. 5 vols. Florence, 1965–83. Vols. 1, 5.

———, Kathleen Loach Bramanti, and Renzo Ristori, eds. *Il carteggio indiretto di Michelangelo*. 2 vols. Florence, 1988–95.

Barolsky, Paul. *The Faun in the Garden: Michelangelo and the Poetic Origins of Italian Renaissance Art*. University Park, PA, 1994.

Barzaghi, Antonio. *Donne o cortigiane? La prostituzione a Venezia: Documenti di costume dal XVI al XVIII secolo*. Verona, 1980.

Barzman, Karen-edis. *The Florentine Academy and the Early Modern State: The Discipline of Disegno*. New York, 2000.

Battaglia, Salvatore, ed. See *Grande Dizionario della Lingua Italiana*.

Battiffera, Laura degli Ammannati. *Il Primo Libro dell'Opere Toscane di Madonna Laura Battiffera degli Ammannati*. Florence, 1560.

———. *Il Primo libro delle opere toscane*. Ed. Enrico Maria Guidi. Urbino, 2000.

Baxandall, Michael. *Painting and Experience in Fifteenth-Century Italy*. 2nd ed. 1988; Oxford, 1991.

Bec, Christian. *Les livres des Florentins (1413–1608)*. Florence, 1984.

———. *Les marchands écrivains a Florence 1375–1434*. Paris, 1967.

Beccaria, Gian Luigi. *Spagnolo e spagnoli in Italia. Riflessi ispanici sulla lingua italiana del Cinque e del Seicento*. Turin, 1985.

Bell, Rudolph M. and Judith C. Brown. "Renaissance Sexuality and the Florentine Archives: An Exchange." *Renaissance Quarterly* 40 (1987): 96–100.

Bembo, Pietro. *Prose della volgar lingua. Prose e Rime*. Ed. Carlo Dionisotti. Turin, 1960.

Berchtold, Jacques. "Le séjour en prison dans l'autobiographie d'artiste: Mythification de l'expérience vécue dans la *Vita* de Benvenuto Cellini." In *Le Moyen Âge dans la Modernité. Mélanges offerts à Roger Dragonetti*. Ed. Jean R. Scheidegger. Paris, 1996. 73–91.

Berger, Maurice, Brian Wallis, and Simon Watson, eds. *Constructing Masculinity*. New York, 1995.

Berner, Samuel. "The Florentine Patriciate in the Transition from Republic to Principato, 1530–1609." *Studies in Medieval and Renaissance History* 9 (1972): 3–15.

———. "Florentine Society in the late Sixteenth and early Seventeenth Centuries." *Studies in the Renaissance* 18 (1971): 203–46.

Berni, Francesco. *Rime*. Ed. Danilo Romei. Milan, 1985.
Berra, Claudia. "Il Galateo fatto per scherzo." In *Per Giovanni della Casa.*
Ricerche e contributi. Eds. Gennaro Barbarisi and Claudia Berra. Bologna,
1997. 271–335.
Biagi, Guido. *Due lettere di Benvenuto Cellini sul portar l'armi.* Florence, 1911.
Bimbenet-Privat, Michèle. *Les Orfèvres Parisiens de la Renaissance (1506–1620).*
Paris, 1992.
Blunt, Anthony. *Artistic Theory in Italy 1450–1600.* Oxford, 1966.
Boccaccio, Giovanni. *Decameron.* Ed. Vittore Branca. Turin, 1980.
Boehrer, Bruce Thomas. "Early Modern Syphilis." *Journal of the History of
Sexuality* 1, no. 2 (1990): 197–214.
Borsellino, Antonino. "Cellini scrittore." *Convegno sul tema Benvenuto Cellini
artista e scrittore.* Rome, 1972. 17–31.
Borsellino, Nino. "Benvenuto Cellini." *Dizionario Biografico degli Italiani* 23
(1979): 440–51.
Bossy, John. "The Social History of Confession in the Age of the Reformation."
Transactions of the Royal Historical Society, 5th ser., 25 (1975): 21–38.
Boswell, John. "Revolutions, Universals, and Sexual Categories." *Salmagundi* 58
(1982): 89–113.
Boughner, Daniel Cliness. *The Braggart in Renaissance Comedy: A Study in
Comparative Drama from Aristophanes to Shakespeare.* Minneapolis, 1954.
Bourdieu, Pierre. *Outline of a Theory of Practice.* Trans. Richard Nice.
Cambridge, 1977.
Bowman, Frank. "Of Food and the Sacred: Cellini, Teresa, Montaigne." *L'Esprit
Créateur* 16, no. 4 (1976): 111–33.
Brackett, John K. *Criminal Justice and Crime in Late Renaissance Florence
1537–1609.* Cambridge, 1992.
———. "The Florentine Onestà and the Control of Prostitution, 1403–1680."
Sixteenth Century Journal 24 (1993): 273–300.
Bradley, John William. *Dictionary of Miniaturists, Illuminators, Calligraphers, and
Copyists with References to Their Works, and Notices of Their Patrons, Compiled
from Sources, Hitherto Inedited, from the Establishment of Christianity to the
18th Century.* 3 vols. New York, 1958.
Brand, C.P. *Ludovico Ariosto: A Preface to the Orlando Furioso.* Edinburgh, 1974.
Bray, Alan. "Homosexuality and the Signs of Male Friendship in Elizabethan
England." In *Queering the Renaissance.* Ed. Jonathan Goldberg. Duke, 1994.
40–61.
Briquet, C.M. *Les filigranes: Dictionanaire historique des marques du papier des
leur apparition vèrs 1282 jusqu'en 1600. A Facsimile of the 1907 edition with
supplementary material.* Ed. Allan Stevenson. 4 vols. Amsterdam, 1968.
Brucker, Gene A. *Florence, The Golden Age, 1138–1737.* 1984; Berkeley,
1998.
———. *Two memoirs of Renaissance Florence: The Diaries of Buonaccorso Pitti and
Gregorio Dati.* Trans. Julia Martines. 2nd ed. Prospect Heights, IL, 1991.
———. *Renaissance Florence.* Berkeley, 1969.
———, ed. *Society of Renaissance Florence: A Documentary Study.* New York, 1971.
Bruscagli, Riccardo, ed. *Trionfi e canti carnascialeschi toscani del Rinascimento.*
2 vols. Rome, 1986.

Bruss, Elizabeth. *Autobiographical Acts: The Changing Situation of a Literary Genre*. Baltimore, 1976.

Bryce, Judith. "The oral world of the Accademia Fiorentina." *Renaissance Studies* 9, no. 1 (1995): 77–103.

Bryson, Frederick R. *The Point of Honor in Sixteenth-Century Italy: An Aspect in the Life of a Gentleman*. Chicago, 1935.

Bullock, Walter LL. "Some Notes on the Circulation of Lyric Poems in Sixteenth-Century Italy." In *Essays in Honor of Carleton Brown*. New York, 1940. 220–41.

Bullough, Vern L. "On Being a Man in the Middle Ages." In *Medieval Masculinities: Regarding Men in the Middle Ages*. Ed. Clare S. Lees. Minnesota, 1994. 31–45.

Buonsignori, Francesco di Andrea. *Francesco di Andrea Buonsignori, Memorie (1530–1565)*. Eds. Sandro Bertelli and Gustavo Bertoli. Florence, 2000.

Burckhardt, Jacob. *The Civilization of the Renaissance in Italy*. Trans. S.G.C. Middlemore. Repr. Harmondsworth, England, 1990.

Burke, Peter. *The Historical Anthropology of Early Modern Italy. Essays on Perception and Communication*. New York, 1987.

———. "Representations of the Self from Petrarch to Descartes." In *Rewriting the Self: Histories from the Renaissance to the Present*. Ed. Roy Porter. London, 1997. 17–28.

Butler, Judith. *Bodies that Matter: On the Discursive Limits of "Sex."* New York, 1993.

Butters, H.C. *Governors and Government in Early Sixteenth-Century Florence 1502–19*. New York, 1985.

Butters, Suzanne B. *The Triumph of Vulcan: Sculptors' Tools, Porphyry, and the Prince in Ducal Florence*. Florence, 1996.

Bynum, Caroline Walker. "Faith Imagining the Self: Somatomorphic Soul and Resurrection Body in Dante's *Divine Comedy*." In *Faithful Imagining: Essays in Honor of Richard R. Niebuhr*. Eds. Sang Hyun Lee et al. Atlanta, 1995. 81–104.

———. *Holy Feast and Holy Fast: The Religious Significance of Food to Medieval Women*. Berkeley, 1988.

Cady, Joseph. " 'Masculine Love,' Renaissance Writing, and the 'New Invention' of Homosexuality." *Journal of Homosexuality* 23 (1992): 9–40.

Cairns, Christopher. *Pietro Aretino and the Republic of Venice: Researches on Aretino and his Circle 1527–1556*. Florence, 1985.

Calamandrei, Piero. *Scritti e inediti Celliniani*. Ed. Carlo Cordié. Florence, 1971.

———. "Sulle relazioni tra Giorgio Vasari e Benvenuto Cellini." In *Studi Vasariani/Convegno Internazionale Vasariano*. Florence, 1952. 195–214.

———. "Inediti celliniani: nascita e vicenda del 'Mio Bel Cristo.' " *Il Ponte* 6 (1950): 378–93, 487–99.

Cambon, Glauco. *Michelangelo's Poetry: Fury of Form*. Princeton, 1985.

———. "L'autobiografia, poesia e verità." *Forum Italicum* 11 (1977): 155–63.

Cantini, Lorenzo, ed. *Legislazione toscana raccolta e illustrata*. 32 vols. Florence, 1800–08. Vol. 1.

Cappello, Mary. " 'Rappaccini's Daughter' as Translation." *Philological Quarterly* 5, no. 2 (1986): 263–77.

Caro, Annibal. *Lettere familiari.* Ed. Aulo Greco. 3 vols. Florence, 1957–61. Vol. 1.

Carrara, Enrico. "Manierismo letterario in Benvenuto Cellini." *Studi Romanzi* 19 (1928): 171–200.

Casanova, Eugenio. "La liberazione di Benvenuto Cellini dalle carceri di Castel Sant'Angelo." *Miscellanea Fiorentina di erudizione e storia.* Rome, 1978. 22–23.

Castiglione, Baldassare. *Il Libro del Cortigiano.* Ed. Ettore Bonora. Milan, 1976.

Castiglioni, Arturo. "Le malatie e i medici di Benvenuto Cellini." In *Il volto di Ippocrate: Istorie di medici e medicine d'altri tempi.* Milan, 1925. 213–51.

Cellini, Benvenuto. *Due Trattati, uno intorno alle otto principali arti dell'Oreficeria. L'altro in materia dell'Arte della Scultura; dove si veggono infiniti segreti nel lavorar le Figure di Marmo e nel gettarle di Bronzo. Composti da M. Benvenuto Cellini scultore fiorentino.* Florence, 1568.

———. *Vita di Benvenuto Cellini orefice e scultore fiorentino, da lui medesimo scritta, nella quale molte curiose particolarità si toccano appartenenti alle Arti ed all'Italia del suo tempo, tratta da un'ottimo manoscritto, e dedicata all'Eccellenza di Mylord Riccardo Boyle.* Colonia [Naples]: Pietro Martello [Paulo Kuhzio], n.d. [1728].

———. *Vita di Benvenuto Cellini orefice e scultore fiorentino . . .* Ed. Francesco Tassi. 3 vols. Florence, 1829.

———. *Le Opere di Benvenuto Cellini.* Florence, 1843.

———. *I Trattati dell'Oreficeria e della Scultura di Benvenuto Cellini.* Ed. Carlo Milanesi. Florence, 1857.

———. *Vita.* Ed. Brunone Bianchi. 1852; Florence, 1924.

———. *Vita.* Milan, 1873.

———. *Vita.* Ed. Orazio Bacci. Florence, 1901.

———. *Vita.* Ed. Orazio Bacci. Florence, 1920.

———. *The Life of Benvenuto Cellini.* Trans. John Addington Symonds. Repr. London, 1925.

———. *The Life of Benvenuto Cellini.* Trans. Anne MacDonell. Repr. New York, 1926.

———. *The Autogiography of Benvenuto Cellini.* Trans. John Addington Symonds. 2 vols. Repr. Garden City, NY, 1948.

———. *The Autobiography of Benvenuto Cellini.* Trans. George Bull. Harmondsworth, England, 1956.

———. *Benvenuto Cellini, La Vita, I Trattati, I Discorsi.* Ed. Pietro Scarpellini. 1967; Milan, 1987.

———. *Benvenuto Cellini, Opere.* Ed. Bruno Maier. Milan, 1968.

———. *L'opera completa del Cellini.* Eds. Charles Avery and Susanne Barbaglia. Milan, 1981.

———. *Benvenuto Cellini. La Vita.* Ed. Lorenzo Bellotto. Parma, 1996.

———. *Benvenuto Cellini. La Vita.* Ed. Carlo Cordié. Milan, 1996.

———. *The Autobiography of Benvenuto Cellini.* Trans. George Bull. Repr. 1956; Harmondsworth, England, 1998.

Cellini, Benvenuto. *Benvenuto Cellini, Rime*. Ed. Vittorio Gatto. Rome, 2001.

Cervigni, Dino Sigismondo. *The Vita of Benvenuto Cellini: Literary Tradition and Genre*. Ravenna, 1979.

———. "Cellini's *Vita* and Cervantes' *Don Quixote*: An Inquiry into Prose Narrative and Genre." In *Il Rinascimento*. Ed. Vittore Branca. Florence, 1979. 275–98.

La Chanson de Roland. Ed. Cesare Segre. 2nd ed. Geneva, 1989.

Chambers, David and Brian Pullan, eds. *Venice: A Documentary History, 1450–1630*. Oxford, 1992.

Chao, Yemin. "Two Renaissance lives: Benvenuto Cellini and Teresa of Jesus." *Renaissance and Reformation* new ser., 23, no. 2 (1999): 29–44.

Chiorando, Emilio. "Le prigioni di Benvenuto Cellini in Castel S. Angelo." *Nuova Antologia* 6th ser., 196, no. 1115 (1918): 31–46.

Churchill, Sidney J.A. "Bibliografia celliniana." *La Bibliofilia* 9 (1907): 173–77, 262–69.

Cione, Edmondo. "Benvenuto Cellini." In *Il dramma religioso dello spirito moderno e la Rinascenza*. Naples, 1929. 97–106.

Clubb, Louise George. *Italian Drama in Shakespeare's Time*. New Haven, 1989.

Cochrane, Eric. *Florence in the Forgotten Centuries 1527–1800: A History of Florence and the Florentines in the Age of the Grand Dukes*. Chicago, 1973.

Cohen, Thomas V. and Elizabeth S. Cohen. "Open and Shut: The Social Meanings of the Cinquecento Roman House." *Studies in the Decorative Arts* 9, no. 1 (2001–02): 61–84.

———. *Words and Deeds in Renaissance Rome: Trials Before the Papal Magistrates*. Toronto, 1993.

Cole, Michael W. *Cellini and the Principles of Sculpture*. Cambridge, 2002.

———. "Grazzini, Allori and Judgment in the Montauti Chapel." *Mitteilungen des Kunsthistorischen Institutes in Florenz* 45 (2001): 302–12.

———. "Cellini's Blood." *Art Bulletin* 81, no. 2 (1999): 215–35.

———. "Benvenuto Cellini's designs for his tomb." *The Burlington Magazine* 140, no. 1149 (1998): 798–803.

Colie, Rosalie L. *Resources of Kind: Genre-theory in the Renaissance*. Berkeley, 1973.

Concordanza del Decameron. See Barbina, Alfredo, ed.

Concordanza della Commedia *di Dante Alighieri*. See Lovera, Luciano, ed.

Cordié, Carlo. "Nota agli 'Scritti e inediti celliniani' di Piero Calamandrei." *Rassegna della letteratura italiana* 7th ser., 76, no. 1 (1972): 71–79.

———. "Benvenuto Cellini." *Cultura e Scuola* 2, no. 7 (1963): 26–34.

———. "Maidè e dienaì." *Lingua nostra* 24 (1963): 117.

Cosenza, Mario Emilio. *Biographical and Bibliographical Dictionary of the Italian Printers and of Foreign Printers in Italy from the Introduction of the Art of Printing into Italy to 1800*. 1967; Boston, 1968.

Courbon, Paul. *Étude Psychiatrique sur Benvenuto Cellini*. Paris, 1906.

Crescimbeni, Giovan Mario. *L'istoria della volgar poesia*. Vol. 1. Venice, 1730.

Croce, Benedetto. "Sul Cellini scrittore." In *Poeti e scrittori del pieno e tardo Rinascimento*. Vol. 3. Bari, 1952. 168–70.

———. *La Spagna nella vita italiana durante la Rinascita*. Bari, 1917.

Currie, Stuart, ed. *Drawing 1400–1600. Invention and Innovation*. Brookfield, VT, 1998.

—— and Peta Motture, eds. *The Sculpted Object 1400–1700*. Brookfield, VT, 1997.

da Bisticci,Vespasiano. *The Vespasiano Memoirs: Lives of Illustrious Men of the XVth Century*. Trans. William George and Emily Waters. 1963; Toronto, 1997.

Dacos, Nicole. *La découverte de la Domus Aurea et la formation des grotesques à la Renaissance*. London, 1969.

Dale, Philip Marshall. *Medical Biographies: The Ailments of Thirty-Three Famous Persons*. Norman, OK, 1952.

Dandelet, Thomas James. *Spanish Rome, 1500–1700*. New Haven, 2001.

Davico-Bonino, Guido. *Lo Scrittore, il Potere, la Maschera: Tre Studi sul Cinquecento*. Padua, 1979.

Davis, Charles. "Benvenuto Cellini and the Scuola Fiorentina." *North Carolina Museum of Art Bulletin* 13, no. 4 (1976): 1–70.

Davis, Natalie Zemon. "Fame and Secrecy: Leon Modena's *Life* as an early modern autobiography." In *Essays in Jewish Historiography*. Ed. Ada Rapoport-Albert. Atlanta, 1991. 103–18.

——. *Society and Culture in Early Modern France*. Stanford, 1975.

de Certeau, Michel. *The Practice of Everyday Life*. Trans. Steven F. Rendall. Berkeley, 1984.

de Frede, Carlo. *La fuga del Cellini da Roma nel 1532*. Rome, 1964.

de Gaetano, Armand L. *Giambattista Gelli and the Florentine Academy: The Rebellion Against Latin*. Florence, 1976.

de Givry, Grillot. *Witchcraft, Magic, and Alchemy*. Trans. by J. Courtenay Locke. 1931; New York, 1971.

de Sanctis, Francesco. *Storia della letteratura italiana*. Ed. Gianfranco Contini. Milan, 1989.

dell'Aquila, Giulia. "Benvenuto Cellini lirico." *Rivista di letteratura italiana* 18 (2000): 47–69.

Dean, Trevor. "Marriage and Mutilation: Vendetta in late medieval Italy." *Past and Present* 157 (1997): 3–36.

Del Vita, Alessandro. "Giorgio Vasari e Benvenuto Cellini." *Il Vasari* 15, no. 4, n.s. (1957): 124–34.

——. "Benvenuto Cellini e Leone Leoni." *Il Vasari* 15, no. 4, n.s. (1957): 21–30.

Della Casa, Giovanni. *Galateo overo de' costumi*. Ed. Giancarlo Rati. Rome, 1993.

Dempsey, Charles. "Some observations on the education of artists in Florence and Bologna during the late sixteenth century." *Art Bulletin* 62, no. 4 (1980): 552–69.

Derrida, Jacques. "The Violence of the Letter. From Lévi-Strauss to Rousseau." In *Of Grammatology*. Trans. Gayatri C. Spivak. Baltimore, 1976. 101–40.

Devoto, Giacomo and Gian Carlo Oli, eds. *Dizionario della lingua italiana*. Florence, 1971.

Diaz, F. *Il Granducato di Toscana—i Medici*. Turin, 1976.

Dionisotti, Carlo. "Fortuna e sfortuna del Boiardo nel Cinquecento." In *Il Boiardo e la critica contemporanea: Atti del convegno di studi su Matteo Maria Boiardo, Scandiano-Reggio Emilia 25–27 aprile 1969.* Ed. Giuseppe Anceschi. Florence, 1970. 221–41.

Dizionario della lingua italiana. See Devoto, Giacomo.

Doni, Anton Francesco. *La Libraria.* Ed. Vanni Bramanti. Milan, 1972.

Dorris, George E. *Paolo Rolli and the Italian Circle in London, 1715–1744.* The Hague, 1967.

Dronke, Peter. *Verse with Prose from Petronius to Dante: The Art and Scope of the Mixed Form.* Cambridge, MA, 1994.

Dubost, Jean-François. *La France italienne XVIe–XVIIe siècle.* Paris, 1997.

Dunn, Peter N. *Spanish Picaresque Fiction: A New Literary History.* Ithaca, 1993.

Duprè dal Poggetto, Maria Grazia Ciardi. "Nuove Ipotesi sul Cellini." In *Essays Presented to Myron P. Gilmore.* Eds. S. Bertelli and G. Ramakus. Florence, 1978. 95–106.

Duranton-Mallet, Françoise. "Propositions pour une lecture analytique de la *Vita* de Benvenuto Cellini." *Revues des Etudes Italiennes* 29, no. 4 (1983): 223–31.

Durling, Robert. *The Figure of the Poet in Renaissance Epic.* Cambridge, MA, 1962.

Eakin, Paul. *Fictions in Auobiography.* Princeton, 1985.

Eamon, William. *Science and the Secrets of Nature: Books of Secrets in Medieval and Early Modern Culture.* Princeton, 1994.

Edgerton, Samuel Y. *Pictures and Punishment: Art and Criminal Prosecution During the Florentine Renaissance.* Ithaca, 1985.

Eggenschwyler, Renata. *Saggio sullo stile di Benvenuto Cellini.* Vercelli, 1940.

Eisenbichler, Konrad. "Nativity and Magi plays in Renaissance Florence." *Comparative Drama* 29, no. 3 (1995): 319–33.

Elam, Caroline. "Art in the Service of Liberty: Battista della Palla. An Agent for Francis I." *I Tatti Studies* 5 (1993): 33–110.

Elias, Norbert. *The Civilizing Process. I: The History of Manners.* Trans. Edmund Jephcott. New York, 1978.

Ellis, Havelock. *Casanova in Rome, in Venice, and in Paris: An Appreciation.* Boston, 1924.

Enciclopedia Dantesca. 6 vols. Rome, 1970–76.

Erspamer, Francesco. *La Biblioteca di Don Ferrante: Duello e Onore nella Cultura del Cinquecento.* Rome, 1982.

Even, Yael. "The Loggia dei Lanzi: A Showcase of Female Subjugation." *Women's Art Journal* 12 (1991): 10–14.

Fadiman, Anne. "Randolph Johnston: Cellini meets Crusoe." *Life* 9 (1986): 21–26.

Faggi, Adolfo. "Postilla celliniana." *Giornale Storico della Letteratura Italiana* 84 (1924): 209–22.

Farago, Claire, ed. *Reframing the Renaissance: Visual Culture in Europe and Latin America, 1450–1650.* New Haven, 1995.

Fasano Guarini, Elena. *Lo stato mediceo di Cosimo I.* Florence, 1973.

Ferguson, Margaret W. *Trials of Desire: Renaissance Defences of Poetry.* New Haven, 1983.

——, Maureen Quilligan, and Nancy Vickers, eds. *Rewriting the Renaissance: Discourses of Sexual Difference in Early Modern Europe.* Chicago, 1986.

Ferrante, Lucia. "L'onore ritrovato: Donne nella Casa del Soccorso di San Paolo a Bologna." *Quaderni Storici* 53 (1983): 499–527.

Ferroni, Giulio. "Dalla Faresina a Fountainbleau: Il confronto con la donna nella *Vita* del Cellini." In *Culture et Société en Italie: Du moyen-age à la Renaissance, Hommage à Andre Rochon.* Paris, 1985. 311–27.

Finucci, Valeria, ed. *Renaissance Transactions: Ariosto and Tasso.* Durham, NC, 1999.

Fisher, Richard. " 'Ein Repräsentant seines Jahrhunderts': A Portrait of the Artist in Goethe's *Anhang* to the Autobiography of Benvenuto Cellini." *Michigan Germanic Studies* 14, no. 2 (1988): 85–105.

Foa, Anna. "Il nuovo e il vecchio: l'insorgere della sifilide." *Quaderni Storici* 55 (1984): 11–34.

Fontes Baratto, Anna. "La grande illusion: Les rapports entre le monarque et l'artiste dans la *Vita* de Benvenuto Cellini." In *Le Pouvoir Monarchique et ses rapports idéologiques aux XVIe–XVIIe siècles.* Eds. Jean Dufournet, Adelin Fiorato, and Augustin Redondo. Paris, 1990. 231–43.

Foucault, Michel. *Discipline and Punish: The Birth of the Prison.* Trans. Alan Sheridan. New York, 1979.

——. "Politics and the Study of Discourse." Trans. Colin Gordon. *Ideology and Consciousness* 3 (1978): 7–26.

——. "A Preface to Transgression." In *Language, Counter-Memory, Practice: Selected Essays and Interviews,* 29–52. Ed. Donald F. Bouchard. Trans. D. Bouchard and Sherry Simon. Ithaca, 1977.

——. "Sexual Choice, Sexual Act: In Interview with Michel Foucault." Conducted and Trans. James O'Higgins. *Salmagundi (Homosexuality: Sacrilege, Vision, Politics).* Eds. Robert Boyers and George Steiner. 58–59 (1982–83): 10–24.

——. "Technologies of the Self." *Technologies of the Self.* Amherst, MA, 1988. 16–49.

——. *A History of Sexuality. Volume One: An Introduction.* Trans. Robert Hurley. New York, 1980.

Fracastoro, Girolamo. *Hieronymi Fracastorii Syphilis sive Morbus Gallicus.* Rome, 1531.

Franco, Veronica. *Poems and Letters, Veronica Franco.* Eds. and trans. Ann Rosalind Jones and Margaret F. Rosenthal. Chicago, 1998.

Frati, Carlo. *Dizionario bio-bibliografico dei bibliotecari e bibliofili italiani dal sec. XIV al XIX: raccolto e pubblicato da Albano Sorbelli.* Florence, 1933.

Freccero, John. "The Fig Tree and the Laurel: Petrarch's Poetics." *Diacritics* 5 (1975): 34–40.

——. "Autobiography and Narrative." In *Reconstructing Individualism: Autonomy, Individuality, and the Self in Western Thought.* Eds. Thomas C. Heller, Morton Sosna, and David. E. Wellbery. Stanford, 1986. 16–29.

Freedman, Luca. "'Rilievo' as an Artistic Term in Renaissance Art Theory." *Rinascimento* 29 (1989): 217–47.

Fumagalli, Giuseppina. *Leonardo omo sanza lettere.* 2nd ed. Florence, 1970.

Galetta, Maria. "Tradizione ed innovazione nella *Vita* di Benvenuto Cellini." *Romance Review* 5, no. 1 (1995): 65–72.

Gallucci, Margaret A. "Benvenuto Cellini as Pop Icon." Forthcoming in *Benvenuto Cellini 1500–71: Sculptor, Goldsmith, Writer.* Eds. Margaret A. Gallucci and Paolo L. Rossi. Cambridge, 2004.

———. "Cellini's Trial for Sodomy: Power and Patronage at the Court of Cosimo I." In *The Cultural Politics of Duke Cosimo I de' Medici.* Ed. Konrad Eisenbichler. Aldershot, England, 2001. 37–46.

———. "A New Look at Benvenuto Cellini's Poetry." *Forum Italicum* 34, no. 2 (2000): 323–71.

———. "Intervista a Stephen Greenblatt: Il Nuovo Storicismo e Il Futuro della Letteratura." *Allegoria,* n.s., 8, no. 24 (1996): 130–43.

———. "The Unexamined *Life* of Benvenuto Cellini: Poetic Deviation and Sexual Transgression in Sixteenth-Century Italy." Ph.D. diss., University of California, Berkeley, 1995.

Gardiner, Eileen, ed. *Visions of Heaven and Hell Before Dante.* New York, 1989.

Gardner, Victoria C. "*Homines non nascuntur, sed figuntur*: Benvenuto Cellini's *Vita* and Self-Presentation of the Renaissance Artist." *Sixteenth Century Journal* 28, no. 2 (1997): 447–65.

Gaspari, Gianmarco. "La *Vita* del Cellini e le origini dell'autobiografia." *Versants* 21 (1992): 103–17.

Gatto, Vittorio. *La protesta di un irregolare: Benvenuto Cellini.* Naples, 1988.

Gavitt, Philip. "Charity and State Building in Cinquecento Florence: Vincenzio Borghini as Administrator of the Ospedale degli Innocenti." *Journal of Modern History* 69 (1997): 230–70.

The Gay and Lesbian Literary Heritage. See Summers, Claude J., ed.

Gelli, Jacopo. *Bibliografia generale dello scherma con note critiche biografice e storiche.* Milan, 1895.

Gentile, Luigi, ed. *Indici e cataloghi, IV: I codici palatini della R. Biblioteca Nazionale Centrale di Firenze.* 2 vols. Rome, 1890.

Ghiberti, Lorenzo. *I Commentari.* Ed. Ottaviano Morisani. Naples, 1947.

Giamatti, A. Bartlett. *The Earthly Paradise and the Renaissance Epic.* Princeton, 1966.

Gil, Antonio C.M. "Truth and Form in Autobiography: Some Notes on Cellini's *Vita.*" *Proceedings of the Pacific Northwest Conference on Foreign Languages* 29, no. 1 (1978): 77–80.

Ginzburg, Carlo. "Titian, Ovid, and Sixteenth-Century Codes for Erotic Illustration." In *Clues, Myths, and Historical Method.* Trans. John and Anne C. Tedeschi. Baltimore, 1989. 77–95, 197–200.

Godard, Alain. "Sur quelques passages de la *Vita* de Cellini du danger du développement romanesque dans l'autobiographie." *Filigrana* 4 (1997): 49–70.

Goldberg, Jonathan, ed. *Queering the Renaissance.* Durham, NC, 1994.

———. *Sodometries: Renaissance Texts, Modern Sexualities.* Stanford, 1992.

——. "Cellini's *Vita* and the Convention of Early Autobiography." *MLN* 89 (1974): 71–83.

Gombrich, E.H. "Leonardo and the Magicians: Polemics and Rivalry." In *New Light on Old Masters, Studies in the Art of the Renaissance IV*. Chicago, 1986. 61–88, 181–82.

Grande Dizionario della Lingua Italiana. Ed. Salvatore Battaglia. 20 vols. to date. Turin, 1961–2000. Vols. 1, 2, 4, 6, 7, 11, 12, 13, 14, 17, 19, 20.

Grazzini, Anton Francesco. *Le rime burlesche edite e inedite di Antonfrancesco Grazzini detto il Lasca*. Ed. Carlo Verzone. Florence, 1882.

——. "A Trick played by the Scheggia on Gian Simone Berrettaio." In *Renaissance Comic Tales of Love, Treachery, and Revenge*. Eds. and trans. Valerie Martone and Robert L. Martone. New York, 1994. 174–99.

——. *Opere di Anton Francesco Grazzini*. Ed. Guido Davico Bonino. Turin, 1974.

Greci, Luigi. "Benvenuto Cellini nei delitti e nei processi fiorentini ricostruiti attraverso le leggi del tempo." *Archivio di Antropologia Criminale* 2nd ser., 50 (1930): 342–85, 509–42.

Green, Roland. *Post-Petrarchism: Origins and Innovations of the Western Lyric Sequence*. Princeton, 1991.

Greenblatt, Stephen. *Renaissance Self-Fashioning: From More to Shakespeare*. Chicago, 1980.

Greene, Thomas M. *The Light in Troy: Imitation and Discovery in Renaissance Poetry*. New Haven, 1982.

Grendler, Paul F. "Chivalric Romances in the Italian Renaissance." *Studies in Medieval and Renaissance History*. Eds. J.A.S. Evans and R.W. Unger, n.s., 10 (1988): 59–102.

——. *Schooling in Italy: Literacy and Learning 1300–1600*. Baltimore, 1989.

Grote, Andreas. "Cellini in gara." *Il Ponte* 19 (1963): 73–94.

Guarini, Battista. *Opere di Battista Guarini*. Ed. Marziano Guglielminetti. Turin, 1971.

Guglielminetti, Marziano. *Memoria e scrittura. L'autobiografia da Dante a Cellini*. Turin, 1977.

Guicciardini, Francesco. *Consolatoria, Accusatoria, Defensoria. Autodifesa di un politico*. Ed. Ugo Dotti. Bari, 1993.

Hale, J.R., ed. *Encyclopaedia of the Italian Renaissance*. Repr. London, 1989.

Halperin, David M. "Questions of Evidence: Commentary on Koehl, DeVries, and Williams." In *Queer Representations: Reading Lives, Reading Cultures*. Ed. Martin Duberman. New York, 1997. 39–54.

——. *One Hundred Years of Homosexuality and Other Essays on Greek Love*. New York, 1990.

Hathaway, Baxter. *Marvels and Commonplaces: Renaissance Literary Criticism*. New York, 1968.

Healy, Margaret. "Bronzino's London *Allegory* and the Art of Syphilis." *Oxford Art Journal* 20, no. 1 (1997): 3–11.

Heikamp, Detlef. "Rapporti fra accademici ed artisti nella Firenze del '500." *Il Vasari* 15 (1957): 139–63.

——. "Poesie in vituperio del Bandinelli." *Paragone* 15, no. 175 (1964): 59–68.

Henderson, Dave. "Power unparalleled: Gunpowder weapons and the early *Furioso.*" *Schifanoia* 13–14 (1992): 109–31.

Hendrix, Scott. "Masculinity and Patriarchy in Reformation Germany." *Journal of the History of Ideas* 56, no. 2 (1995): 177–93.

Herlihy, David. "Some Pyschological and Social Roots of Violence in Tuscan Cities." In *Violence and Civic Disorder in Italian Cities 1200–1500.* Ed. Lauro Martines. Berkeley, 1972. 129–54.

Hibbert, Christopher. *The Rise and Fall of the House of Medici.* 1974; Harmondsworth, England, 1979.

Hollander, Robert. "Dante's Harmonious Homosexuals." www.princeton.edu/ ~dante/rh.html.

Holsinger, Bruce W. "Sodomy and Resurrection: The Homoerotic Subject of the *Divine Comedy.*" In *Premodern Sexualities.* Eds. Louise Fradenburg and Carla Freccero. New York, 1996. 243–74.

Howard, Jean E. "The New Historicism in Renaissance Studies." *English Literary Renaissance* 16, no. 1 (1986): 13–43.

Howarth, William L. "Some Principles of Autobiography." In *Autobiography: Essays Theoretical and Critical.* Ed. James Olney. Princeton, 1980. 84–114.

Hunt, Lynn, ed. *The New Cultural History.* Berkeley, 1989.

IUPI: Incipitario Unificato della Poesia Italiana. See Santagata, Marco, ed.

Jagose, Annemarie. *Queer Theory: An Introduction.* Washington Square, NY, 1996.

Javitch, Daniel. *Proclaiming a Classic: The Canonization of Orlando Furioso.* Princeton, 1991.

Jones, Ann Rosalind and Peter Stallybrass. *Renaissance Clothing and the Materials of Memory.* New York, 2001.

———. See also Franco, Veronica.

Jones, William B. Jr. *Classics Illustrated: A Cultural History, with Illustrations.* Jefferson, NC, 2002.

Jordan, Mark. *The Invention of Sodomy in Christian Theology.* Chicago, 1997.

Karras, Ruth Mazo and David Lorenzo Boyd. "'Ut cum muliere': A Male Transvestite Prostitute in Fourteenth-Century London." In *Premodern Sexualities.* Eds. Louise Fradenburg and Carla Freccero. New York, 1996. 99–116.

Keen, Maurice. *Nobles, Knights, and Men-at-Arms in the Middle Ages.* London, 1996.

Keller, Hans-Erich, ed. *Romance Epic: Essays on a Medieval Literary Genre.* Kalamazoo, MI, 1987.

Kelly-Gadol, Joan. *Women, History, and Theory.* Chicago, 1984.

Kennedy, Ruth Wedgwood. "Cellini and Vincenzo de' Rossi." *Renaissance News* 4, no. 3 (1951): 33–39.

Kennedy, William J. *Authorizing Petrarch.* Ithaca, 1994.

Kenner, Hugh. "The Inside Story—First Prize: Cellini's Satyr, the Start of Ian Woodner's Lifetime of Collecting." *Art and Antiques* 7 (1990): 192.

Kent, F.W. and Patricia Simons. *Patronage, Art, and Society in Renaissance Italy.* New York, 1987.

Kirkham, Victoria, ed. and trans. *Laura Battiferra degli Ammannati and her Renaissance Circle. An Anthology with Translations, Introduction, and Commentary.* Chicago, 2004.

——. "Creative Partners: The Marriage of Laura Battiferra and Bartolomeo Ammannati." *Renaissance Quarterly* 60, no. 2 (2002): 498–558.

——. "Laura Battiferra degli Ammannati's First Book of Poetry: A Renaissance Holograph Comes Out of Hiding." *Rinascimento* 36, 2nd ser. (1996): 351–91.

Kisacky, Julia. "Chaos and Order: Magical and Anti-Magical Books in Boiardo and Ariosto." *Romance Languages Annual* 8 (1996): 207–12.

Klopp, Charles. *The Memoirs and Letters of Italian Political Prisoners from Benvenuto Cellini to Aldo Moro.* Toronto, 1999.

Knecht, R.J. *Renaissance Warrior and Patron: The Reign of Francis I.* Cambridge, 1996.

Koenigsberger, Dorothy. "*Leben des Benvenuto Cellini*: Goethe, Cellini and Transformation." *European History Quarterly* 22, no. 1 (1992): 7–37.

Kriegbaum, Friedrich. "Marmi di Cellini ritrovati." *L'arte* 11, n.s., (1940): 3–25.

Kris, Ernst and Otto Kurz. *Legend, Myth, and Magic in the Image of the Artist: A Historical Experiment.* New Haven, 1979.

Labalme, Patricia H. "Personality and Politics in Venice: Pietro Aretino." In *Titian: His World and His Legacy.* Ed. David Rosand. New York, 1982. 119–32.

Landi, Ann. "It's a Cellini." *Art News* 94 (1995): 35.

Larivaille, Paul. *Pietro Aretino fra Rinascimento e manierismo.* Trans. Mariella Di Maio and Maria Luisa Rispoli. Rome, 1980.

——. *La vita quotidiana delle cortigiane nell'Italia del Rinascimento. Roma e Venezia nei secoli XV e XVI.* Trans. Maura Pizzorno. 1975; Milan, 1983.

Lawner, Lynne. *I modi: The Sixteen Pleasures—An Erotic Album of the Italian Renaissance.* Evanston, IL, 1988.

Le Goff, Jacques. *The Birth of Purgatory (Naissance du purgatoire).* Trans. Arthur Goldhammer. Chicago, 1984.

Lejeune, Philippe. *On Autobiography.* Trans. Katherine M. Leary. Minneapolis, 1989.

Leonardo da Vinci. *Leonardo, I codici.* Eds. Carlo Pedretti and Marco Cianchi. Florence, 1995.

Levi, Giorgio Enrico. *Bibliografia del duello.* Milan, 1903.

Levi, Giovanni. "Les usages de la biographie." *Annales E.S.C.* 6 (1989): 1325–36.

Lévi-Strauss, Claude. "A Writing Lesson." Trans. John Russell. In *Tristes Tropiques.* 1963; New York, 1971. 286–97.

Litchfield, R. Burr. *The Emergence of a Bureaucracy: The Florentine Patricians, 1530–1790.* Princeton, 1986.

Looney, Dennis. *Compromising the Classics: Romance Epic Narrative in the Italian Renaissance.* Detroit, 1996.

Lorenzoni, Piero. *Erotismo e Pornografia nella letteratura italiana.* Milan, 1976.

Lovera, Luciano, ed. *Concordanza della* Commedia *di Dante Alighieri*. 3 vols. Turin, 1975.

Lucas, Corinne. "L'artiste et l'écriture: *il dire* et *il fare* dans les écrits de Cellini." In *Culture et Professions en Italie (fin XVe–début XVIIe siècles)*. Ed. Adelin Charles Fiorato. Paris, 1989. 67–96.

Lucente, Gregory L. "Lyric Tradition and the Desires of Absence: Rudel, Dante, and Michelangelo ('Vorrei uoler')." *Canadian Review of Comparative Literature* 10, no. 3 (1983): 305–32.

Mabellini, Adolfo. *Delle Rime di Benvenuto Cellini*. Florence, 1885.

———. ed. *Le rime di Benvenuto Cellini pubblicate ed annotate*. Turin, 1891.

Machiavelli, Niccolò. *Tutte le opere storiche e letterarie di Niccolò Machiavelli*. Eds. G. Massoni and M. Casella. Florence, 1929.

———. *The Portable Machiavelli*. Eds. Peter Bondanella and Mark Musa. Harmondsworth, England, 1979.

Maclean, Ian. *The Renaissance Notion of Woman: A Study in the Fortunes of Scholasticism and Medical Science in European Intellectual Life*. Cambridge, 1980.

Maier, Bruno. "Le Rime di Benvenuto Cellini." *Annali Triestini* 22 (1952): 307–58.

———. "Wolfgango Goethe traduttore e critico della *Vita* del Cellini." *Tesaur* 2, no. 1 (1950): 10–12.

———. *Umanità e stile di Benvenuto Cellini scrittore*. Milan, 1952.

———. "Il frammento autobiografico di Raffaello da Montelupo e la *Vita* di Benvenuto Cellini." In *Problemi ed esperienze di critica letteraria*. Siena, 1950. 41–50.

The Malleus Maleficarum of Heinrich Kramer and Jacob Sprenger. See Summers, Montague.

Mancini, Albert N. "Writing the Self: Forms of Autobiography in the Late Italian Renaissance." *Canadian Journal of Italian Studies* 14 (1991): 11–22.

Mandel, Corinne. "Perseus and the Medici: Political Iconography of Benvenuto Cellini's *Perseus and the Medusa*." *Storia dell'arte* 87 (1996): 168–87.

Manetti, Antonio di Tuccio. *The Life of Brunelleschi*. Ed. Howard Saalman. Trans. Catherine Enggass. University Park, PA, 1970.

———. *Vita di Filippo di ser Brunelleschi*. Ed. Domenicho De Robertis. Milan, 1976.

Manganelli, Giorgio, ed. *Il Novellino: Libro di novelle e di bel parlar gentile*. 3rd ed. Milan, 1989.

Martelli, Mario. "Schede sulla cultura di Machiavelli." *Interpres* 6 (1985–86): 283–330.

Martin, John. "Inventing Sincerity, Refashioning Prudence: The Discovery of the Individual in Renaissance Europe." *American Historical Review* 102 (1997): 1309–42.

Martin, Ruth. *Witchcraft and the Inquisition in Venice, 1550–1650*. New York, 1989.

Martines, Lauro. *Power and Imagination: City-States in Renaissance Italy*. New York, 1979.

Marucci, Valerio et al. *Pasquinate romane del Cinquecento*. Rome, 1983.

Marzocco 5, no. 44 (1900). Special issue on Cellini.

Mauss, Marcel. "Une categorie de l'esprit humain: La notion de personne, celle de 'moi.'" *Sociologie et anthropologie*, 9th ed. Paris, 1985. 333–62.

May, Georges. *L'autobiographie*. Paris, 1979.

McCoy, Richard C. *The Rites of Knighthood: The Literature and Politics of Elizabethan Chivalry*. Berkeley, 1989.

McGee, Timothy J. "In the Service of the Commune: The Changing Role of Florentine Civic Musicians, 1450–1532." *Sixteenth Century Journal* 30, no. 3 (1999): 727–43.

———. "Giovanni Cellini, piffero di Firenze," *Rivista italiana di musicologia* 32, no. 2 (1997): 201–21.

McHam, Sarah Blake. *Looking at Italian Renaissance Sculpture*. Cambridge, 1998.

McLaughlin, Thomas and Frank Lentricchia, eds. *Critical Terms for Literary Study*. 2nd ed. Chicago, 1995.

McLucas, John C. "'Faccio o nol faccio?' Cross-dressing initiatives in the *Orlando furioso*." *Italian Culture* 14 (1996): 35–46.

Melzi, Gaetano. *Bibliografia dei romanzi e poemi cavallereschi italiani*. 2nd ed. Ed. Paolo Antonio Tosi. Milan, 1838.

Migiel, Marilyn. "Gender Studies and the Italian Renaissance." In *Interpreting the Renaissance: Literary Perspectives*. Ed. A. Toscano. Stony Brook, NY, 1991. 29–41.

Mirollo, James V. "The Lives of Saints Teresa of Avila and Benvenuto of Florence." *Texas Studies in Literature and Language* 29, no. 1 (1987): 54–73.

Mitchell, Mark, ed. *The Penguin Book of International Gay Writing*. Harmondsworth, England, 1995.

Monga, Luigi. "Odeporico celliniano: Il viaggiare nella *Vita*." *Annali d'Italianistica* 4 (1986): 73–79.

Montrose, Louis Adrian. "Renaissance Literary Studies and the Subject of History." *English Literary Renaissance* 16 (1986): 5–12.

Monumenta ordinis servorum Sanctae Mariae a PP. Augustino Morini et Peregrino Soulier edita. 20 vols. Brussels, 1897–1926. Vol. 6.

Morgan, David. "Masculinity, Autobiography, and History." *Gender and History* 2 (1990): 34–39.

Mori, Barbara. "Le vite ariostesche del Fornari, Pigna e Garofalo." *Schifanoia* 17–18 (1997): 135–39.

Morsberger, Robert E. "Melville's *The Bell-Tower* and Benvenuto Cellini." *American Literature* 44, no. 3 (1972): 459–62.

Muir, Edward. *Mad Blood Stirring: Vendetta and Factions in Friuli During the Renaissance*. Baltimore, 1993.

———. "The Double Binds of Manly Revenge in Renaissance Italy." In *Gender Rhetorics: Postures of Dominance and Submission in History*. Ed. Richard C. Trexler. Binghamton, NY, 1994. 65–82.

Murrin, Michael. *History and Warfare in the Renaissance Epic*. Chicago, 1994.

Mussio, Thomas E. "The Augustinian Conflict in the Lyrics of Michelangelo: Michelangelo Reading Petrarch." *Italica* 74 (1997): 339–59.

Muxfeldt, Kristina. "Political Crimes and Liberty, or Why would Schubert eat a peacock?" *Nineteenth-Century Music* 17 (1993): 47–64.

Najemy, James M. *Between Friends: Discourses of Power and Desire in the Machiavelli-Vettori Letters of 1513–1515.* Princeton, 1993.

Nardelli, Franca Petrucci. "Riproduzione o interpretazione? Note sull'edizione dei documenti" *Arte Documento* 4 (1992): 266–67.

———. *La legatura italiana: Storia, descrizione, techniche (XV–XIX secolo).* Rome, 1989.

Negri, Giulio. *Istoria degli scrittori fiorentini.* Ferrara, 1722.

Olney, James, ed. *Autobiography: Essays Theoretical and Critical.* Princeton, 1980.

Orsino, Margherita. "Il fuoco nella *Vita* di Benvenuto Cellini: Aspetti di un mito dell'artista-fabbro." *Italian Studies* 52 (1997): 94–110.

Orvieto, Enzo. "Un raro esemplare delle *Esequie* di Michelangelo nella Biblioteca dell'Università di Pennsylvania." *Library Chronicle* 39 (1973): 76–80.

Ovid. *Metamorphoses.* Trans. Frank Justus Miller. 2 vols. 3rd ed. Cambridge, MA, 1976–77.

The Oxford English Dictionary. Eds. J.A. Simpson and E.S.C. Weiner. 2nd ed. 20 vols. Oxford, 1989. Vol. 19.

Paolini, Paolo. "Le Rime di Benvenuto Cellini." *Rivista di letteratura italiana* 18 (2000): 71–89.

Paris, Renzo and Antonio Veneziani, eds. *L'amicizia amorosa: Antologia della poesia omosessuale italiana dal tredicesimo secolo a oggi.* Milan, 1982.

Parker, Deborah. *Bronzino: Renaissance Painter as Poet.* New York, 2000.

———. "Towards a Reading of Bronzino's Burlesque Poetry." *Renaissance Quarterly* 50 (1997): 1011–44.

———. *Commentary and Ideology: Dante in the Renaissance.* Durham, NC, 1993.

Partridge, Loren. See Starn, Randolph.

Patch, Howard Rollin. *The Other World, According to Descriptions in Medieval Literature.* Cambridge, MA, 1950.

Paxson, James J. *The Poetics of Personification.* New York, 1994.

The Penguin Book of International Gay Writing. See Mitchell, Mark, ed.

Pequigney, Joseph. "Sodomy in Dante's *Inferno* and *Purgatorio*." *Representations* 36 (1991): 22–42.

Perini, Leandro. "Libri e lettori nella Toscana del Cinquecento." In *Firenze e la Toscana dei Medici nell'Europa del '500. I: Strumenti e veicoli della cultura, Relazioni politiche ed economiche.* 3 vols. Florence, 1983. 1: 109–131.

Petrarch. *Canzoniere.* Ed. Gianfranco Contini. Turin, 1964.

———. *Petrarch's Lyric Poems: The Rime Sparse and Other Lyrics.* Trans. and ed. Robert M. Durling. 1976; Cambridge, MA, 1995.

Petrucci, Armando. *La Descrizione del Manoscritto: Storia, Problemi, Modelli.* Rome, 1984.

——— and Franca Petrucci Nardelli. "Lettere di artisti italiani del Rinascimento: Osservazioni paleografiche ed ecdotiche." Public lecture at the University of California, Berkeley. 8 September 1993.

Piccinini, A. Maria Manetti. "Will Perseus come in from the cold?" *Art Newspaper* 7 (1996): 27.

Plaisance, Michel. "Une première affirmation de la politique culturelle de Côme Ier: La transformation de l'Académie des 'Humidi' en Académie Florentine (1540–1542)." In *Les écrivains et le pouvoir en Italie à l'époque de la Renaissance*. 1st ser. Ed. André Rochon. Paris, 1973. 361–438.

———. "Culture et politique à Florence de 1542 a 1551: Lasca et les *Humidi* aux prises avec l'Académie Florentine." In *Les écrivains et le pouvoir en Italie à l'époque de la Renaissance*. 2nd ser. Ed. André Rochon. Paris, 1974. 149–242.

Plato. *The Works of Plato*. Trans. Henry Cary. Vol. 1. London, 1848.

Plon, Eugène. *Benvenuto Cellini, orfèvre, médailleur, sculpteur: Recherches sur sa vie, sur son oeuvre, et sur les pièces qui lui sont attribuées*. Paris, 1883.

Pon, Lisa. "Michelangelo's Lives: Sixteenth-Century Books by Vasari, Condivi, and Others." *Sixteenth Century Journal* 27 (1996): 1015–37.

Pontormo, Jacopo. *Il mio libro*. Ed. Salvatore S. Nigro. Genoa, 1984.

Pope-Hennessy, John. *Cellini*. London, 1985.

———. "A Bronze Satyr by Cellini." *The Burlington Magazine* 124 (1982): 406–12.

Prandi, Stefano. *Il cortigiano ferrarese: I Discorsi di Annibale Romei e la cultura nobiliare nel Cinquecento*. Florence, 1990.

Praz, Mario. "De Foe e Cellini." In *Studi e svaghi inglesi*. Florence, 1937. 27–53.

Price, George E. "A Sixteenth-Century Paranoic: His Story and his Autobiography." *New York Medical Journal* 99 (1914): 727–31.

Prodi, Paolo. *Una storia della Giustizia: Dal Pluralismo dei Fori al Moderno Dualismo tra Coscienza e Diritto*. Bologna, 2000.

Pulci, Luigi. *Il Morgante*. Ed. Raffaello Ramat. Milan, 1961.

Querenghi, Francesco. *La psiche di Benvenuto Cellini*. Bergamo, 1913.

Quétel, Claude. *History of Syphilis*. Trans. Judith Braddock and Brian Pike. Baltimore, 1990.

Quint, David. *Origin and Originality in Renaissance Literature: Versions of the Source*. New Haven, 1983.

———. "The Figure of Atlante: Ariosto's and Boiardo's Poem." *MLN* 94 (1979): 77–91.

Quondam, Amedeo, ed. *Archivio della tradizione lirica da Petrarca a Marino*. Rome, 1997. CD-ROM.

Rabinow, Paul, ed. *The Foucault Reader*. New York, 1984.

Radcliffe, Anthony. "Cellini review article." *The Burlington Magazine* 130 (1988): 929–32.

Raeder Taraldsen, Ingrid. "Un'analisi delle costruzioni participiali assolute nella *Vita* del Cellini." *Revue Romane* 10 (1975): 306–27.

Ramaut, Alban. "Benvenuto Cellini: Un opera Jeune-France?" *Bulletin de la Société Theophile Gautier* 15, no. 1 (1993): 219–29.

Reizov, Boris. "Stendhal et Benvenuto Cellini (Sur les problèmes des sources de la *Chartreuse de Parme*)." *Stendhal-Club* 8, no. 32, new ser. (1966): 325–38.

Renier, Rodolfo. "La psicopatia di Benvenuto Cellini." *Svaghi Critici*. Bari, 1910. 71–91.

Rey, Michel. "Communauté et individu: L'amitié comme lien social à la Renaissance." *Revue du Histoire Moderne et Contemporaine* 38 (1991): 617–25.

Richards, David. "Benvenuto Cellini and Goethe's Autobiography." *Carleton Germanic Papers* 2 (1974): 89–104.

Richardson, Brian. *Print Culture in Renaissance Italy: The Editor and the Vernacular Text, 1470–1600.* Cambridge, 1994.

Ridolfi, Roberto. *Vita di Niccolò Machiavelli.* 5th ed. 2 vols. Florence, 1972.

Riggs, Don. "Was Michelangelo Born under Saturn?" *Sixteenth Century Journal* 26 (1995): 99–121.

Rocke, Michael J. *Forbidden Friendships: Homosexuality and Male Culture in Renaissance Florence.* New York, 1996.

Roncoroni, Luigi. "Benvenuto Cellini (Contributo allo studio delle parafrenie)." *Minerva Medicolegale (Archivio di Psichiatria)* 26 (1905): 271–97.

Rosen, David. *The Changing Fictions of Masculinity.* Urbana, IL, 1993.

Rosenthal, Margaret F. *The Honest Courtesan: Veronica Franco, Citizen and Writer in Sixteenth-Century Venice.* Chicago, 1992.

—— and Ann Rosalind Jones, eds. and trans. *Poems and Letters, Veronica Franco.* Chicago, 1998.

Rossi, Paolo L. "*Sprezzatura*, Patronage, and Fate: Benvenuto Cellini and the World of Words." In *Vasari's Florence: Artists and Literati at the Medicean Court.* Ed. Philip Jacks. Cambridge, 1998. 55–69, 263–65.

——. "The Writer and the Man. Real Crimes and Mitigating Circumstances: Il caso Cellini." In *Crime, Society and the Law in Renaissance Italy.* Eds. T. Dean and K.J.P. Lowe. Cambridge, 1994. 157–83.

Rowland, Ingrid. "The Real Caravaggio." *New York Review of Books* 46, no. 15 (1999): 11–14.

Rubin, Patricia Lee. *Giorgio Vasari: Art and History.* New Haven, 1995.

Rubinstein, Nicolai. "The Beginnings of Political Thought in Florence." *JWCI* 5 (1942): 198–227.

Ruff, Julius R, ed. *Violence in Early Modern Europe, 1500–1800.* Cambridge, 2001.

Ruggiero, Guido. *The Boundaries of Eros: Sex Crime and Sexuality in Renaissance Venice.* New York, 1985.

——. "Marriage, Love, Sex and Civic Morality." In *Sexuality and Gender in Early Modern Europe: Institutions, Texts, Images.* Ed. James Grantham Turner. Cambridge, 1993. 10–30.

——. "'More Dear to Me than Life Itself': Marriage, Honor, and a Woman's Reputation in the Renaissance." *Binding Passions: Tales of Magic, Marriage, and Power at the End of the Renaissance.* New York, 1993. 57–87.

——. *Violence in Early Renaissance Venice.* New Brunswick, NJ, 1980.

Russo, Luigi. *Compendio storico della letteratura italiana.* 2nd ed. Messina, 1967.

Ryan, Christopher. *Michelangelo, The Poems. A New Translation.* London, 1996.

Sacchetti, Franco. *Il Trecentonovelle.* Ed. Valerio Marucci. Rome, 1996.

Saltini, Guglielmo Enrico. *Tragedie medicee domestiche (1557–87) narrate sui documenti da G. E. Saltini, premessavi una introduzione sul governo di Cosimo I.* Florence, 1898.

Santagata, Marco, ed. *IUPI: Incipitario Unificato della Poesia Italiana.* 3 vols. Modena, 1988–90.

Santangelo, Salvatore. *Le tenzoni poetiche nella letteratura italiana delle origini.* Geneva, 1928.

Saslow, James M. *Ganymede in the Renaissance*. New Haven, 1986.
——. "Homosexuality in the Renaissance: Behavior, Identity, and Artistic Expression." In *Hidden from History: Reclaiming the Gay and Lesbian Past*. Eds. Martin B. Duberman et al. New York, 1989. 90–105.
——. "'A Veil of Ice Between my Heart and the Fire:' Michelangelo's Sexual Identity and Early Modern Constructs of Homosexuality." *Genders* 2 (1988): 77–90.
Scala, Flaminio. *Il Teatro delle Favole Rappresentative*. Ed. F. Marotti. Milan, 1976.
Scalini, Mario. *Benvenuto Cellini*. Florence, 1995.
Schiesari, Juliana. *The Gendering of Melancholia: Feminism, Psychoanalysis, and the Symbolics of Loss in Renaissance Literature*. Ithaca, 1992.
Schleiner, Winfried. "Male Cross-dressing and Transvestism in Renaissance Romances." *Sixteenth Century Journal* 19 (1988): 605–19.
Schlosser, Julius Magnino. *La letteratura artistica: manuale delle fonti della storia dell'arte moderna*. Trans. Filippo Rossi. 3rd ed. 1924; Florence, 1964.
Scott, Joan Wallach. "Gender: A Useful Category of Historical Analysis." *American Historical Review* 91 (1986): 1053–75.
Scritti d'Arte del Cinquecento. See Barocchi, Paola, ed.
Scrivano, Riccardo. "Commitenza e alienzione: casi celliniani nella Roma del 1500." *Letteratura e Filologia*. Foggia, 1985. 139–53.
Sedgwick, Eve Kosofsky. *Between Men: English Literature and Male Homosocial Desire*. 1985; New York, 1992.
Segni, Bernardo. *Istorie fiorentine dall'anno MDXXVII al MDLV*. Florence, 1857.
Shanley, John Patrick. *Cellini. Adapted from the Autobiography of Benvenuto Cellini translated by J. Addington Symonds*. Dramatists Play Service, Inc. 2002.
Shearman, John. *Only Connect . . . Art and the Spectator in the Italian Renaissance*. Princeton, 1992.
Shemek, Deanna. *Ladies Errant: Wayward Women and Social Order in Early Modern Italy*. Durham, NC, 1998.
Short-title catalogue of books printed in Italy and of Italian books printed in other countries from 1465 to 1600 now in the British Library. London, 1986.
Silverman, Kaja. *Male Subjectivity at the Margins*. London, 1992.
Simonetta, Bono. "Le medaglie di Benvenuto Cellini." *Rivista Italiana di Numismatica e Scienze Affini* 63, 5th ser. (1961): 69–78.
Simons, Patricia. "Alert and Erect: Masculinity in Some Italian Renaissance Portraits of Fathers and Sons." In *Gender Rhetorics: Postures of Dominance and Submission in History*. Ed. Richard C. Trexler. Binghamton, NY, 1994. 163–86.
Solomon, Maynard. "Franz Schubert and the Peacocks of Benvenuto Cellini." *19th Century Music* 12 (1989): 193–206.
Somigli, Guglielmo, ed. *Sulla fusione del Perseo. Notizie storiche, con alcuni documenti inediti di Benvenuto Cellini*. Milan, 1958.
Spiegel, Gabrielle M. "Genealogy: Form and Function in Medieval Historical Narrative." *History and Theory* 22 (1983): 43–53.
Stallybrass, Peter and Allon White. *The Politics and Poetics of Transgression*. Ithaca, 1986.

Starn, Randolph. "The Early Modern Muddle." Unpublished ts. 2002. Forthcoming in the *Journal of early modern History*.

—— and Loren Partridge. *Arts of Power: Three Halls of State in Italy 1300–1600*. Berkeley, 1992.

——. "Francesco Guicciardini and His Brothers." In *Renaissance Studies in Honor of Hans Baron*. Eds. Anthony Molho and John Tedeschi. Florence, 1971. 409–44.

Stefanini, Ruggero. "Tenzone sì e tenzone no." *Lectura Dantis* 18–19 (1996): 111–28.

Stern, Laura Ikins. *The Criminal Law System of Medieval and Renaissance Florence*. Baltimore, 1994.

Stewart, Alan. *Close Readers: Humanism and Sodomy in Early Modern England*. Princeton, 1997.

Stewart, Alison G. *Unequal Lovers: A Study of Unequal Couples in Northern Art*. 1977; New York, 1979.

Stoppani, Fernando. "L'avventurosa vita di Benvenuto Cellini." *Urbe: Rivista Romana di Storia, Arte, Lettere, Costumanze* 25 (1962): 4–10.

Strozier, Robert M. "Renaissance Humanist Theory: Petrarch and the Sixteenth Century." *Rinascimento* 26 (1986): 193–229.

Sturrock, John. "Fame and Fortune: Cellini, Cardano." In *The Language of Autobiography: Studies in the First Person Singular*. Cambridge, 1993. 64–74.

Summers, Claude J., ed. *The Gay and Lesbian Literary Heritage: A Reader's Companion to the Writers and Their Works, from Antiquity to the Present*. New York, 1995.

Summers, David. *Michelangelo and the Language of Art*. Princeton, 1981.

Summers, Montague, trans. *The Malleus Maleficarum of Heinrich Kramer and Jacob Sprenger*. 1921; New York, 1971.

Switzer, Richard. "Berlioz, Dumas, and the Foundry." *Nineteenth-Century French Studies* 8 (1980): 252–57.

Talvacchia, Bette. *Taking Positions: On the Erotic in Renaissance Culture*. Princeton, 1999.

Tarsia, Giovanni Maria. *Oratione o vero Discorso di M. Giovan Maria Tarsia. Fatto nell'Essequie del divino Michelagnolo Buonarroti. Con alcuni sonetti, e prose latine e volgari di diversi, circa il disparare occorso tra gli Scultori, e Pittori*. Florence, 1564.

Tedeschi, John A. "Toward a Statistical Profile of the Italian Inquisitions, Sixteenth to Eighteenth Centuries (with William Monter)." In *The Prosecution of Heresy: Collected Studies on the Inquisition in Early Modern Italy*. Binghamton, NY, 1991. 89–126.

Tentler, Thomas. *Sin and Confession on the Eve of the Reformation*. Princeton, 1977.

Teza, E. "La *Vita* di Benvenuto Cellini nelle mani del Goethe." *Atti del R. Istituto Veneto di Scienze, Lettere ed Arti*, 7th ser., 6 (1895): 299–307.

Todorov, Tzvetan. *Genres in Discourse*. Trans. Catherine Porter. Cambridge, 1990.

Tognetti, Giampaolo. "Criteri per la trascrizione di testi medievali latini e italiani." *Quaderni della Rassegna degli Archivi di Stato* 51 (1982): 1–66.

Tognozzi, Elissa Ann. "The Heterodoxy of Cellini: Emblematic Symbol of the Renaissance or Isolated Case of Excessive Indulgence." Ph.D. diss., University of California, Los Angeles, 1993.

Toscan, Jean. *Le Carnaval du langue: Le lexique érotique des poètes de l'équivoque de Burchiello à Marino (XVᵉ–XVIIᵉ siècles)*. 4 vols. Lille, 1981.

Toschi, Paolo, ed. *Sacre Rappresentazioni toscane dei secoli XV e XVI*. 9 vols. Florence, 1969.

Trento, Dario. *Benvenuto Cellini, Opere non esposte e Documenti notarili*. Florence, 1984.

Tristan and Yseut: Old French Text with Facing English Translation. Ed. and trans. Guy R. Mermier. New York, 1987.

Trottein, Gwendolyn. "Battling Fortune in Sixteenth-Century Italy: Cellini and the Changing Faces of Fortuna." *Artful Armies, Beautiful Battles: Art and Warfare in Early Modern Europe*. Ed. Pia Cuneo. Leiden, 2002. 213–34.

Turner, James Grantham, ed. *Sexuality and Gender in Early Modern Europe*. Cambridge, 1993.

Tylus, Jane. "The Merchant of Florence: Benvenuto Cellini, Cosimo de' Medici, and the *Vita*." In *Writing and Vulnerability in the Late Renaissance*. Stanford, 1993. 31–53.

Vallone, Giancarlo. "Contributo allo studio dell'arte del ferro tra Italia e Francia: Due chiavi già attribuite al Cellini." *Bollettino d'Arte* 78 (1993): 63–78.

Van Veen, Henk Th. *Letteratura artistica e arte di corte nella Firenze granducale: Studi vari*. Florence, 1986.

Varchi, Benedetto. *Sonetti spirituali di M. Benedetto Varchi. Con alcune risposte, et proposte di diversi eccellentissimi ingegni. Nuovamente stampati*. Florence, 1573.

Vasari, Giorgio. *Le Vite de' più eccellenti pittori, scultori e architettori nelle redazioni del 1550 e 1568*. Eds. Rosanna Bettarini and Paola Barocchi. 6 vols. Florence, 1966. Vol. 6.

——. *Le Vite de' più eccellenti pittori scultori e architettori: Nelle redazioni del 1550 e 1568. Indice di frequenza*. Ed. Paola Barocchi. 2 vols. Pisa, 1994.

——. *Il Carteggio di Giorgio Vasari*. Ed. Karl Frey. Munich, 1923.

——. *Il Carteggio di Giorgio Vasari dal 1563 al 1565*. Ed. Karl Frey. Arezzo, 1941.

——. *Lives of the Painters, Sculptors, and Architects*. Trans. Gaston du C. de Vere. 2 vols. New York, 1996. Vol. 2.

Vecellio, Cesare. *Degli Habiti Antichi et Moderni di Diverse Parti del Mondo*. Venice, 1590.

Venturi, Adolfo. "Benvenuto Cellini nel quarto centenario della nascita." *Nuova Antologia* 90, 4th ser. (1900): 107–20.

Verrecchia, Anacleto. "La Vita di Benvenuto Cellini." *Ausonia* 18 (1963): 148–50.

Vettori, Vittorio. "Dante nel Rinascimento." In *Il Rinascimento: Aspetti e problemi attuali*. Eds. Vittore Branca et al. Florence, 1982. 667–70.

Vickers, Nancy K. "The Mistress in the Masterpiece." In *The Poetics of Gender*. New York, 1986. 19–41.

Vico, Enea. *Discorso sopra le medaglie de gli antichi*. 2 vols. Venice, 1555.

Viglionese, Paschal. "Leonardo and the Nature of Writing: A Page from His Notebooks." *Canadian Journal of Italian Studies* 15 (1992): 11–16.

Villani, Giovanni. *Nuova Cronica*. In *Cronisti del Trecento*. Ed. R. Palmarocchi. Milan, 1935. 159–61.

Virgil. *The Aeneid*. Ed. J.W. MacKail. Oxford, 1930.

Vocabolario degli Accademici della Crusca. See Accademia della Crusca.

Waddington, Raymond B. "The Bisexual Portrait of Francis I: Fontainebleau, Castiglione, and the Tone of Courtly Mythology." In *Playing with Gender: A Renaissance Pursuit*. Eds. Jean R. Brink, Maryanne C. Horowitz, and Allison P. Coudert. Urbana, IL, 1991. 99–132.

Waldman, Louis Alexander. "Bandinelli and the Opera di Santa Maria del Fiore: Patronage, Privilege, and Pedagogy." In *Santa Maria del Fiore. The Cathedral and Its Sculpture*. Ed. Margaret Haines. Fiesole, 2001. 221–56.

——. "'Miracol Novo et Raro:' Two Unpublished Contemporary Satires on Bandinelli's 'Hercules.'" *Mitteilungen Des Kunsthistorischen Institutes in Florenz* 38 (1994): 419–27.

Walkowitz, Judith R. *City of Dreadful Delight: Narratives of Sexual Danger in Late-Victorian London*. Chicago, 1992.

Wallace, William E. *Michelangelo: The Complete Sculpture, Painting, and Architecture*. New York, 1998.

Ward, Roger B. "New Drawings by Bandinelli and Cellini." *Master Drawings* 31 (1993): 395–99.

Wazbinski, Zygmunt. "Artisti e pubblico nella Firenze del Cinquecento: A proposito del topos del 'cane abbaiante.'" *Paragone* 28 (1997): 3–24.

Webber, Ruth House. "Towards the Morphology of the Romance Epic." In *Romance Epic: Essays on a Medieval Literary Genre*. Ed. Hans-Erich Keller. Kalamazoo, MI, 1987. 1–10.

Weinberg, Bernard. *A History of Literary Criticism in the Italian Renaissance*. 2 vols. Chicago, 1961. Vol. 2.

Weinstein, Donald. "The Myth of Florence." In *Florentine Studies*. Ed. Nicolai Rubenstein. Evanston, IL, 1968. 15–44.

Weintraub, Karl J. *The Value of the Individual: Self and Circumstance in Autobiography*. Chicago, 1978.

Weissman, Ronald. *Ritual Brotherhood in Renaissance Florence*. New York, 1982.

Weller, Barry. "The Rhetoric of Friendship in Montaigne's Essais." *New Literary History* 9 (1978): 503–23.

White, John. "*Paragone*: Aspects of the Relationship Between Painting and Sculpture." In *Art, Science, and History in the Renaissance*. Ed. Charles S. Singleton. Baltimore, 1967. 43–109.

Wiesner, Merry E. "Beyond Women and the Family: Toward a Gender Analysis of the Reformation." *Sixteenth Century Journal* 18 (1987): 311–21.

Wilde, Oscar. *The Portable Oscar Wilde*. Rev. ed. Eds. Robert Arlington and Stanley Weintraub. New York, 1981.

Wittkower, Rudolf and Margot. *Born under Saturn: The Character and Conduct of Artists, A Documentary History from Antiquity to the French Revolution*. 1963; New York, 1969.

———, trans. *The Divine Michelangelo: The Florentine Academy's Homage on His Death in 1564, a Facsimile Edition of* Esequie del divino Michelagnolo Buonarroti, *Florence 1564*. London, 1964.

Wolfgang, Marvin E. "A Florentine Prison: Le Carceri delle Stinche." *Studies in the Renaissance* 7 (1960): 148–66.

Wolfthal, Diane. *Images of Rape: The "Heroic" Tradition and its Alternatives*. Cambridge, 1999.

Woods, Gregory. *A History of Gay Literature: The Male Tradition*. New Haven, 1998.

Woods-Marsden, Joanna. *Renaissance Self-Portraiture: The Visual Construction of Identity and the Social Status of the Artist*. New Haven, 1998.

Zatti, Sergio. *Il Furioso fra epos e romanzo*. Lucca, 1990.

———. *L'ombra del Tasso: Epica e romanzo nel Cinquecento*. Milan, 1996.

Zimmerman, T.C. Price. "Confession and Autobiography in the Early Renaissance." In *Renaissance Studies in Honor of Hans Baron*. Eds. Anthony Molho and John A. Tedeschi. 3 vols. Dekalb, IL, 1971. 1: 119–40.

Zorach, Rebecca E. "The Matter of Italy: Sodomy and the Scandal of Style in Sixteenth-Century France." *The Journal of Medieval and Early Modern Studies* 28, no. 3 (1998): 581–609.

Zumthor, Paul. "Autobiography in the Middle Ages?" Trans. Sherry Simon. *Genre* 6 (1973): 29–48.

INDEX